GANDHI IN NATIONAL MOVEMENT

Encyclopaedic History of India Series

GANDHI IN NATIONAL MOVEMENT

Dr. Mahesh Vikram Singh
Professor, Deptt. of History
Mahatma Gandhi Kashi Vidyapeeth
Varanasi (UP)

Dr. Brij Bhushan Shrivastava
Head of Deptt., Ancient History, Archeology & Culture
SMMTPG College, Ballia (UP)

CENTRUM PRESS
NEW DELHI-110002 (INDIA)

CENTRUM PRESS
H.O.: 4360/4, Ansari Road, Daryaganj,
New Delhi-110002 (India)
Tel: 23278000, 23261597, 23255577, 23286875
B.O.: No. 1015, Ist Main Road, BSK IIIrd Stage,
IIIrd Phase, IIIrd Block, Bangalore-560085 (INDIA)
Tel: 080-41723429
Email: centrumpress@gmail.com
Visit us at: www.centrumpress.com

Gandhi in National Movement

First Edition, 2011

ISBN 978-93-80836-92-8

PRINTED IN INDIA

Printed at Mehra Offset Press, Delhi

प्रो. विपिन चंद्रा
अध्यक्ष
Prof. Bipan Chandra
Chairman

नेशनल बुक ट्रस्ट, इंडिया
नेहरू भवन
5 इंस्टीट्यूशनल एरिया, फेज़-II, वसंत कुंज, नई दिल्ली-110 070
फोन/ Phone: 011-26121880 फैक्स/ Fax: 011-26121883
NATIONAL BOOK TRUST, INDIA
Nehru Bhawan
5 Institutional Area, Phase II, Vasant Kunj, New Delhi-110 070
ई-मेल / E-mail: chairman@nbtindia.org.in
वेबसाइट / Website: www.nbtindia.org.in

FOREWORD

The term 'history' is derived from the Greek word 'historia' that means knowledge acquired through investigation. Obviously, this knowledge can be correct if the method of investigation is objective and not vitiated by any kind of bias. In other words, if the study of human past is comprehensive and obtained through scientific inquiry, it can provide perspective on the present day problems and help one plan for the future.

A true historian has to identify the sources that can be most useful in a given context. Documents, coins, archaeology, anthropology, geography, travel accounts, oral traditions, mythology and so on can be useful but they can be used only after their veracity is tested and they are critically examined. They should be checked and counter-checked.

Over the centuries, one finds the study and writing of history vitiated by biases. There are numerous instances in which historical data have been distorted to support or oppose certain preconceived ideas and purposes. Strictly speaking such history is just like fiction to accord with preconceived notions and serve some ulterior purposes.

The study of the past has never been static. Conclusions go on changing because of the discovery of new materials and tools of investigation. To give a concrete example, the carbon 14 or radiocarbon dating test has revolutionized the study of civilizations and settlements, especially of prehistoric times, for which written documents, coins, etc. are seldom available. This method has enabled historians to determine more accurately than before the time period of a particular civilization or settlement. This method was discovered only 70 years ago by American scientists.

In our country, excavations brought to light the Indus Valley Civilization and its various features, hitherto unknown. Similarly, no complete text of Kautilya's Arthashastra was available before it was discovered by Shamasastry, the chief of the Mysore Government Oriental Library in the first decade of the last century. Likewise, people's knowledge of the history of the Buddhist period got extended after excavations at Sarnath and the ruins of the Asokan period at Patna. In the future, if the Harappan inscriptions are deciphered, our knowledge of the Indus Valley Civilization will increase enormously. All these instances underline the fact that our knowledge of history is never static and its frontiers go on extending.

In the light of what has been said above the encyclopedic history is going to be of great help to students interested in Indian history. It is comprehensive and as far as possible free from biases. It includes the latest materials, and objective conclusions.

Prof . Bipan Chandra

Professor Emeritus, JNU

Chairman, National Book Trust, India

Contents

Preface

The people of India have had a continuous civilization since 2500 B.C., when the inhabitants of the Indus River valley developed an urban culture based on commerce and sustained by agricultural trade. This civilization declined around 1500 B.C., probably due to ecological changes. During the second millennium B.C., pastoral, Aryan-speaking tribes migrated from the northwest into the subcontinent. As they settled in the middle Ganges River valley, they adapted to antecedent cultures.

The political map of ancient and medieval India was made up of myriad kingdoms with fluctuating boundaries. In the 4th and 5th centuries A.D., northern India was unified under the Gupta Dynasty. During this period, known as India's Golden Age, Hindu culture and political administration reached new heights. Islam spread across the Indian subcontinent over a period of 500 years. In the 10th and 11th centuries, Turks and Afghans invaded India and established sultanates in Delhi. In the early 16th century, descendants of Genghis Khan swept across the Khyber Pass and established the Mughal (Mogul) Dynasty, which lasted for 200 years. From the 11th to the 15th centuries, southern India was dominated by Hindu Chola and Vijayanagar Dynasties. During this time, the two systems—the prevailing Hindu and Muslim—mingled, leaving lasting cultural influences on each other.

The first British outpost in South Asia was established in 1619 at Surat on the northwestern coast. Later in the century, the East India Company opened permanent trading stations at Madras, Bombay, and Calcutta, each under the protection of native rulers. The British expanded their influence from these footholds until, by the 1850s, they controlled most of present-day India, Pakistan, and Bangladesh. In 1857, a rebellion in north India led by mutinous Indian soldiers caused the British Parliament to transfer all political power from the East India Company to the Crown. Great Britain began administering most of India directly while controlling the rest through treaties with local rulers.

In the late 1800s, the first steps were taken toward self-government in British India with the appointment of Indian councillors to advise the British viceroy and the establishment of provincial councils with Indian members; the British subsequently widened participation in legislative councils. Beginning in 1920, Indian leader Mohandas K. Gandhi transformed the Indian National Congress political party into a mass movement to campaign against British colonial rule.

—Authors

1

Introduction

Mohandas Karamchand Gandhi; 2 October 1869 – 30 January 1948) was the pre-eminent political and spiritual leader of India during the Indian independence movement. He was the pioneer of *satyagraha*—resistance to tyranny through mass civil disobedience, a philosophy firmly founded upon *ahimsa* or total nonviolence—which led India to independence and inspired movements for civil rights and freedom across the world. Gandhi is commonly known around the world as Mahatma Gandhi, and in India also as Bapu. He is officially honoured in India as the *Father of the Nation*; his birthday, 2 October, is commemorated there as *Gandhi Jayanti*, a national holiday, and worldwide as the International Day of Non-Violence.

Gandhi first employed nonviolent civil disobedience while an expatriate lawyer in South Africa, during the resident Indian community's struggle for civil rights. After his return to India in 1915, he organized protests by peasants, farmers, and urban labourers concerning excessive land-tax and discrimination. After assuming leadership of the Indian National Congress in 1921, Gandhi led nationwide campaigns to ease poverty, expand women's rights, build religious and ethnic amity, end untouchability, and increase economic self-reliance.

Above all, he aimed to achieve *Swaraj* or the independence of India from foreign domination. Gandhi famously led his followers in the Non-cooperation movement that protested the British-imposed salt tax with the 400 km (240 mi) Dandi Salt March in 1930. Later, in 1942, he launched the *Quit India* civil disobedience movement demanding immediate independence for India. Gandhi spent a number of years in jail in both South Africa and India.

As a practitioner of *ahimsa,* he swore to speak the truth and advocated that others do the same. Gandhi lived modestly in a self-sufficient residential community and wore the traditional Indian *dhoti* and shawl, woven with yarn he had hand spun on a *charkha.* He ate simple vegetarian food, eventually adopting a fruitarian diet, and also undertook long fasts as a means of both self-purification and social protest.

Early Life and Background

Mohandas Karamchand Gandhi was born on 2 October 1869 in Porbandar, a coastal town in present-day Gujarat, India. His father, Karamchand Gandhi (1822–1885), who belonged to the Hindu Modh community, was the *diwan* (Prime Minister) of Porbander state, a small princely state in the Kathiawar Agency of British India.

His grandfather's name was Uttamchand Gandhi, fondly called Utta Gandhi. His mother, Putlibai, who came from the Hindu Pranami Vaishnava community, was Karamchand's fourth wife, the first three wives having apparently died in childbirth.

Growing up with a devout mother and the Jain traditions of the region, the young Mohandas absorbed early the influences that would play an important role in his adult life; these included compassion for sentient beings, vegetarianism, fasting for self-purification, and mutual tolerance between individuals of different creeds.

The Indian classics, especially the stories of Shravana and Maharaja Harishchandra from the Indian epics, had a great impact on Gandhi in his childhood. The story of Harishchandra, a well known tale of an ancient Indian king and a truthful hero, haunted Gandhi as a boy. Gandhi in his autobiography admits that it left an indelible impression on his mind. He writes: "It haunted me and I must have acted Harishchandra to myself times without number." Gandhi's early self-identification with Truth and Love as supreme values is traceable to his identification with these epic characters.

In May 1883, the 13-year old Mohandas was married to 14-year old Kasturbai Makhanji (her first name was usually shortened to "Kasturba," and affectionately to "Ba") in an arranged child marriage, as was the custom in the region. Recalling about the day of their marriage he once said that " As we didn't know much about marriage, for us it meant only wearing new clothes, eating sweets and playing with relatives."

However, as was also the custom of the region, the adolescent bride was to spend much time at her parents' house, and away from her husband. In 1885, when Gandhi was 15, the couple's first child was born, but survived only a few days; Gandhi's father, Karamchand Gandhi, had died earlier that year. Mohandas and Kasturba had four more children, all sons: Harilal, born in 1888; Manilal, born in 1892; Ramdas, born in 1897; and Devdas, born in 1900. At his middle school in Porbandar and high school in Rajkot, Gandhi remained an average student academically. He passed the matriculation exam for Samaldas College at Bhavnagar, Gujarat with some difficulty. While there, he was unhappy, in part because his family wanted him to become a barrister.

On 4 September 1888, less than a month shy of his 19th birthday, Gandhi travelled to London, England, to study law at University College London and to train as a barrister. His time in London, the Imperial capital, was influenced by a vow he had made to his mother in the presence of the Jain monk Becharji, upon leaving India, to observe the Hindu precepts of abstinence from meat, alcohol, and promiscuity. Although Gandhi experimented with adopting "English" customs—taking dancing lessons for example—he could not stomach the bland vegetarian food offered by his landlady and he was always hungry until he found one of London's few vegetarian restaurants.

Influenced by Salt's book, he joined the Vegetarian Society, was elected to its executive committee, and started a local Bayswater chapter. Some of the vegetarians he met were members of the Theosophical Society, which had been founded in 1875 to further universal brotherhood, and which was devoted to the study of Buddhist and Hindu literature. They encouraged Gandhi to join them in reading the *Bhagavad Gita* both in translation as well as in the original. Not having shown a particular interest in religion before, he became interested in religious thought and began to read both Hindu as well as Christian scriptures.

Gandhi was called to the bar on June 10, 1891 and left London for India on June 12, 1891, where he learned that his mother had died while he was in London, his family having kept the news from him. His attempts at establishing a law practice in Mumbai failed and, later, after applying and being turned down for a part-time job as a high school teacher, he ended up returning to Rajkot to make a modest living drafting petitions for litigants, a business he was forced to close when he ran afoul of a British officer. In his autobiography, he refers to this incident as an unsuccessful attempt to lobby on behalf of his older brother. It was in this climate that, in April 1893, he accepted a year-long contract from Dada Abdulla & Co., an Indian firm, to a post in the Colony of Natal, South Africa, then part of the British Empire.

Civil Rights Movement in South Africa (1893–1914)

In South Africa, Gandhi faced discrimination directed at Indians. He was thrown off a train at Pietermaritzburg after refusing to move from the first class to a third class coach while holding a valid first class ticket. Travelling farther on by stagecoach he was beaten by a driver for refusing to travel on the foot board to make room for a European passenger. He suffered other hardships on the journey as well, including being barred from several hotels. In another incident, the magistrate of a Durban court ordered Gandhi to remove his turban-which he refused to do. These events were a turning point in his life, awakening him to social injustice and influencing his subsequent social activism. It was through witnessing firsthand the racism, prejudice and injustice against Indians in South Africa that Gandhi started to question his people's status within the British Empire, and his own place in society.

Gandhi extended his original period of stay in South Africa to assist Indians in opposing a bill to deny them the right to vote. Though unable to halt the bill's passage, his campaign was successful in drawing attention to the grievances of Indians in South Africa. He helped found the Natal Indian Congress in 1894, and through this organization, he moulded the Indian community of South Africa into a homogeneous political force. In January 1897, when Gandhi landed in Durban he was attacked by a mob of white settlers and escaped only through the efforts of the wife of the police superintendent. He, however, refused to press charges against any member of the mob, stating it was one of his principles not to seek redress for a personal wrong in a court of law.

In 1906, the Transvaal government promulgated a new Act compelling registration of the colony's Indian population. At a mass protest meeting held in Johannesburg on 11 September that year, Gandhi adopted his still evolving methodology of *satyagraha* (devotion to the truth), or nonviolent protest, for the first time, calling on his fellow Indians to defy the new law and suffer the punishments for doing so, rather than resist through violent means. This plan was adopted, leading to a seven-year struggle in which thousands of Indians were jailed (including Gandhi), flogged, or even shot, for striking, refusing to register, burning their registration cards or engaging in other forms of nonviolent resistance. While the government was successful in repressing the Indian protesters, the public outcry stemming from the harsh methods employed by the South African government in the face of peaceful Indian protesters finally forced South African General Jan Christiaan Smuts to negotiate a compromise with Gandhi. Gandhi's ideas took shape and the concept of *satyagraha* matured during this struggle.

Racism and Controversy

Some of Gandhi's early South African articles are controversial. On 7 March 1908, Gandhi wrote in the *Indian Opinion* of his time in a South African prison: "Kaffirs are as a rule uncivilized-the convicts even more so. They are troublesome, very dirty and live almost like animals." Writing on the subject of immigration in 1903, Gandhi commented: "We believe as much in the purity of race as we think they do... We believe also that the white race in South Africa should be the predominating race." During his time in South Africa, Gandhi protested repeatedly about the social classification of blacks with Indians, who he described as "undoubtedly infinitely superior to the Kaffirs". Remarks such as these have led some to accuse Gandhi of racism.

Two professors of history who specialize in South Africa, Surendra Bhana and Goolam Vahed, examined this controversy in their text, *The Making of a Political Reformer: Gandhi in South*

Africa, 1893–1914. (New Delhi: Manohar, 2005). "Gandhi, Africans and Indians in Colonial Natal" on the relationship between the African and Indian communities under "White rule" and policies which enforced segregation (and, they argue, inevitable conflict between these communities). Of this relationship they state that, "the young Gandhi was influenced by segregationist notions prevalent in the 1890s." At the same time, they state, "Gandhi's experiences in jail seemed to make him more sensitive to their plight...the later Gandhi mellowed; he seemed much less categorical in his expression of prejudice against Africans, and much more open to seeing points of common cause. His negative views in the Johannesburg jail were reserved for hardened African prisoners rather than Africans generally."

Former President of South Africa Nelson Mandela is a follower of Gandhi, despite efforts in 2003 on the part of Gandhi's critics to prevent the unveiling of a statue of Gandhi in Johannesburg. Bhana and Vahed commented on the events surrounding the unveiling in the conclusion to *The Making of a Political Reformer: Gandhi in South Africa, 1893–1914*. In the section "Gandhi's Legacy to South Africa," they note that "Gandhi inspired succeeding generations of South African activists seeking to end White rule. This legacy connects him to Nelson Mandela...in a sense Mandela completed what Gandhi started."

Role in Zulu War of 1906

In 1906, after the British introduced a new poll-tax, Zulus in South Africa killed two British officers. In response, the British declared a war against the Zulus. Gandhi actively encouraged the British to recruit Indians. He argued that Indians should support the war efforts in order to legitimize their claims to full citizenship. The British, however, refused to commission Indians as army officers. Nonetheless, they accepted Gandhi's offer to let a detachment of Indians volunteer as a stretcher bearer corps to treat wounded British soldiers. This corps was commanded by Gandhi. On 21 July 1906, Gandhi wrote in *Indian Opinion*: "The corps had been formed at the instance of the Natal Government by way of experiment, in connection with the operations against the Natives consists of twenty three Indians". Gandhi urged the Indian population in South Africa to join the war through his columns in *Indian Opinion*: "If the Government only realized what reserve force is being wasted, they would make use of it and give Indians the opportunity of a thorough training for actual warfare."

In Gandhi's opinion, the Draft Ordinance of 1906 brought the status of Indians below the level of Natives. He therefore urged Indians to resist the Ordinance along the lines of *satyagraha* by taking the example of "Kaffirs". In his words, "Even the half-castes and kaffirs, who are less advanced than we, have resisted the government. The pass law applies to them as well, but they do not take out passes."

In 1927 Gandhi wrote of the event: "The Boer War had not brought home to me the horrors of war with anything like the vividness that the [Zulu] 'rebellion' did. This was no war but a man-hunt, not only in my opinion, but also in that of many Englishmen with whom I had occasion to talk."

Struggle for Indian Independence (1915–1945)

In 1915, Gandhi returned from South Africa to live in India. He spoke at the conventions of the Indian National Congress, but was primarily introduced to Indian issues, politics and the Indian people by Gopal Krishna Gokhale, a respected leader of the Congress Party at the time.

Role in World War I

In April 1918, during the latter part of World War I, Gandhi was invited by the Viceroy to a War Conference in Delhi. Perhaps to show his support for the Empire and help his case for India's independence, Gandhi agreed to actively recruit Indians for the war effort. In contrast to the Zulu War of 1906 and the outbreak of World War I in 1914, when he recruited volunteers for the Ambulance Corps, this time Gandhi attempted to recruit combatants. In a June 1918 leaflet entitled "Appeal for Enlistment", Gandhi wrote "To bring about such a state of things we should have the ability to defend ourselves, that is, the ability to bear arms and to use them...If we want to learn the use of arms with the greatest possible despatch, it is our duty to enlist ourselves in the army." He did however stipulate in a letter to the Viceroy's private secretary that he "personally will not kill or injure anybody, friend or foe." Gandhi's war recruitment campaign brought into question his consistency on nonviolence as his friend Charlie Andrews confirms, "Personally I have never been able to reconcile this with his own conduct in other respects, and it is one of the points where I have found myself in painful disagreement." Gandhi's private secretary also acknowledges that "The question of the consistency between his creed of 'Ahimsa' (non-violence) and his recruiting campaign was raised not only then but has been discussed ever since."

Champaran and Kheda

Gandhi's first major achievements came in 1918 with the Champaran agitation and *Kheda Satyagraha*, although in the latter it was indigo and other cash crops instead of the food crops necessary for their survival. Suppressed by the militias of the landlords (mostly British), they were given measly compensation, leaving them mired in extreme poverty. The villages were kept extremely dirty and unhygienic; and alcoholism, untouchability and purdah were rampant. Now in the throes of a devastating famine, the British levied a tax which they insisted on increasing. The situation was desperate. In Kheda in Gujarat, the problem was the same. Gandhi established an ashram there, organizing scores of his veteran supporters and fresh volunteers from the region. He organized a detailed study and survey of the villages, accounting for the atrocities and terrible episodes of suffering, including the general state of degenerate living. Building on the confidence of villagers, he began leading the clean-up of villages, building of schools and hospitals and encouraging the village leadership to undo and condemn many social evils, as accounted above.

But his main impact came when he was arrested by police on the charge of creating unrest and was ordered to leave the province. Hundreds of thousands of people protested and rallied outside the jail, police stations and courts demanding his release, which the court reluctantly granted. Gandhi led organized protests and strikes against the landlords who, with the guidance of the British government, signed an agreement granting the poor farmers of the region more compensation and control over farming, and cancellation of revenue hikes and its collection until the famine ended. It was during this agitation, that Gandhi was addressed by the people as *Bapu* (Father) and *Mahatma* (Great Soul). In

Kheda, Sardar Patel represented the farmers in negotiations with the British, who suspended revenue collection and released all the prisoners. As a result, Gandhi's fame spread all over the nation. He is also now called as "Father of the nation" in Indian.

Non-cooperation

Gandhi employed non-cooperation, non-violence and peaceful resistance as his "weapons" in the struggle against British. In Punjab, the Jallianwala Bagh massacre of civilians by British troops (also known as the Amritsar Massacre) caused deep trauma to the nation, leading to increased public anger and acts of violence. Gandhi criticized both the actions of the British Raj and the retaliatory violence of Indians. He authored the resolution offering condolences to British civilian victims and condemning the riots which, after initial opposition in the party, was accepted following Gandhi's emotional speech advocating his principle that all violence was evil and could not be justified. But it was after the massacre and subsequent violence that Gandhi's mind focused upon obtaining complete self-government and control of all Indian government institutions, maturing soon into *Swaraj* or complete individual, spiritual, political independence.

In December 1921, Gandhi was invested with executive authority on behalf of the Indian National Congress. Under his leadership, the Congress was reorganized with a new constitution, with the goal of *Swaraj*. Membership in the party was opened to anyone prepared to pay a token fee. A hierarchy of committees was set up to improve discipline, transforming the party from an elite organization to one of mass national appeal. Gandhi expanded his non-violence platform to include the *swadeshi* policy – the boycott of foreign-made goods, especially British goods. Linked to this was his advocacy that *khadi* (homespun cloth) be worn by all Indians instead of British-made textiles. Gandhi exhorted Indian men and women, rich or poor, to spend time each day spinning *khadi* in support of the independence movement. This was a strategy to inculcate discipline and dedication to weed out the unwilling and ambitious, and to include women in the movement at a time when many thought that such activities were not respectable activities for women. In addition to boycotting British products, Gandhi urged the people to boycott British educational institutions and law courts, to resign from government employment, and to forsake British titles and honours.

"Non-cooperation" enjoyed widespread appeal and success, increasing excitement and participation from all strata of Indian society. Yet, just as the movement reached its apex, it ended abruptly as a result of a violent clash in the town of Chauri Chaura, Uttar Pradesh, in February 1922. Fearing that the movement was about to take a turn towards violence, and convinced that this would be the undoing of all his work, Gandhi called off the campaign of mass civil disobedience. Gandhi was arrested on 10 March 1922, tried for sedition, and sentenced to six years' imprisonment. He began his sentence on 18 March 1922. He was released in February 1924 for an appendicitis operation, having served only 2 years.

Without Gandhi's uniting personality, the Indian National Congress began to splinter during his years in prison, splitting into two factions, one led by Chitta Ranjan Das and Motilal Nehru favouring party participation in the legislatures, and the other led by Chakravarti Rajagopalachari and Sardar Vallabhbhai Patel, opposing this move. Furthermore, cooperation among Hindus and Muslims, which had been strong at the height of the non-violence campaign, was breaking down. Gandhi attempted to bridge these differences through many means, including a three-week fast in the autumn of 1924, but with limited success.

Salt Satyagraha (Salt March)

Gandhi stayed out of active politics and, as such, the limelight for most of the 1920s. He focused instead on resolving the wedge between the Swaraj Party and the Indian National Congress, and expanding initiatives against untouchability, alcoholism, ignorance and poverty. He returned to the fore in 1928. In the preceding year, the British government had appointed a new constitutional reform commission under Sir John Simon, which did not include any Indian as its member. The result was a boycott of the commission by Indian political parties. Gandhi pushed through a resolution at the Calcutta Congress in December 1928 calling on the British government to grant India dominion status or face a new campaign of non-cooperation with complete independence for the country as its goal. Gandhi had not only moderated the views of younger men like Subhas Chandra Bose and Jawaharlal Nehru, who sought a demand for immediate independence, but also reduced his own call to a one year wait, instead of two. The British did not respond. On 31 December 1929, the flag of India was unfurled in Lahore. 26 January 1930 was celebrated as India's Independence Day by the Indian National Congress meeting in Lahore. This day was commemorated by almost every other Indian organization. Gandhi then launched a new satyagraha against the tax on salt in March 1930. This was highlighted by the famous Salt March to Dandi from 12 March to 6 April, where he marched 388 kilometres (241 miles) from Ahmedabad to Dandi, Gujarat to make salt himself. Thousands of Indians joined him on this march to the sea. This campaign was one of his most successful at upsetting British hold on India; Britain responded by imprisoning over 60,000 people.

The government, represented by Lord Edward Irwin, decided to negotiate with Gandhi. The Gandhi–Irwin Pact was signed in March 1931. The British Government agreed to free all political prisoners, in return for the suspension of the civil disobedience movement. Also as a result of the pact, Gandhi was invited to attend the Round Table Conference in London as the sole representative of the Indian National Congress. The conference was a disappointment to Gandhi and the nationalists, because it focused on the Indian princes and Indian minorities rather than on a transfer of power. Furthermore, Lord Irwin's successor, Lord Willingdon, began a new campaign of controlling and subduing the nationalist movement. Gandhi was again arrested, and the government tried to negate his influence by completely isolating him from his followers. But this tactic failed.

In 1932, through the campaigning of the Dalit leader B. R. Ambedkar, the government granted untouchables separate electorates under the new constitution. In protest, Gandhi embarked on a six-day fast in September 1932. The resulting public outcry successfully forced the government to adopt a more equitable arrangement via negotiations mediated by the Dalit cricketer turned political leader Palwankar Baloo. This was the start of a new campaign by Gandhi to improve the lives of the untouchables, whom he named Harijans, the children of God. On 8 May 1933, Gandhi began a 21-day fast of self-purification to help the Harijan movement. This new campaign was not universally embraced within the Dalit community, as prominent leader B. R. Ambedkar condemned Gandhi's use of the term *Harijans* as saying that Dalits were socially immature, and that privileged caste Indians played a paternalistic role. Ambedkar and his allies also felt Gandhi was undermining Dalit political rights. Gandhi, although born into the Vaishya caste, insisted that he was able to speak on behalf of Dalits, despite the presence of Dalit activists such as Ambedkar.

In the summer of 1934, three unsuccessful attempts were made on Gandhi's life.

When the Congress Party chose to contest elections and accept power under the Federation scheme, Gandhi resigned from party membership. He did not disagree with the party's move, but felt that if he resigned, his popularity with Indians would cease to stifle the party's membership, that actually varied from communists, socialists, trade unionists, students, religious conservatives, to those with pro-business convictions and that these various voices would get a chance to make themselves heard. Gandhi also wanted to avoid being a target for Raj propaganda by leading a party that had temporarily accepted political accommodation with the Raj.

Gandhi returned to active politics again in 1936, with the Nehru presidency and the Lucknow session of the Congress. Although Gandhi wanted a total focus on the task of winning independence and not speculation about India's future, he did not restrain the Congress from adopting socialism as its goal. Gandhi had a clash with Subhas Bose, who had been elected president in 1938. Their main points of contention were Bose's lack of commitment to democracy, and lack of faith in non-violence. Bose won his second term despite Gandhi's criticism, but left the Congress when the All-India leaders resigned en masse in protest of his abandonment of the principles introduced by Gandhi.

World War II and *Quit India*

World War II broke out in 1939 when Nazi Germany invaded Poland. Initially, Gandhi favoured offering "nonviolent moral support" to the British effort, but other Congressional leaders were offended by the unilateral inclusion of India in the war, without consultation of the people's representatives. All Congressmen resigned from office. After long deliberations, Gandhi declared that India could not be party to a war ostensibly being fought for democratic freedom, while that freedom was denied to India itself. As the war progressed, Gandhi intensified his demand for independence, drafting a resolution calling for the British to *Quit India*. This was Gandhi's and the Congress Party's most definitive revolt aimed at securing the British exit from India.

Gandhi was criticized by some Congress party members and other Indian political groups, both pro-British and anti-British. Some felt that not supporting Britain more in its life or death struggle against the evil of Nazism was unethical. Others felt that Gandhi's refusal for India to participate in the war was insufficient and more direct opposition should be taken, while Britain fought against Nazism yet continued to contradict itself by refusing to grant India Independence. *Quit India* became the most forceful movement in the history of the struggle, with mass arrests and violence on an unprecedented scale. Thousands of freedom fighters were killed or injured by police gunfire, and hundreds of thousands were arrested. Gandhi and his supporters made it clear they would not support the war effort unless India were granted immediate independence. He even clarified that this time the movement would not be stopped if individual acts of violence were committed, saying that the *"ordered anarchy"* around him was *"worse than real anarchy."* He called on all Congressmen and Indians to maintain discipline via ahimsa, and *Karo Ya Maro* ("Do or Die") in the cause of ultimate freedom.

Gandhi and the entire Congress Working Committee were arrested in Bombay by the British on 9 August 1942. Gandhi was held for two years in the Aga Khan Palace in Pune. It was here that Gandhi suffered two terrible blows in his personal life. His 50-year old secretary Mahadev Desai died of a heart attack 6 days later and his wife Kasturba died after 18 months imprisonment in 22 February 1944; six weeks later Gandhi suffered a severe malaria attack. He was released before the end of the war on 6 May 1944 because of his failing health and necessary surgery; the Raj did not want him to die in prison and enrage the nation. Although the Quit India movement had moderate success in its objective, the ruthless suppression of the movement brought order to India by the end of 1943. At the end of the war, the British gave clear indications that power would be transferred to Indian hands. At this point Gandhi called off the struggle, and around 100,000 political prisoners were released, including the Congress's leadership.

Freedom and Partition of India

As a rule, Gandhi was opposed to the concept of partition as it contradicted his vision of religious unity. Of the partition of India to create Pakistan, he wrote in *Harijan* on 6 October 1946:

[The demand for Pakistan] as put forth by the Moslem League is un-Islamic and I have not hesitated to call it sinful. Islam stands for unity and the brotherhood of mankind, not for disrupting the oneness of the human family. Therefore, those who want to divide India into possibly warring groups are enemies alike of India and Islam. They may cut me into pieces but they cannot make me subscribe to something which I consider to be wrong [...] we must not cease to aspire, in spite of [the] wild talk, to befriend all Moslems and hold them fast as prisoners of our love.

However, as Homer Jack notes of Gandhi's long correspondence with Jinnah on the topic of Pakistan: "Although Gandhi was personally opposed to the partition of India, he proposed an agreement...which provided that the Congress and the Moslem League would cooperate to attain independence under a provisional government, after which the question of partition would be decided by a plebiscite in the districts having a Moslem majority."

These dual positions on the topic of the partition of India opened Gandhi up to criticism from both Hindus and Muslims. Muhammad Ali Jinnah and contemporary Pakistanis condemned Gandhi for undermining Muslim political rights. Vinayak Damodar Savarkar and his allies accused him of politically appeasing Muslims while turning a blind eye to their atrocities against Hindus, and for allowing the creation of Pakistan, despite having publicly declared that "before partitioning India, my body will have to be cut into two pieces".

This continues to be politically contentious: some, like Pakistani-American historian Ayesha Jalal argue that Gandhi and the Congress's unwillingness to share power with the Muslim League hastened partition; others, like Hindu nationalist politician Pravin Togadia indicated that excessive weakness on Gandhi's part led to the division of India.

Gandhi also expressed his dislike for partition during the late 1930s in response to the topic of the partition of Palestine to create Israel. He stated in *Harijan* on 26 October 1938:

> Several letters have been received by me asking me to declare my views about the Arab-Jew question in Palestine and persecution of the Jews in Germany. It is not without hesitation that I venture to offer my views on this very difficult question. My sympathies are all with the Jews. I have known them intimately in South Africa. Some of them became life-long companions. Through these friends I came to learn much of their age-long persecution. They have been the untouchables of Christianity [...] But my sympathy does not blind me to the requirements of justice. The cry for the national home for the Jews does not make much appeal to me. The sanction for it is sought in the Bible and the tenacity with which the Jews have hankered after return to Palestine. Why should they not, like other peoples of the earth, make that country their home where they are born and where they earn their livelihood? Palestine belongs to the Arabs in the same sense that England belongs to the English or France to the French. It is wrong and inhuman to impose the Jews on the Arabs. What is going on in Palestine today cannot be justified by any moral code of conduct.

Gandhi advised the Congress to reject the proposals the British Cabinet Mission offered in 1946, as he was deeply suspicious of the *grouping* proposed for Muslim-majority states—Gandhi viewed this as a precursor to partition. However, this became one of the few times the Congress broke from Gandhi's advice (though not his leadership), as Nehru and Patel knew that if the Congress did not approve the plan, the control of government would pass to the Muslim League. Between 1946 and 1948, over 5,000 people were killed in violence. Gandhi was vehemently opposed to any plan that partitioned India into two separate countries. But an overwhelming majority of Muslims living in India, alongside Hindus and Sikhs, favoured partition. Additionally Muhammad Ali Jinnah, the leader of the Muslim League, commanded widespread support in West Punjab, Sindh, North-West Frontier Province and East Bengal. The partition plan was approved by the Congress leadership as the only way to prevent a wide-scale Hindu-Muslim civil war. Congress leaders knew that Gandhi would viscerally oppose partition, and it was impossible for the Congress to go ahead without his agreement, for Gandhi's support in the party and throughout India was strong. Gandhi's closest colleagues had accepted partition as the best way out, and Sardar Patel endeavoured to convince Gandhi that it was the only way to avoid civil war. A devastated Gandhi gave his assent.

He conducted extensive dialogue with Muslim and Hindu community leaders, working to cool passions in northern India, as well as in Bengal. Despite the Indo-Pakistani War of 1947, he was troubled when the Government decided to deny Pakistan the 55 crores (550 million Indian rupees) due as per agreements made by the Partition Council. Leaders like Sardar Patel feared that Pakistan would use the money to bankroll the war against India. Gandhi was also devastated when demands resurged for all Muslims to be deported to Pakistan, and when Muslim and Hindu leaders expressed frustration and an inability to come to terms with one another. Gandhi's arrival in Delhi, turned out to an important intervention in ending the rioting, he even visited Muslims *mohallas* to restore faith of the Muslim populace. He launched his last fast-unto-death on January 12, 1948, in Delhi, asking that all communal violence be ended once and for all, Muslims homes be restored to them and that the payment of 550 million rupees be made to Pakistan. Gandhi feared that instability and insecurity in Pakistan would increase their anger against India, and violence would spread across the borders. He further feared that Hindus and Muslims would renew their enmity and that this would precipitate open civil war. After emotional debates with his life-long colleagues, Gandhi refused to budge, and the Government rescinded its policy and made the payment to Pakistan. Hindu, Muslim and Sikh community leaders, including the Rashtriya Swayamsevak Sangh and Hindu Mahasabha assured him that they would renounce violence and call for peace. Gandhi thus broke his fast by sipping orange juice.

Assassination

On 30 January 1948, Gandhi was shot while having his nightly public walk on the grounds of the *Birla Bhavan* (Birla House) in New Delhi. The assassin, Nathuram Godse, was a Hindu nationalist with links to the extremist Hindu Mahasabha, who held Gandhi responsible for weakening India by insisting upon a payment to

Pakistan. Godse and his co-conspirator Narayan Apte were later tried and convicted; they were executed on 15 November 1949. Gandhi's memorial (or *Samâdhi*) at Râj Ghât, New Delhi, bears the epigraph "Hç Ram", which may be translated as "Oh God". These are widely believed to be Gandhi's last words after he was shot, though the veracity of this statement has been disputed. Jawaharlal Nehru addressed the nation through radio:

"Friends and comrades, the light has gone out of our lives, and there is darkness everywhere, and I do not quite know what to tell you or how to say it. Our beloved leader, Bapu as we called him, the father of the nation, is no more. Perhaps I am wrong to say that; nevertheless, we will not see him again, as we have seen him for these many years, we will not run to him for advice or seek solace from him, and that is a terrible blow, not only for me, but for millions and millions in this country."-Jawaharlal Nehru's address to Gandhi

Gandhi's ashes were poured into urns which were sent across India for memorial services. Most were immersed at the Sangam at Allahabad on 12 February 1948 but some were secretly taken away. In 1997, Tushar Gandhi immersed the contents of one urn, found in a bank vault and reclaimed through the courts, at the Sangam at Allahabad.

On 30 January 2008 the contents of another urn were immersed at Girgaum Chowpatty by the family after a Dubai-based businessman had sent it to a Mumbai museum. Another urn has ended up in a palace of the Aga Khan in Pune (where he had been imprisoned from 1942 to 1944) and another in the Self-Realization Fellowship Lake Shrine in Los Angeles. The family is aware that these enshrined ashes could be misused for political purposes but does not want to have them removed because it would entail breaking the shrines.

Gandhi's Principles

Truth

Gandhi dedicated his life to the wider purpose of discovering truth, or *Satya*. He tried to achieve this by learning from his own mistakes and conducting experiments on himself. He called his autobiography *The Story of My Experiments with Truth*.

Gandhi stated that the most important battle to fight was overcoming his own demons, fears, and insecurities. Gandhi summarized his beliefs first when he said "God is Truth". He would later change this statement to "Truth is God". Thus, *Satya* (Truth) in Gandhi's philosophy is "God".

Nonviolence

Although Mahatama Gandhi was not the originator of the principle of non-violence, he was the first to apply it in the political field on a huge scale. The concept of nonviolence (*ahimsa*) and nonresistance has a long history in Indian religious thought and has had many revivals in Hindu, Buddhist, Jain, Jewish and Christian contexts. Gandhi explains his philosophy and way of life in his autobiography *The Story of My Experiments with Truth*. He was quoted as saying:

"When I despair, I remember that all through history the way of truth and love has always won. There have been tyrants and murderers and for a time they seem invincible, but in the end, they always fall — think of it, always."

"What difference does it make to the dead, the orphans, and the homeless, whether the mad destruction is wrought under the name of totalitarianism or the holy name of liberty and democracy?"

"An eye for an eye makes the whole world blind."

"There are many causes that I am prepared to die for but no causes that I am prepared to kill for."

In applying these principles, Gandhi did not balk from taking them to their most logical extremes in envisioning a world where even government, police and armies were nonviolent. The quotations below are from the book "For Pacifists."

The science of war leads one to dictatorship, pure and simple. The science of non-violence alone can lead one to pure democracy...Power based on love is thousand times more effective and permanent than power derived from fear of punishment....It is a blasphemy to say non-violence can be practiced only by individuals and never by nations which are composed of individuals...The nearest approach to purest anarchy would be a democracy based on non-violence...A society organized and run on the basis of complete non-violence would be the purest anarchy. I have conceded that even in a nonviolent state a police force may be necessary...Police ranks will be composed of believers in non-violence. The people will instinctively render them every help and through mutual cooperation they will easily deal with the ever decreasing disturbances...Violent quarrels between labour and capital and strikes will be few and far between in a nonviolent state because the influence of the nonviolent majority will be great as to respect the principle elements in society. Similarly, there will be no room for communal disturbances....

A nonviolent army acts unlike armed men, as well in times of peace as in times of disturbances. Theirs will be the duty of bringing warring communities together, carrying peace propaganda, engaging in activities that would bring and keep them in touch with every single person in their parish or division. Such an army should be ready to cope with any emergency, and in order to still the frenzy of mobs should risk their lives in numbers sufficient for that purpose....Satyagraha (truth-force) brigades can be organized in every village and every block of buildings in the cities. [If the nonviolent society is attacked from without] there are two ways open to non-violence. To yield possession, but non-cooperate with the aggressor...prefer death to submission. The second way would be nonviolent resistance by the people who have been trained in the nonviolent way...The unexpected spectacle of endless rows upon rows of men and women simply dying rather than surrender to the will of an aggressor must ultimately melt him and his soldiery...A nation or group which has made non-violence its final policy cannot be subjected to slavery even by the atom bomb.... The level of non-violence in that nation, if that even happily comes to pass, will naturally have risen so high as to command universal respect.

In accordance with these views, in 1940, when invasion of the British Isles by Nazi Germany looked imminent, Gandhi offered the following advice to the British people (*Non-Violence in Peace and War*):

"I would like you to lay down the arms you have as being useless for saving you or humanity. You will invite Herr Hitler and Signor Mussolini to take what they want of the countries you call your possessions...If these gentlemen choose to occupy your homes, you will vacate them. If they do not give you free passage out, you will allow yourselves, man, woman, and child, to be slaughtered, but you will refuse to owe allegiance to them."

In a post-war interview in 1946, he offered a view at an even further extreme:

"Hitler," Gandhi said, "killed five million Jews. It is the greatest crime of our time. But the Jews should have offered themselves to the butcher's knife. They should have thrown themselves into the sea from cliffs… It would have aroused the world and the people of Germany… As it is they succumbed anyway in their millions."

However, Gandhi was aware that this level of nonviolence required incredible faith and courage, which he realized not everyone possessed. He therefore advised that everyone need not keep to nonviolence, especially if it were used as a cover for cowardice:

"Gandhi guarded against attracting to his *satyagraha* movement those who feared to take up arms or felt themselves incapable of resistance. 'I do believe,' he wrote, 'that where there is only a choice between cowardice and violence, I would advise violence.'"

"At every meeting I repeated the warning that unless they felt that in non-violence they had come into possession of a force infinitely superior to the one they had and in the use of which they were adept, they should have nothing to do with non-violence and resume the arms they possessed before. It must never be said of the Khudai Khidmatgars that once so brave, they had become or been made cowards under Badshah Khan's influence. Their bravery consisted not in being good marksmen but in defying death and being ever ready to bare their breasts to the bullets."

Gandhi also came under some political fire for his criticism of those who attempted to achieve independence through more violent means. His refusal to protest against the hanging of Bhagat Singh, Sukhdev, Udham Singh and Rajguru were sources of condemnation among some parties.

Of this criticism, Gandhi stated, "There was a time when people listened to me because I showed them how to give fight to the British without arms when they had no arms...but today I am told that my non-violence can be of no avail against the [Hindu–Moslem riots] and, therefore, people should arm themselves for self-defence."

Winston Churchill said that it was "nauseating" to see Gandhi, "a seditious Middle Temple lawyer, now posing as a fakir of a type well-known in the Middle East, striding half-naked up the steps of the Vice-regal palace... to parley on equal terms with the representative of the King-Emperor".

He continued this argument in a number of articles reprinted in Homer Jack's *The Gandhi Reader: A Sourcebook of His Life and Writings*. In the first, "Zionism and Anti-Semitism," written in 1938, Gandhi commented upon the 1930s persecution of the Jews in Germany within the context of Satyagraha. He offered non-violence as a method of combating the difficulties Jews faced in Germany, stating,

If I were a Jew and were born in Germany and earned my livelihood there, I would claim Germany as my home even as the tallest Gentile German might, and challenge him to shoot me or cast me in the dungeon; I would refuse to be expelled or to submit to discriminating treatment. And for doing this I should not wait for the fellow Jews to join me in civil resistance, but would have confidence that in the end the rest were bound to follow my example. If one Jew or all the Jews were to accept the prescription here offered, he or they cannot be worse off than now. And suffering voluntarily undergone will bring them an inner strength and joy...the calculated violence of Hitler may even result in a general massacre of the Jews by way of his first answer to the declaration of such hostilities. But if the Jewish mind could be prepared for voluntary suffering, even the massacre I have imagined could be turned into a day of thanksgiving and joy that Jehovah had wrought deliverance of the race even at the hands of the tyrant. For to the God-fearing, death has no terror.

Gandhi was highly criticized for these statements and responded in the article "Questions on the Jews" with "Friends have sent me two newspaper cuttings criticizing my appeal to the Jews. The two critics suggest that in presenting non-violence to the Jews as a remedy against the wrong done to them, I have suggested nothing new...what I have pleaded for is renunciation of violence of the heart and consequent active exercise of the force generated by the great renunciation.

Gandhi's statements regarding Jews facing the impending Holocaust have attracted criticism from a number of commentators. Martin Buber wrote a sharply critical open letter to Gandhi on 24 February 1939. Buber asserted that the comparison between British treatment of Indian subjects and Nazi treatment of Jews was inappropriate; moreover, he noted that when Indians were the victims of persecution, Gandhi had, on occasion, supported the use of force.

Gandhi commented upon the 1930s persecution of the Jews in Germany within the context of Satyagraha. In the November 1938 article on the Nazi persecution of the Jews quoted above, he offered non-violence as a solution:

The German persecution of the Jews seems to have no parallel in history. The tyrants of old never went so mad as Hitler seems to have gone. And he is doing it with religious zeal. For he is propounding a new religion of exclusive and militant nationalism in the name of which any inhumanity becomes an act of humanity to be rewarded here and hereafter.

The crime of an obviously mad but intrepid youth is being visited upon his whole race with unbelievable ferocity. If there ever could be a justifiable war in the name of and for humanity, a war against Germany, to prevent the wanton persecution of a whole race, would be completely justified. But I do not believe in any war. A discussion of the pros and cons of such a war is therefore outside my horizon or province. But if there can be no war against Germany, even for such a crime as is being committed against the Jews, surely there can be no alliance with Germany. How can there be alliance between a nation which claims to stand for justice and democracy and one which is the declared enemy of both?"

Vegetarianism

As a young child, Gandhi experimented with meat-eating. This was due partially to his inherent curiosity as well as his rather persuasive peer and friend Sheikh Mehtab. The idea of vegetarianism is deeply ingrained in Hindu and Jain traditions in India, and, in his native land of Gujarat, most Hindus are vegetarian and so are almost all Jains. The Gandhi family was no exception. Before leaving for his studies in London, Gandhi made a promise to his mother, Putlibai and his uncle, Becharji Swami that he would abstain from eating meat, taking alcohol, and engaging in promiscuity. He held fast to his promise and gained more than a diet: he gained a basis for his life-long philosophies. As Gandhi grew into adulthood, he became a strict vegetarian. He wrote the book *The Moral Basis of Vegetarianism* and several articles on the subject, some of which were published in the London Vegetarian Society's publication, *The Vegetarian*. During this period, the young Gandhi became inspired by many great minds and was befriended by the chairman of the London Vegetarian Society, Dr. Josiah Oldfield.

Having also read and admired the work of Henry Stephens Salt, the young Mohandas met and often corresponded with the vegetarian campaigner. Gandhi spent much time advocating vegetarianism during and after his time in London. To Gandhi, a vegetarian diet would not only satisfy the requirements of the body, it would also serve an economic purpose as meat was, and still is, generally more expensive than grains, vegetables, and fruits. Also, many Indians of the time struggled with low income, thus vegetarianism was seen not only as a spiritual practice but also a practical one. He abstained from eating for long periods, using fasting as a form of political protest. He refused to eat until his death or his demands were met. It was noted in his autobiography that vegetarianism was the beginning of his deep commitment to Brahmacharya; without total control of the palate, his success in Bramacharya would likely falter.

For much of his adult life, Gandhi was a fruitarian, stating in his autobiography, "I decided to live on a pure fruit diet, and that too composed of the cheapest fruit possible... Raw groundnuts, bananas, dates, lemons and olive oil composed our usual diet." However, late in life he broke his discipline and started taking goat's milk on the advice of his doctor. This lapse of discipline bothered him to his dying day, and he wrote, "The memory of this action even now rankles my breast and fills me with remorse, and I am constantly thinking how to give up goat's milk." He never took dairy products obtained from cows because of his view initially that milk is not the natural diet of man, disgust for cow blowing, and, specifically, because of a vow to his late mother.

Brahmacharya

When Gandhi was 16 his father became very ill. Being very devoted to his parents, he attended to his father at all times during his illness. However, one night, Gandhi's uncle came to relieve Gandhi for a while. He retired to his bedroom where carnal desires overcame him and he made love to his wife. Shortly afterward a servant came to report that Gandhi's father had just died. Gandhi felt tremendous guilt and never could forgive himself. He came to refer to this event as "double shame." The incident had significant influence in Gandhi becoming celibate at the age of 36, while still married.

This decision was deeply influenced by the philosophy of Brahmacharya — spiritual and practical purity — largely associated with celibacy and asceticism. Gandhi saw Brahmacharya as a means of becoming close with God and as a primary foundation for self realization. In his autobiography he tells of his battle against lustful urges and fits of jealousy with his childhood bride, Kasturba. He felt it his personal obligation to remain celibate so that he could learn to love, rather than lust. For Gandhi, Brahmacharya meant "control of the senses in thought, word and deed.".

Towards the end of his life, it became public knowledge that Gandhi had been sharing his bed for a number of years with young women. He explained that he did this for bodily warmth at night and termed his actions as "nature cure". Later in his life he started experimenting with Brahmacharya in order to test his self control. His letter to Birla in April, 1945 referring to 'women or girls who have been naked with me' indicates that several women were part of his experiments. He wrote five editorials in *Harijan* discussing the practice of Brahmacharya.

As part of these experiments, he initially slept with his women associates in the same room but at a distance. Afterwards he started to lie in the same bed with his women disciples and later took to sleeping naked alongside them. According to Gandhi active-celibacy meant perfect self control in the presence of opposite sex. Gandhi conducted his experiments with a number of women such as Abha, the sixteen year old wife of his grandnephew Kanu Gandhi. Gandhi acknowledged "that this experiment is very dangerous indeed", but thought "that it was capable of yielding great results". His nineteen year old grandniece, Manu Gandhi, too was part of his experiments. Gandhi had earlier written to her father, Jaisukhlal Gandhi, that Manu had started to share his bed so that he may "correct her sleeping posture". Gandhi saw himself as a mother to these women and would refer to Abha and Manu as "my walking sticks".

Gandhi called Sarladevi, a married woman with children and a devout follower, his "spiritual wife". He later said that he had come close to having sexual relations with her. He had told a correspondent in March, 1945 that "sleeping together came with my taking up of bramhacharya or even before that"; he said he had experimented with his wife "but that was not enough". Gandhi felt satisfied with his experiments and wrote to Manu that "I have successfully practiced the eleven vows taken by me. This is the culmination of my striving for last thirty six years. In this yajna I got a glimpse of the ideal truth and purity for which I have been striving".

Gandhi had to take criticism for his experiments by many of his followers and opponents. His stenographer, R. P. Parasuram, resigned when he saw Gandhi sleeping naked with Manu. Gandhi insisted that he never felt aroused while he slept beside her, or with Sushila or Abha. "I am sorry" Gandhi said to Parasuram, "you are at liberty to leave me today." Nirmal Kumar Bose, another close associate of Gandhi, parted company with him in April, 1947 post Gandhi's tour of Noakhali, where some sort of altercation had taken place between Gandhi and Sushila Nayar in his bedroom at midnight that caused Gandhi to slap his forehead. Bose had stated that the nature of his experiments in bramhacharya still remained unknown and unstated.

N. K. Bose, who stayed close to Gandhi during his Noakhali tour, testified that "there was no immorality on part of Gandhi. Moreover Gandhi tried to conquer the feeling of sex by consciously endeavouring to convert himself into a mother of those who were under his case, whether men or women". Dattatreya Balkrishna Kalelkar, a revolutionary turned disciple of Gandhi, used to say that Gandhi's "relationships with women were, from beginning to end, as pure as mother's milk"..

Simplicity

Gandhi earnestly believed that a person involved in public service should lead a simple life. He first displayed this principle when he gave up wearing western-style clothing, which he associated with wealth and success. When he returned to India he renounced the western lifestyle he lead in South Africa, where he had enjoyed a successful legal practice.

Gandhi dressed to be accepted by the poorest person in India, advocating the use of homespun cloth (*khadi*). He and his followers adopted the practice of weaving their own clothes from thread they themselves spun, and encouraged others to do so. While Indian workers were often idle due to unemployment, they had often bought their clothing from industrial manufacturers owned by British interests.

It was Gandhi's view that if Indians made their own clothes, it would deal an economic blow to the British establishment in India. Consequently, the spinning wheel was later incorporated into the flag of the Indian National Congress. He subsequently wore a dhoti for the rest of his life to express the simplicity of his life.

The practice of giving up unnecessary expenditure, embracing a simple lifestyle and washing his own clothes, Gandhi called "reducing himself to zero". On one occasion he returned the gifts bestowed to him from the Natals for his diligent service to the community.

Gandhi spent one day of each week in silence. He believed that abstaining from speaking brought him inner peace. This influence was drawn from the Hindu principles of *mauna* and *shanti*. On such days he communicated with others by writing on paper. For three and a half years, from the age of 37, Gandhi refused to read newspapers, claiming that the tumultuous state of world affairs caused him more confusion than his own inner unrest.

After reading John Ruskin's *Unto This Last,* he decided to change his lifestyle and create a commune called *Phoenix Settlement.*

Faith

Gandhi was born a Hindu and practised Hinduism all his life, deriving most of his principles from Hinduism. As a common Hindu, he believed all religions to be equal, and rejected all efforts to convert him to a different faith. He was an avid theologian and read extensively about all major religions. He had the following to say about Hinduism:

Hinduism as I know it entirely satisfies my soul, fills my whole being...When doubts haunt me, when disappointments stare me in the face, and when I see not one ray of light on the horizon, I turn to the *Bhagavad Gita,* and find a verse to comfort me; and I immediately begin to smile in the midst of overwhelming sorrow. My life has been full of tragedies and if they have not left any visible and indelible effect on me, I owe it to the teachings of the *Bhagavad Gita.*

Gandhi wrote a commentary on the *Bhagavad Gita* in Gujarati. The Gujarati manuscript was translated into English by Mahadev Desai, who provided an additional introduction and commentary. It was published with a Foreword by Gandhi in 1946.

Gandhi believed that at the core of every religion was truth and love (compassion, nonviolence and the Golden Rule). He also questioned what he saw as hypocrisy, malpractices, and dogma in all religions, including his own, and he was a tireless advocate for social reform in religion. Some of his comments on various religions are:

Thus if I could not accept Christianity either as a perfect, or the greatest religion, neither was I then convinced of Hinduism being such. Hindu defects were pressingly visible to me. If untouchability could be a part of Hinduism, it could but be a rotten part or an excrescence. I could not understand the *raison d'être* of a multitude of sects and castes. What was the meaning of saying that the Vedas were the inspired Word of God? If they were inspired, why not also the Bible and the Koran? As Christian friends were endeavouring to convert me, so were Muslim friends. Abdullah Seth had kept on inducing me to study Islam, and of course he had always something to say regarding its beauty. – Gandhi's autobiography

As soon as we lose the moral basis, we cease to be religious. There is no such thing as religion over-riding morality. Man, for instance, cannot be untruthful, cruel or incontinent and claim to have God on his side.

The sayings of Muhammad are a treasure of wisdom, not only for Muslims but for all of mankind.

I like your Christ, I do not like your Christians.

Later in his life, when he was asked whether he was a Hindu, he replied, "Yes I am. I am also a Christian, a Muslim, a Buddhist and a Jew."

In spite of their deep reverence to each other, Gandhi and Rabindranath Tagore engaged in protracted debates more than once. These debates exemplify the philosophical differences between the two most famous Indians at the time. On 15 January 1934, an earthquake hit Bihar and caused extensive damage and loss of life. Gandhi maintained this was because of the sin committed by upper caste Hindus by not letting untouchables in their temples (Gandhi was committed to the cause of improving the fate of untouchables, referring to them as Harijans, people of Krishna). Tagore vehemently opposed Gandhi's stance, maintaining that an earthquake can only be caused by natural forces, not moral reasons, however repugnant the practice of untouchability may be.

Gandhi took a keen interest in theosophy. He empathized with theosophy's message of "universal brotherhood and consequent toleration", as he put it in 1926.

Swaraj

Gandhi was a self-described philosophical anarchist, and his vision of India meant India without an underlying government. He once said that "the ideally nonviolent state would be an ordered anarchy." While political systems are largely hierarchical, with each layer of authority from the individual to the central government have increasing levels of authority over the layer below, Gandhi believed that society should be the exact opposite, where nothing is done without the consent of anyone, down to the individual. His idea was that true self-rule in a country means that every person rules his or herself and that there is no state which enforces laws upon the people. This would be achieved over time with nonviolent conflict mediation, as power is divested from layers of hierarchical authorities, ultimately to the individual, which would come to embody the ethic of nonviolence. Rather than a system where rights are enforced by a higher authority, people are self-governed by mutual responsibilities. On returning from South Africa, when Gandhi received a letter asking for his participation in writing a world charter for human rights, he responded saying, "in my experience, it is far more important to have a charter for human duties." A free India for him meant the existence of thousands of self sufficient small communities (an idea possibly from Tolstoy) who rule themselves without hindering others. It did not mean merely transferring a British established administrative structure into Indian hands which he said was just *making Hindustan into Englistan*. He wanted to ultimately dissolve the Congress Party after independence and establish a system of direct democracy in India, having no faith in the British styled parliamentary system.

Literary works

Young India, A Journal Published by Gandhi

Gandhi was a prolific writer. For decades he edited several newspapers including *Harijan* in Gujarati, Hindi and English; *Indian Opinion* while in South Africa and, *Young India*, in English, and Navajivan, a Gujarati monthly, on his return to India. Later Navajivan was also published in Hindi. In addition, he wrote letters almost every day to individuals and newspapers.

Gandhi also wrote several books including his autobiography, *An Autobiography of My Experiments with Truth*, *Satyagraha in South Africa* about his struggle there, *Hind Swaraj or Indian Home Rule*, a political pamphlet, and a paraphrase in Gujarati of John Ruskin's *Unto This Last*. This last essay can be considered his program on economics. He also wrote extensively on vegetarianism, diet and health, religion, social reforms, etc. Gandhi usually wrote in Gujarati, though he also revised the Hindi and English translations of his books. Gandhi's complete works were published by the Indian government under the name *The Collected Works of Mahatma Gandhi* in the 1960s. The writings comprise about 50,000 pages published in about a hundred volumes. In 2000, a revised edition of the complete works sparked a controversy, as Gandhian followers argue that the government incorporated the changes for political purposes. The Indian government later withdrew the revised edition.

Legacy and Depictions in Popular Culture

The word *Mahatma,* while often mistaken for Gandhi's given name in the West, is taken from the Sanskrit words *maha* meaning *Great* and *atma* meaning *Soul.* Rabindranath Tagore is said to have accorded or popularised the title for Gandhi. In his autobiography, Gandhi nevertheless explains that he never valued the title, and was often pained by it.

Followers and Influence

Gandhi influenced important leaders and political movements. Leaders of the civil rights movement in the United States, including Martin Luther King and James Lawson, drew from the writings of Gandhi in the development of their own theories about non-violence. Anti-apartheid activist and former President of South Africa, Nelson Mandela, was inspired by Gandhi. Others include Khan Abdul Ghaffar Khan, Steve Biko, Aung San Suu Kyi and Philippine opposition leader during the dictatorship of Ferdinand Marcos, Benigno Aquino, Jr.

"Christ gave us the goals and Mahatma Gandhi the tactics."-Martin Luther King Jr, 1955

Gandhi's life and teachings inspired many who specifically referred to Gandhi as their mentor or who dedicated their lives to spreading Gandhi's ideas. In Europe, Romain Rolland was the first to discuss Gandhi in his 1924 book *Mahatma Gandhi,* and Brazilian anarchist and feminist Maria Lacerda de Moura wrote about Gandhi in her work on pacifism. In 1931, notable European physicist Albert Einstein exchanged written letters with Gandhi, and called him "a role model for the generations to come" in a later writing about him. Lanza del Vasto went to India in 1936 intending to live with Gandhi; he later returned to Europe to spread Gandhi's philosophy and founded the Community of the Ark in 1948 (modelled after Gandhi's ashrams). Madeleine Slade (known as "Mirabehn") was the daughter of a British admiral who spent much of her adult life in India as a devotee of Gandhi.

In addition, the British musician John Lennon referred to Gandhi when discussing his views on non-violence. At the Cannes Lions International Advertising Festival in 2007, former U.S. Vice-President and environmentalist Al Gore spoke of Gandhi's influence on him. Finally, prior to becoming President of the United States, then-Senator Barack Obama noted that:

Throughout my life, I have always looked to Mahatma Gandhi as an inspiration, because he embodies the kind of transformational change that can be made when ordinary people come together to do extraordinary things. That is why his portrait hangs in my Senate office: to remind me that real results will come not just from Washington – they will come from the people.

Obama at the Wakefield High School speech in Sept 2009, said that his biggest inspiration came from Mahatma Gandhi. It was when a question posed on him as 'who was the one person, dead or live, that he would choose to dine with?' and his quick reply was 'Gandhi!'. He continued and said that-"He's somebody I find a lot of inspiration in. He inspired Dr. King with his message of nonviolence. He ended up doing so much and changed the world just by the power of his ethics".

National Holidays

Gandhi's birthday, 2 October, is a national holiday in India, Gandhi Jayanti. On 15 June 2007, it was announced that the "United Nations General Assembly" has "unanimously adopted" a resolution declaring 2 October as "the International Day of Non-Violence." India observes January 30, the day of his assassination, as Martyr's Day, to commemorate those who gave up their lives in service of the Indian nation.

On 30 January every year, on the anniversary of the death of Mahatma Gandhi, in schools of many countries is observed the School Day of Non-violence and Peace (DENIP), founded in Spain in 1964. In countries with a Southern Hemisphere school calendar, it can be observed on 30 March or thereabouts.

Awards

Time magazine named Gandhi the Man of the Year in 1930. Gandhi was also the runner-up to Albert Einstein as "Person of the Century" at the end of 1999. Time Magazine named The 14th Dalai Lama, Lech Wa³êsa, Dr. Martin Luther King, Jr., Cesar Chavez, Aung San Suu Kyi, Benigno Aquino, Jr., Desmond Tutu, and Nelson Mandela as *Children of Gandhi* and his spiritual heirs to non-violence. The Government of India awards the annual Mahatma Gandhi Peace Prize to distinguished social workers, world leaders and citizens. Nelson Mandela, the leader of South Africa's struggle to eradicate racial discrimination and segregation, is a prominent non-Indian recipient.

Gandhi never received the Nobel Peace Prize, although he was nominated five times between 1937 and 1948, including the first-ever nomination by the American Friends Service Committee, though he made the short list only twice, in 1937 and 1947. Decades later, the Nobel Committee publicly declared its regret for the omission, and admitted to deeply divided nationalistic opinion denying the award. Gandhi was nominated in 1948 but was assassinated before nominations closed. That year, the committee chose not to award the peace prize stating that "there was no suitable living candidate" and later research shows that the possibility of awarding the prize posthumously to Gandhi was discussed and that the reference to no suitable living candidate was to Gandhi. When the 14th Dalai Lama was awarded the Prize in 1989, the chairman of the committee said that this was "in part a tribute to the memory of Mahatma Gandhi."

Film and Literature

Mahatma Gandhi has been portrayed in film, literature, and in the theatre. Ben Kingsley portrayed Gandhi in the 1982 film *Gandhi.* Gandhi is also a central theme in the 2006 Bollywood film *Lage Raho Munna Bhai.* The 2007 film, *Gandhi, My Father* explores the relationship between Gandhi and his son Harilal. The 1996 film, *The Making of the Mahatma,* documents Gandhi's 21 years in South Africa.

Several biographers have undertaken the task of describing Gandhi's life. Among them are: D. G. Tendulkar with his *Mahatma.*

Life of Mohandas Karamchand Gandhi in eight volumes, and Pyarelal and Sushila Nayar with their *Mahatma Gandhi* in 10 volumes.

Rise of Gandhi

Rise to Power

"The ancient texts are unclear. It appears we were invaded by a race that was more powerful than us. We called on the gods for protection, and they came to our aid in the form of a stick figure, providing us with the knowledge we needed to convert our small children to weapons. We defeated the threat, and, empowered by our victory, we gradually became conquerors of other ethnicities and civilizations" ~ Yann Martel on The Life of Pi.

Before the British conquered India, the country was a peaceful utopia, ruled by a mandate from the masses, but afterwards India became little more than a large factory for producing war machines for the greedy white bastards. One day, while rooting through a dumpster for some needles, a little boy discovered a grimy copy of "Das Kapital" by Karl Marx. Fascinated by the author's large vocabulary and bushy beard, the young Gandhi decided to work for the good of his people and become their leader against the British.

"They're not so tough! Look at their teeth!"

Gandhi on the British

Sadly, the Indian people were loath to leave their crack houses and kitten dens, and publicly humiliated by insulting the young man's loincloth (a deadly insult, in those days.) Mad with rage, Gandhi swore that one day, he would become king of the Indians. He quickly organized a resistance front, Male Indian Liberation Front, or M.I.L.F. These youths, especially known for the pink banana hammocks they wore, were famous for opposing British parliament by blocking bills and acts such as the Child Molesting ban of 1934 and the Anti-Baby Seal Clubbing Act of 1939. British lawmakers, politicians, military officers, government workers, workers, teachers, students, citizens, men, women, children, babies, pets and other barmy British bastards were the subject of endless pranks, jokes, beatings and surprise sex. Gandhi gloated as his political opponents lost power overnight or became pregnant, even while he gained power.

A Changing Regime

Orignially, Gandhi's rise to power was due to his best mate Adolf Hitler during World War II. Once Gandhi was at the top he deserted Hitler and left him in such a horny state that he was aroused but yet angry, searching for grief. This caused millions of Jews to die, cheers Gandhi. Anyway, Gandhi's powers were proved when he drastically healed a young boy with a disastrous odour problem, excessive cellulite and a very good looking mother. Which primarily was the main reason after she mysteriously disappeared September 1997 (Gandhi isn't dead, I heard it on the radio). The boy was healed of the cellulite disaster but the body odour problem didn't seem to disappear, this was Gandhi's death. UL.

"We are an India ruled by the majority! An India ruled by a new Constitution! An India of laws, not of politicians! An India devoted to the preservation of a just society. Of a safe and secure society! We are an India that will stand ten thousand years!"

The more political and executive power Gandhi gained, the more his sanity seemed to suffer. A combination of his Epicurean lifestyle, kitten huffing, a low-carbon diet and his tendency to inhale exhaust fumes from the tailpipe on his car through a rubber hose resulted in extreme brain damage. Gandhi would accuse members of his own party of crimes ranging from "looking funny" to "breathing too heavily," and were promptly executed by having battery acid pumped up their anuses. Gandhi outlawed many species of animal, especially the Sciuridae, Cricetidae and Castor families, declaring them to be "disgusting, perverted and monstrous creatures" and called upon the League of Nations to accept his "final solution to the Woodland Question." Gandhi's hatred was not limited to small animals, however. When a bank of cumulus clouds massed near Gandhi's palace in New Delhi, he accused them of being "Enemies of the People" and ordered them to be shot, resulting in what is now known as the Cloud Wars.

2

Gandhi and Satyagraha

Mahatma Gandhi's entry and meteoric rise in the Indian political scenario following his return from South Africa in 1918, has been variously equated with the emergence of a guiding light to a breath of fresh air. Indian national Congress was the single most popular party, spearheading India's war for independence when Gandhi returned, having led two successful revolutions in South Africa. They were conducted on the lines of Satyagraha, Gandhi's personal mode of nonviolent resistance. Indian National Congress (INC), at that point was dominated by the combative policies of the extremists. Bal Gangadhar Tilak, Lala Lajpat Rai and Bipin Chandra Pal were the chief propagators of these extremist tendencies within the ranks of the INC. Gandhi's modes and ideologies were markedly different, and were slow to gain acceptance. However, he soon became a member of the Indian National Congress, and then embarked in a nationwide journey under the command and wish of Sri Gopal Krishna Gokhale, his political mentor. What he saw reaffirmed in his mind his already firm faith in the ideals of satyagraha. The Home Rule movement under Tilak and Annie Besant were far from successful, and Gandhi knew that no mode of armed revolution could make India free from the clutches of the British rule.

Satyagraha at Champaran and Kheda

Gandhi's political career took a head start when he went to lead satyagraha against the indigo merchants at Champaran in Bihar. He raised his voice against the unbearable exploitation of the indigo farmers of the region. His methods, as always, were based on non-violence, and he met with success. The British authorities were forced to accept to the demandes of the indigo workers. He repeated his success at Kheda in Gujarat against the increasing revenues and taxed imposed by the government on the farmers at rural Gujarat. Once again, the processes were nonviolent. With these successes, Gandhi was hailed as the new light in the Indian political scenario. He gained the appellation of the Mahatma (the great soul) and Bapu (father). Soon Rowlatt Act and the subsequent massacre at Jalianwallah Bagh at Amritsar in Punjab considerably heated up the scenario of Indian politics. Gandhiji assumed the responsibilities of the president of Indian National Congress in 1921, and unleashed a series of reforms in the party ranks, thereby giving impetus to the non-cooperation movement, that by that time took the entire nation in its grip.

Mahatma Gandhi as the President of Indian National Congress

Mahatma Gandhi was elected as the president of the Indian National Congress in 1921. He immediately introduced a number of reforms within the party ranks. The first responsibility that Gandhi undertook as the president of the Indian National Congress was to increase the reach of the party among the masses who reside in the remote corners in order to eradicate its elitist status. Gandhi famously stated that rural India was the very backbone of the country, both in economic and in logistical terms. Therefore no movement can be truly successful unless whole-heartedly supported by the inhabitants of the Indian villages. The first step that he took was to considerably reduce the membership fee of the party. Then he restructured the entire party hierarchy, and opened new party branches at various provinces and princely states of India. Soon congress took a national dimension with membership multiplied manifold. Gandhi became the new guiding star of Indian politics, operating under the umbrella of the Indian National Congress.

As the president of the Indian National Congress, Mahatma Gandhi introduced the tenets and the ideals of Satyagraha, and the party saw the emergence of many new and charismatic leaders with great public appeals, who were loyal followers of Gandhi. By then, Lala Lajpat Rai also became an admirer of Gandhi in spite of former differences. With such great following, non-cooperation movement against the Rowlatt Act and the Amritsar tragedy naturally took massive national dimension.

Gandhi's Contribution towards Unification of the Congress

Gandhi called off the non-cooperation movement abruptly following the unfortunate violence at Chauri Chaura. It was even condemned by many of his most loyal followers as a historic blunder, with the likes of Sri CR Das among them. Gandhi's arrest in 1922 was the beginning of a stormy period for the Indian National Congress. Two factions under CR Das and Chakraborty Rajagopalachari gathered force, and the entire coherent fabric of the INC was on the point of breaking down, thereby bringing down the impetus of the Indian nationalist movement and also tarnishing the image of the Congress in the public eye. Gandhi tried hard to bridge the differences. He undertook a fast in a bid to unite the warring factions. However, success was limited and Gandhi had to come back and hold the reins in order to guide Congress in the proper direction.

Gandhi returned from a brief hibernation following his imprisonment and in the Calcutta Conference of 1928, announced his arrival with aplomb, daring the British government with a one year deadline to free India. He was influenced by the enthusiasm of younger Congressmen like Jawaharlal Nehru and Subhash Chandra Bose. The government did not respond and the INC celebrated Indian independence on 26th January, 1930, following the proposals undertaken Lahore Congress the year before. The Civil Disobedience movement ensued with Gandhi at the helm, defying government orders.

Gandhi arrives in India

Mohandas Gandhi (also known as Mahatma Gandhi), had been a prominent leader of the anti-Apartheid movement in South Africa, and had been a vocal opponent of basic discrimination and abusive labour treatment as well as suppressive police control such as the Rowlatt Acts. During these protests, Gandhi had perfected the concept of *satyagraha*, which had been inspired by the philosophy of Baba Ram Singh (famous for leading the Kuka Movement in the Punjab in 1872). The end of the protests in South

Africa saw oppressive legislation repealed and the release of political prisoners by General Jan Smuts, head of the South African Government of the time.

Gandhi, a stranger to India and its politics after twenty years, had initially entered the fray not with calls for a nation-state, but in support of the unified commerce-oriented territory that the Congress Party had been asking for. Gandhi believed that the industrial development and educational development that the Europeans had brought with them were required to alleviate many of India's problems. Gopal Krishna Gokhale, a veteran Congressman and Indian leader, became Gandhi's mentor. Gandhi's ideas and strategies of nonviolent civil disobedience initially appeared impractical to some Indians and Congressmen. In Gandhi's own words, "civil disobedience is civil breach of unmoral statutory enactments." It had to be carried out non-violently by withdrawing cooperation with the corrupt state. Gandhi's ability to inspire millions of common people became clear when he used satyagraha during the anti-Rowlatt Act protests in Punjab.

Gandhi's vision would soon bring millions of regular Indians into the movement, transforming it from an elitist struggle to a national one. The nationalist cause was expanded to include the interests and industries that formed the economy of common Indians. For example, in Champaran, Bihar, the Congress Party championed the plight of desperately poor sharecroppers and landless farmers who were being forced to pay oppressive taxes and grow cash crops at the expense of the subsistence crops which formed their food supply. The profits from the crops they grew were insufficient to provide for their sustenance.

The positive impact of reform was seriously undermined in 1919 by the Rowlatt Act, named after the recommendations made the previous year to the Imperial Legislative Council by the Rowlatt Commission, which had been appointed to investigate what was termed the "seditious conspiracy" and the German and Bolshevik involvement in the millitant movements in India. The Rowlatt Act, also known as the Black Act, vested the Viceroy's government with extraordinary powers to quell sedition by silencing the press, detaining the political activists without trial, and arresting any individuals suspected of sedition or treason without a warrant. In protest, a nationwide cessation of work (*hartal*) was called, marking the beginning of widespread, although not nationwide, popular discontent. The agitation unleashed by the acts culminated on 13 April 1919, in the Jallianwala Bagh massacre (also known as the Amritsar Massacre) in Amritsar, Punjab. The British military commander, Brigadier-General Reginald Dyer, blocked the main entrance, and ordered his soldiers to fire into an unarmed and unsuspecting crowd of some 5,000 men, women and children. They had assembled at Jallianwala Bagh, a walled in courtyard in defiance of the ban. A total of 1,651 rounds were fired, killing 379 people (as according to an official British commission; Indian estimates ranged as high as 1,499) and wounding 1,137 in the episode, which dispelled wartime hopes of home rule and goodwill in a frenzy

Mahatma Gandhi

Mohandas Karamchand Gandhi was born in the town of Porbander in the state of what is now Gujarat on 2 October 1869. He had his schooling in nearby Rajkot, where his father served as the adviser or prime minister to the local ruler. Though India was then under British rule, over 500 kingdoms, principalities, and states were allowed autonomy in domestic and internal affairs: these were the so-called 'native states'. Rajkot was one such state.

Gandhi later recorded the early years of his life in his extraordinary autobiography, *The Story of My Experimentswith Truth.* His father died before Gandhi could finish his schooling, and at thirteen he was married to Kasturba [or Kasturbai], who was even younger. In 1888 Gandhi set sail for England, where he had decided to pursue a degree in law. Though his elders objected, Gandhi could not be prevented from leaving; and it is said that his mother, a devout woman, made him promise that he would keep away from wine, women, and meat during his stay abroad. Gandhi left behind his son Harilal, then a few months old.

In London, Gandhi encountered theosophists, vegetarians, and others who were disenchanted not only with industrialism, but with the legacy of Enlightenment thought. They themselves represented the fringe elements of English society. Gandhi was powerfully attracted to them, as he was to the texts of the major religious traditions; and ironically it is in London that he was introduced to the Bhagavad Gita. Here, too, Gandhi showed determination and single-minded pursuit of his purpose, and accomplished his objective of finishing his degree from the Inner Temple. He was called to the bar in 1891, and even enrolled in the High Court of London; but later that year he left for India.

After one year of a none too successful law practice, Gandhi decided to accept an offer from an Indian businessman in South Africa, Dada Abdulla, to join him as a legal adviser. Unbeknown to him, this was to become an exceedingly lengthy stay, and altogether Gandhi was to stay in South Africa for over twenty years. The Indians who had been living in South Africa were without political rights, and were generally known by the derogatory name of 'coolies'. Gandhi himself came to an awareness of the frightening force and fury of European racism, and how far Indians were from being considered full human beings, when he when thrown out of a first-class railway compartment car, though he held a first-class ticket, at Pietermaritzburg. From this political awakening Gandhi was to emerge as the leader of the Indian community, and it is in South Africa that he first coined the term *satyagraha* to signify his theory and practice of nonviolent resistance. Gandhi was to describe himself preeminently as a votary or seeker of *satya* (truth), which could not be attained other than through *ahimsa* (non-violence, love) and *Brahmacharya* (celibacy, striving towards God). Gandhi conceived of his own life as a series of experiments to forge the use of satyagraha in such a manner as to make the oppressor and the oppressed alike recognize their common bonding and humanity: as he recognized, freedom is only freedom when it is indivisible. In his book *Satyagraha in South Africa* he was to detail the struggles of the Indians to claim their rights, and their resistance to oppressive legislation and executive measures, such as the imposition of a poll tax on them, or the declaration by the government that all non-Christian marriages were to be construed as invalid. In 1909, on a trip back to India, Gandhi authored a short treatise entitled *Hind Swaraj* or Indian Home Rule, where he all but initiated the critique, not only of industrial civilization, but of modernity in all its aspects.

Gandhi returned to India in early 1915, and was never to leave the country again except for a short trip that took him to Europe in 1931. Though he was not completely unknown in India, Gandhi followed the advice of his political mentor, Gokhale, and took it upon himself to acquire a familiarity with Indian conditions. He travelled widely for one year. Over the next few years, he was to become involved in numerous local struggles, such as at Champaran in Bihar, where workers on indigo plantations complained of oppressive working conditions, and at Ahmedabad, where a dispute had broken out between management and workers at textile mills.

His interventions earned Gandhi a considerable reputation, and his rapid ascendancy to the helm of nationalist politics is signified by his leadership of the opposition to repressive legislation (known as the "Rowlatt Acts") in 1919. His saintliness was not uncommon, except in someone like him who immersed himself in politics, and by this time he had earned from no less a person than Rabindranath Tagore, India's most well-known writer, the title of *Mahatma*, or 'Great Soul'. When 'disturbances' broke out in the Punjab, leading to the massacre of a large crowd of unarmed Indians at the Jallianwala Bagh in Amritsar and other atrocities, Gandhi wrote the report of the Punjab Congress Inquiry Committee. Over the next two years, Gandhi initiated the non-cooperation movement, which called upon Indians to withdraw from British institutions, to return honours conferred by the British, and to learn the art of self-reliance; though the British administration was at places paralyzed, the movement was suspended in February 1922 when a score of Indian policemen were brutally killed by a large crowd at Chauri Chaura, a small market town in the United Provinces.

Gandhi himself was arrested shortly thereafter, tried on charges of sedition, and sentenced to imprisonment for six years. At The Great Trial, as it is known to hisOwing to his poor health, Gandhi was released from prison in 1925. Over the following years, he worked hard to preserve Hindu-Muslim relations, and in 1924 he observed, from his prison cell, a 21-day fast when Hindu-Muslim riots broke out at Kohat, a military barracks on the Northwest Frontier.

This was to be of his many major public fasts, and in 1932 he was to commence the so-called Epic Fast unto death, since he thought of "separate electorates" for the oppressed class of what were then called *untouchables* (or Harijans in Gandhi's vocabulary, and dalits in today's language) as a retrograde measure meant to produce permanent divisions within Hindu society.

Gandhi earned the hostility of Ambedkar, the leader of the *untouchables*, but few doubted that Gandhi was genuinely interested in removing the serious disabilities from which they suffered, just as no one doubt that Gandhi never accepted the argument that Hindus and Muslims constituted two separate elements in Indian society. These were some of the concerns most prominent in Gandhi's mind, but he was also to initiate a constructive programme for social reform. Gandhi had ideas — mostly sound — on every subject, from hygiene and nutrition to education and labour, and he relentlessly pursued his ideas in one of the many newspapers which he founded. Indeed, were Gandhi known for nothing else in India, he would still be remembered as one of the principal figures in the history of Indian journalism.

In early 1930, as the nationalist movement was revived, the Indian National Congress, the preeminent body of nationalist opinion, declared that it would now be satisfied with nothing short of complete independence (*purna swaraj*). Once the clarion call had been issued, it was perforce necessary to launch a movement of resistance against British rule. On March 2, Gandhi addressed a letter to the Viceroy, Lord Irwin, informing him that unless Indian demands were met, he would be compelled to break the "salt laws".

Predictably, his letter was received with bewildered amusement, and accordingly Gandhi set off, on the early morning of March 12, with a small group of followers towards Dandi on the sea. They arrived there on April 5th: Gandhi picked up a small lump of natural salt, and so gave the signal to hundreds of thousands of people to similarly defy the law, since the British exercised a monopoly on the production and sale of salt. This was the beginning of the civil disobedience movement: Gandhi himself was arrested, and thousands of others were also hauled into jail. It is to break this deadlock that Irwin agreed to hold talks with Gandhi, and subsequently the British agreed to hold a Round Table Conference in London to negotiate the possible terms of Indian independence. Gandhi went to London in 1931 and met some of his admirers in Europe, but the negotiations proved inconclusive. On his return to India, he was once again arrested.

For the next few years, Gandhi would be engaged mainly in the constructive reform of Indian society. He had vowed upon undertaking the salt march that he would not return to Sabarmati Ashram in Ahmedabad, where he had made his home, if India did not attain its independence, and in the mid-1930s he established himself in a remote village, in the dead centre of India, by the name of Segaon [known as Sevagram]. It is to this obscure village, which was without electricity or running water, that India's political leaders made their way to engage in discussions with Gandhi about the future of the independence movement, and it is here that he received visitors such as Margaret Sanger, the well-known American proponent of birth-control. Gandhi also continued to travel throughout the country, taking him wherever his services were required.

One such visit was to the Northwest Frontier, where he had in the imposing Pathan, Khan Abdul Ghaffar Khan (known by the endearing term of "Frontier Gandhi", and at other times as *Badshah* [King] *Khan*), a fervent disciple. At the outset of World War II, Gandhi and the Congress leadership assumed a position of neutrality: while clearly critical of fascism, they could not find it in themselves to support British imperialism. Gandhi was opposed by Subhas Chandra Bose, who had served as President of the Congress, and who took to the view that Britain's moment of weakness was India's moment of opportunity. When Bose ran for President of the Congress against Gandhi's wishes and triumphed against Gandhi's own candidate, he found that Gandhi still exercised influence over the Congress Working Committee, and that it was near impossible to run the Congress if the cooperation of Gandhi and his followers could not be procured. Bose tendered his resignation, and shortly thereafter was to make a dramatic escape from India to find support among the Japanese and the Nazis for his plans to liberate India.

In 1942, Gandhi issued the last call for independence from British rule. On the grounds of what is now known as *August Kranti Maidan*, he delivered a stirring speech, asking every Indian to lay down their life, if necessary, in the cause of freedom. He gave them this mantra: "Do or Die"; at the same time, he asked the British to 'Quit India'. The response of the British government was to place Gandhi under arrest, and virtually the entire Congress leadership was to find itself behind bars, not to be released until after the conclusion of the war.

A few months after Gandhi and Kasturba had been placed in confinement in the Aga Khan's Palace in Pune, Kasturba passed away: this was a terrible blow to Gandhi, following closely on the heels of the death of his private secretary of many years, the gifted Mahadev Desai. In the period from 1942 to 1945, the Muslim League, which represented the interest of certain Muslims and by now advocated the creation of a separate homeland for Muslims, increasingly gained the attention of the British, and supported them in their war effort. The new government that came to power in Britain under Clement Atlee was committed to the independence of India, and negotiations for India's future began in earnest. Sensing that the political leaders were now craving for power, Gandhi largely distanced himself from the negotiations. He declared his opposition to the vivisection of India. It is generally conceded, even by his detractors, that the last years of his life were in some respects his finest. He walked from village to village in riot-torn Noakhali, where Hindus were being killed in retaliation for the killing of Muslims in Bihar, and nursed the wounded and consoled the widowed; and in Calcutta he came to constitute, in the famous words of the last viceroy, Mountbatten, a "one-man boundary force" between Hindus and Muslims. The ferocious fighting in Calcutta came to a halt, almost entirely on account of Gandhi's efforts, and even his critics were wont to speak of the Gandhi's 'miracle of Calcutta'. When the moment of freedom came, on 15 August 1947, Gandhi was nowhere to be seen in the capital, though Nehru and the entire Constituent Assembly were to salute him as the architect of Indian independence, as the 'father of the nation'.

Mahatma Gandhi

Mohandas Karamchand Gandhi (1869-1948) most reverently known as Mahatma Gandhi was born in Gujarat. He was called by the people 'Mahatma' which means great soul. The people also called him 'Bapu' the father. Gandhi belonged to the business community of Gujarat. He studied law in England. Towards the end of the 19 century he arrived in South Africa to represent an Indian client. In South Africa, Gandhi, once travelling in the first class compartment reserved for whites only was thrown out of a train because he was not white. He started a movement for civil rights in South Africa and succeeded in changing some rules there. He left South Africa in 1915 and returned to India. His actions in South Africa already made him famous in India and on his arrival in India he was welcomed by the Indians as a hero. After his arrival in India, he was introduced to the leader of Indian National Congress, Gopal Gokhale, whom Gandhi considered as his political guru.

Gandhi had developed while in South Africa, a philosophy of struggle for political and human rights through non-violence. He started to convince Indians to use his philosophy to achieve political rights for Indians. At that period the leader of Indian National Congress was Lokmanya Tilak who was militant and was supportive of violent actions against the British. Gandhi opposed to these ideas of Tilak but he admired the other ideas of Tilak. He agreed with Tilak that Indian political struggle was a matter of the people of India and not only of the intellectuals. Gandhi like Tilak supported a cultural and social change in Indian society. In 1920 Tilak died and Gandhi became the leader of Indian National Congress.

Like other Indians whom the British fostered to 'think like the British', Gandhi's family also belonged to this group. Gandhi studied law in England. He dressed like an Englishman. After returning from South Africa (where he was discriminated because of his Indian origin) Gandhi changed his dressing style and began to dress like a simple Indian farmer. He remained in these simple Indian clothes even when he arrived again in England later on as a representative of the Indian National Congress, causing a complete surprise to his British counterparts. His philosophy was that all are equal and everyone should do all kinds of jobs. He built an ashram in which everyone did all different jobs. He even cleaned the toilet, which according to strict Indian customs was the job of the low castes and untouchables. Because of his revolutionary ideas many in the then elitist Indian society mocked at his philosophy. Later on, many of these mockers became his admirers and followers. Gandhi's philosophy of struggle against the British was nonviolent non-cooperation. He demanded from the Indians to restrain even if the British forces physically attacked them. He advised Indians to boycott anything British including British made garments, British universities, British courts and to refuse to follow respect and abide by British laws. He sometimes resorted to hunger strikes. Gandhi succeeded in sweeping the Indian people after him like no other Indian leader ever did before him. One of the famous Gandhi campaigns was the salt march. According to British law Indians could not produce salt, a basic food ingredient, but could only buy it from licensed salt factories, all of them were British owned. Gandhi organized in 1930 a 24-day march to the sea and produced salt from the sea. In this march he gathered behind him the strength of hundred of thousands of people.

Mahatma Gandhi who became the leader of the Indian National Congress in 1920 did not always lead the Indian nationalist movement. There were periods when he was arrested and was completely isolated from the movement. Sometimes he severed from the nationalist movement for other causes. Even when he was the leader of Indian National Congress there were members in the Congress who did not accept his ideas. His opponents, who had other ideas about India even established movements within the Indian National Congress. In the early 1930s Gandhi even resigned from the leadership of the Congress because of growing criticism against his leadership. But from then on Gandhi became the father figure of the Congress. In 1942 Gandhi led the 'Quit India' movement.

Outside the Congress, Mahatma Gandhi also had many rivals who defied his political philosophy. His main rivals outside the Congress were Hindu nationalists. They saw in Mahatma Gandhi pro-Muslim trend. During India's independence there were many riots between Hindus and Muslims. Hundreds of thousands of people died in these riots. During these riots Gandhi, who was a Hindu, tried to be a middleman between Hindus and Muslims. Many Hindus did not like his stand and saw him as a traitor. After India's partition into India and Pakistan, Hindu nationalist blamed the Congress and specially Mahatma Gandhi for the partition. Mahatma Gandhi sometimes even attacked the Indian government as not being fair towards Muslims and towards Pakistan. He even intended to leave India and end his life in Pakistan. On 30 January 1948 a Hindu nationalist, Nathuram Godse shot him to death.

Mahatma Gandhi

That India opted for an entirely original path to solving this crisis and obtaining *swaraj* (independence) was due largely to Gandhi, commonly known as "Mahatma" (or Great Soul) or, as he himself preferred, "Gandhiji" (an honorific term for Gandhi). A native of Gujarat who had been educated in Britain, he was an obscure and unsuccessful provincial lawyer.

Gandhi had accepted an invitation in 1893 to represent indentured Indian labourers in South Africa, where he stayed on for more than twenty years, emerging ultimately as the voice and conscience of thousands who had been subjected to blatant racial discrimination. He returned to India in 1915, virtually a stranger to public life but "fired with a religious vision of a new India, whose *swaraj*... would [be] a moral reformation of a whole people which would either convert the British also or render their Raj impossible by Indian withdrawal of support for it and its modern values," according to historian Judith M. Brown.

Mahatma Gandhi's ideas and strategies of nonviolent civil disobedience (satyagraha), first applied during his South Africa days, initially appeared impractical to many educated Indians. In Gandhi's own words, "Civil disobedience is civil breach of unmoral statutory enactments," but as he viewed it, it had to be carried out nonviolently by withdrawing cooperation with the corrupt state. Observers realized Gandhi's political potential when he used the satyagraha during the anti-Rowlatt Acts protests in Punjab. In 1920, under Gandhi's leadership, the Congress was reorganized and given a new constitution, whose goal was *swaraj*.

Membership in the party was opened to anyone prepared to pay a token fee, and a hierarchy of committees—from district, to province, to all-India—was established and made responsible for discipline and control over a hitherto amorphous and diffuse movement. During his first nationwide satyagraha, Gandhi urged the people to boycott British education institutions, law courts, and products (in favour of *swadeshi*); to resign from government employment; to refuse to pay taxes; and to forsake British titles and honours. The party was transformed from an elite organization to one of mass national appeal.

Mahatma Gandhi's first nationwide satyagraha was too late to influence the framing of the new Government of India Act of 1919, the magnitude of disorder resulting from the movement was unparalleled and presented a new challenge to foreign rule. Gandhi was forced to call off the campaign in 1922 because of atrocities committed against police.

However, the abortive campaign marked a milestone in India's political development. For his efforts, Gandhi was imprisoned until 1924. On his release from prison, he set up an ashram (a rural commune), established a newspaper, and inaugurated a series of reforms aimed at the socially disadvantaged within Hindu society, the rural poor, and the Untouchables. His popularity soared in Indian politics as he reached the hearts and minds of ordinary people, winning support for his causes as no one else had ever done before. By his personal and eclectic piety, his asceticism, his vegetarianism, his espousal of Hindu-Muslim unity, and his firm belief in ahimsa, Gandhi appealed to the loftier Hindu ideals. For Gandhi, moral regeneration, social progress, and national freedom were inseparable.

Emerging leaders within the Congress—Jawaharlal Nehru, Vallabhbhai Patel, Rajendra Prasad, C. Rajagopalachari, Maulana Abdul Kalam Azad, Subhas Chandra Bose, and Jayaprakash (J.P.) Narayan—accepted Gandhi's leadership in articulating nationalist aspirations but disagreed on strategies for wresting more concessions from the British. The Indian political spectrum was further broadened in the mid-1920s by the emergence of both moderate and militant parties, such as the Swaraj Party (sometimes referred to as the Swarajist Party), the Mahasabha Party (literally, great council; an orthodox Hindu communal party), the Unionist Party, the Communist Party of India, and the Socialist Independence for India League. Regional political organizations also continued to represent the interests of non-Brahmans in Madras, Mahars in Maharashtra, and Sikhs in Punjab.

The Congress, however, kept itself aloof from competing in elections. As voices inside and outside the Congress became more strident, the British appointed a commission in 1927, under Sir

John Simon, to recommend further measures in the constitutional devolution of power. The British failure to appoint an Indian member to the commission outraged the Congress and others, and, as a result, they boycotted it throughout India, carrying placards inscribed "Simon, Go Back." In 1929 the Congress responded by drafting its own constitution under the guidance of Motilal Nehru (Jawaharlal's father) demanding full independence (*purna swaraj*) by 1930; the Congress went so far as to observe January 26, 1930, as the first anniversary of the first year of independence.

Mahatma Gandhi reemerged from his long seclusion by undertaking his most inspired campaign, a march of about 400 kilometres from his commune in Ahmadabad to Dandi, on the coast of Gujarat between March 12 and April 6, 1930. At Dandi, in protest against extortionate British taxes on salt, he and thousands of followers illegally but symbolically made their own salt from sea water.

Their defiance reflected India's determination to be free, despite the imprisonment of thousands of protesters. For the next five years, the Congress and government were locked in conflict and negotiations until what became the Government of India Act of 1935 could be hammered out. But by then, the rift between the Congress and the Muslim League had become unbridgeable as each pointed the finger at the other acrimoniously. The Muslim League disputed the claim by the Congress to represent all people of India, while the Congress disputed the Muslim League's claim to voice the aspirations of all Muslims.

The 1935 act, the voluminous and final constitutional effort at governing British India, articulated three major goals: establishing a loose federal structure, achieving provincial autonomy, and safeguarding minority interests through separate electorates. The federal provisions, intended to unite princely states and British India at the centre, were not implemented because of ambiguities in safeguarding the existing privileges of princes. In February 1937, however, provincial autonomy became a reality when elections were held; the Congress emerged as the dominant party with a clear majority in five provinces and held an upper hand in two, while the Muslim League performed poorly. Mahatma Gandhi.

Sabarmati Ashram

Sabarmati Ashram is located in the Ahmedabad suburb of Sabarmati adjoining to famous Ashram Road, at the bank of River Sabarmati, 4 miles away from the city Town Hall. This was one of the residences of Mohandas Karamchand Gandhi. This ashram is now a national monument by the Government of India due to its significance in the Indian independence movement in the form of the Dandi March in 1930.

History

The ashram was originally established at the Kocharab Bungalow of Jivanlal Desai on 25 May 1915. The Ashram was then shifted on 17 June 1917 to a piece of open land on the banks of the river Sabarmati. Reasons for this shift included: Gandhi wanted to do some experiments in living (e.g. farming, animal husbandry, cow breeding, khadi and related constructive activities for which he was in search of this kind of barren land.) It was believed that this was ancient ashram site of Dadhichi Rishi who had donated his bones for a righteous war;, but his actual ashram lies in Naimisharanya, near lucknow, u.p, it is between a jail and a crematorium and he believed that a satyagrahi has invariably to go to either place. Mahatama Gandhi said, "This is the right place for our activities to carry on the search for truth and develop fearlessness, for on one side are the iron bolts of the foreigners, and on the other the thunderbolts of Mother Nature."

While at the Ashram, Gandhi formed a tertiary school that mainly focused on manual labour, agriculture, and literacy to advance his efforts for nation's self-sufficiency. It was also from here on the 12 March 1930 that Gandhi marched towards Dandi,241 miles from the Ashram with 78 companions in protest of the British Salt Law, which taxed Indian salt in an effort to promote sales of British salt in India. This mass awakening filled the British jails with 60 000 freedom fighters. Later the government seized their property, Gandhi, in sympathy with them, responded by asking the Government to forfeit the Ashram. Then Government, however, did not oblige. He had by now already decided on 22 July 1933 to disband the Ashram, which later became asserted place after the detention of many freedom fighters, and then some local citizens decided to preserve it. On 12 March 1930 he vowed that he would not return to the Ashram until India won independence. Although this was won on 15 August 1947, when India was declared a free nation, Gandhi was assassinated in January 1948.

Present day

The ashram now has a museum, Gandhi Smarak Sangrahalay. In 1963 the museum building was erected (designed by architect Charles Correa), and memorial activities were then started here. One of the important activities undertaken is the establishment of a Gandhi Smarak Sangrahalaya. Initially started in 'Hriday Kunj,' Gandhi's own cottage in the Ashram, the Sangrahalaya has now shifted to its own well-designed and well-furnished building which was inaugurated by Jawaharlal Nehru, Prime Minister of India, on 10 May 1963.

Nandini: It is on the right hand side of 'Hridaya Kunj'. It is an old Ashram guest house, where guests from India and abroad are put up.

Vinoba Kutir: Named after Acharya Vinoba Bhave who stayed here, and also known as Mira Kutir after Miraben, Gandhiji's disciple, daughter of a British Admiral.

Upasana Mandir: It is an open-air prayer ground, situated between 'Hridaya Kunj' and 'Magan Kutir' (the hut where Maganlal Gandhi, the ashram manager, used to stay). Here, Gandhiji used to refer to individual questions after prayers and as the head of the family analysed and gave his solutions.

Gandhi Sangrhalaya

- "My life is my message" gallery, consisting of 8 life-size painting and more than 250 photo-enlargements of some of the vivid and historic events of Gandhi's life
- Gandhi in Ahmedabad Gallery, tracking Gandhi's life in Ahmedabad from 1915-1930
- Life-size oil painting gallery
- Gandhi quotations, letters and other relics exhibition
- Library consisting of nearly 35,000 books dealing with Gandhi's life, work, teachings, Indian freedom movement

and allied subjects, and a Reading Room with more than 80 periodicals in English, Gujarati and Hindi

- Archives consisting of nearly 34,117 letters to and from Gandhi both in original and in photocopies, about 8,781 pages of manuscripts of Gandhi's articles appearing in *Harijan*, *Harijansevak*, and *Harijanbandhu* and about 6,000 photographs of Gandhi and his associates
- An important landmark of the Ashram is 'Hridaya Kunj' where some of the personal relics of Gandhi are on display
- Ashram book store, a non-profit book store selling literature and memorabilia related to Gandhi and his life work and also supports local artisans.

Ashram Activities

- The Sabarmati ashram which receives about 7 lakh (700,000) visitors a year houses, photocopies of about 34,000 letters written by Gandhi and about 8000 photographs and 165 films and of course, Hriday Kunj, the house where Gandhi and Kasturba stayed from 1918 to 1930.
- Collecting, processing, preserving and displaying archival materials (writings, photographs, paintings, voice-records, films, personal clothes etc.
- A charkha' used by Gandhi to weave khadi and the writing table he used for writing letters are also few of the priceless items kept here.
- Microfilming, lamination and preservation of negatives
- Arranging exhibitions on aspects of Gandhi's life, literature and activities
- Publication of the "Mahadevbhani Dairy," which chronicles the entire history of the Indian freedom struggle
- The Ashram Trust funds activities that include education for the visitor, the community and routine maintenance of the museum and its surrounding grounds
- Keeping contact with as well as helping and undertaking study and research in Gandhian thought and activities and publishing the results of such study and research and allied literature for the benefit of the people

- Observance in a suitable manner of occasions connected with Gandhi's life
- Maintaining contact with the youth and student community.

The Sabarmati Ashram

A Reflection of Gandhi's Vision

Upon returning from South Africa on January 9, 1915, Mohandas Karamchand Gandhi was in search for a place to settle himself and a small group of relatives and associates who were with him in the African struggle. His political views still unformed, Gandhi chose Ahmedabad in the West Indian state of Gujarat for three reasons, " being a Gujarati, I'll serve my country best through the use of the Gujarati language. As Ahmedabad was the centre of the handloom in early days, the work of spinning wheel (charkha) could be done in a better way, I believed. Being the capital of Gujarat its wealthy persons will also make a larger contribution, I hoped," in his own words.

Gandhi first created Kochrab Ashram, which was located in proper Ahmedabad city; however, in 1917 an epidemic plague broke out that forced them to leave the site. Several visits were made to the Sabarmati sight, which incidentally holds its own glory in Hindu mythology as a famous incident of extreme sacrifice. The land was far from the city of Ahmedabad, surrounded by jungle full of snakes, and situated along the steep rugged cliffs of the Sabarmati River. Nearby, was a British Prison filled with the sounds of iron chains of the inmates engaged in manual labour. Thunder, lightening, and heavy rains marked the day of Gandhi's final decision.

He said, ' This is the right place for our activities to carry on the search for Truth and develop Fearlessness – for, on one side, are the iron bolts of the foreigners, and on the other, thunderbolts of Mother Nature."

Gradually a few dwellings were built, simple but efficient, on the 36 acre Ashram site and activities were begun. The Ashram was a human laboratory where Gandhi could test his moral and spiritual hypotheses. It was a family not linked by blood or property, but by an allegiance to common ideals. These main objectives of Sabarmati were as follows: Education, Truth (Non-Violence and Love), Celibacy, Control of the palate (no liquor or meat), No Stealing, Non-Possession (simple living high thinking), Use of home-made articles, Conquer of Fear, and the eradication of Untouchibility.

The first struggle Gandhi headed from the Sabarmati Ashram was for the textile workers strike. There was a complete deadlock between the mill owners and the inadequately paid workers. It was difficult for the workers not to become angry, as they were starving. However, Gandhi joined with them in fast, and later used the strikers to found a Weavers School at Sabarmati. Gandhi's charkha and untouchability campaign brought the majority of the deprived masses of India into the national mainstream. Also during his time at Sabarmati, Gandhi was jailed for 6 years in the nearby prison and published his now famous autobiography, "My Experiments With Truth", after his release. The most famous and epic chapter of the Sabarmati Ashram came in the way Gandhi bid farewell to it. On March 12, 1930, directed by his 'inner voice,' Gandhiji embarked on a 240 mile walk with 79 selected followers to break the Salt Tax, imposed by the British. This, known in history as The Dandi Salt March, united the country and set into motion the events that would later free a nation. Gandhi was no longer referred to as Mohandas, but as Mahatma, or 'Great Soul.' Gandhi has said he would never return to Sabarmati until India achieved Independence. He did, though on a somber note, see India gain Independence on August 15, 1947; but was unable to return to Sabarmati, as he was assassinated by Vinayak N. Godse, a staunch Hindu fanatic, on January 30, 1948. India's Independence had divided its people into two nations; India and Pakistan.

Ashram History

On his return from South Africa, Gandhi's first Ashram in India was established in the Kochrab area of Ahmedabad on 25 May 1915. The Ashram was then shifted on 17 June 1917 to a piece of open land on the banks of the river Sabarmati. Reasons for this shift included: he wanted to do some experiments in living e.g farming, animal husbandry, cow breeding, Khadi and related constructive activities, for which he was in search of this kind of barren land; mythologically, it was the ashram site of Dadhichi Rishi who had donated his bones for a righteous war; it is between a jail and a crematorium as he believed that a satyagrahi has to invariably go to either place. The Sabarmati Ashram (also known as Harijan Ashram) was home to Mohandas Gandhi from 1917 until 1930 and served as one of the main centres of the Indian freedom struggle. Originally called the Satyagraha Ashram, reflecting the movement toward passive resistance launched by the Mahatma, the Ashram became home to the ideology that set India free. Sabarmati Ashram named for the river on which it sits, was created with a dual mission. To serve as an institution that would carry on a search for truth and a platform to bring together a group of workers committed to non-violence who would help secure freedom for India.

By conceiving such a vision Gandhi and his followers hoped to foster a new social construct of truth and non-violence that would help to revolutionize the existing pattern of like.

While at the Ashram, Gandhi formed a school that focused on manual labour, agriculture, and literacy to advance his efforts for self-sufficiency. It was also from here on the 12 March 1930 that Gandhi launched the famous Dandi march 241 miles from the Ashram (with 78 companions) in protest of the British Salt Law, which taxed Indian salt in an effort to promote sales of British salt in India. This mass awakening filled the British jails with 60 000 freedom fighters. Later the government seized their property, Gandhi, in sympathy with them, responded by asking the Government to forfeit the Ashram. Then Government, however, did not oblige. He had by now already decided on 22 July 1933 to disband the Ashram, which later became asserted place after the detention of many freedom fighters, and then some local citizens decided to preserve it. On 12 March 1930 he vowed that he would not return to the Ashram until India won independence. Although this was won on 15 August 1947, when India was declared a free nation, Gandhi was assassinated in January 1948 and never returned.

Over the years, the Ashram became home to the ideology that set India free. It aided countless other nations and people in their own battles against oppressive forces.

Today, the Ashram serves as a source of inspiration and guidance, and stands as a monument to Gandhi's life mission and a testimony to others who have fought a similar struggle.

Satyagraha

Satyagraha is a philosophy and practice of nonviolent resistance developed by Mohandas Karamchand Gandhi (also known as "Mahatma" Gandhi). Gandhi deployed satyagraha in campaigns for Indian independence and also during his earlier struggles in South Africa. Satyagraha theory also influenced Nelson Mandela and Martin Luther King, Jr. during the campaigns the latter led during the civil rights movement in the United States, and many other social justice and similar movements. Someone who practices satyagraha is a satyagrahi.

Meaning of the Term

Satyagraha is a synthesis of the Sanskrit words *Satya* (meaning "truth") and *Agraha* ("insistence", or "holding firmly to"). For Gandhi, satyagraha went far beyond mere "passive resistance" and became strength in practising nonviolent methods. In his words:

Truth (satya) implies love, and firmness (agraha) engenders and therefore serves as a synonym for force. I thus began to call the Indian movement Satyagraha, that is to say, the Force which is born of Truth and Love or non-violence, and gave up the use of the phrase "passive resistance", in connection with it, so much so that even in English writing we often avoided it and used instead the word "satyagraha"....

In a letter to P.K.Rao, Servants of India Society dated September 10, 1935, quoted in Louis Fischer's, The Life of Mahatma Gandhi, Part I, Gandhi disputes that his idea of Civil Disobedience was adapted from the writings of Thoreau.

"The statement that I had derived my idea of Civil Disobedience phrase to explain our struggle to the English readers. But I found that even "Civil disobedience" failed to convey the full meaning of the struggle. I therefore adopted the phrase "Civil Resistance."

Gandhi described it as follows: I have also called it love-force or soul-force. In the application of satyagraha, I discovered in the earliest stages that pursuit of truth did not admit of violence being inflicted on one's opponent but that he must be weaned from error by patience and compassion.

For what appears to be truth to the one may appear to be error to the other. And patience means self-suffering. So the doctrine came to mean vindication of truth, not by infliction of suffering on the opponent, but on oneself.

Contrast to "Passive Resistance"

Gandhi distinguished between satyagraha and passive resistance in the following letter:

"I have drawn the distinction between passive resistance as understood and practised in the West and satyagraha before I had evolved the doctrine of the latter to its full logical and spiritual extent. Cool is a metaphor for non-violence. I often used "passive resistance" and "satyagraha" as synonymous terms: but as the doctrine of satyagraha developed, the expression "passive resistance" ceases even to be synonymous, as passive resistance has admitted of violence as in the case of suffragettes and has been universally acknowledged to be a weapon of the weak.

Moreover, passive resistance does not necessarily involve complete adherence to truth under every circumstance. Therefore it is different from satyagraha in three essentials: Satyagraha is a weapon of the strong; it admits of no violence under any circumstance whatsoever; and it ever insists upon truth. I think I have now made the distinction perfectly clear."

Satyagraha Theory

Defining Success

In traditional violent and nonviolent conflict, the goal is to defeat the opponent or frustrate the opponent's objectives, or to meet one's own objectives despite the efforts of the opponent to obstruct these. In satyagraha, by contrast, these are not the goals. "The Satyagrahi's object is to convert, not to coerce, the wrong-doer." Success is defined as cooperating with the opponent to meet a just end that the opponent is unwittingly obstructing. The opponent must be converted, at least as far as to stop obstructing the just end, for this cooperation to take place.

Means and Ends

The theory of satyagraha sees means and ends as inseparable. The means used to obtain an end are wrapped up in and attached to that end. Therefore, it is contradictory to try to use unjust means to obtain justice or to try to use violence to obtain peace. As Gandhi wrote: "They say, 'means are, after all, means'. I would say, 'means are, after all, everything'. As the means so the end..."

Gandhi used an example to explain this: If I want to deprive you of your watch, I shall certainly have to fight for it; if I want to buy your watch, I shall have to pay for it; and if I want a gift, I shall have to plead for it; and, according to the means I employ, the watch is stolen property, my own property, or a donation.

Gandhi rejected the idea that injustice should, or even could, be fought against "by any means necessary" — if you use violent, coercive, unjust means, whatever ends you produce will necessarily embed that injustice.

To those who preached violence and called nonviolent actionists cowards, he replied: "I do believe that, where there is only a choice between cowardice and violence, I would advise violence....I would rather have India resort to arms in order to defend her honour than that she should, in a cowardly manner, become or remain a helpless witness to her own dishonour....But I believe that nonviolence is infinitely superior to violence, forgiveness is more manly than punishment."

Satyagraha Versus Duragraha

The essence of Satyagraha is that it seeks to eliminate antagonisms without harming the antagonists themselves, as opposed to violent resistance, which is meant to cause harm to the antagonist. A Satyagrahi therefore does not seek to end or destroy the relationship with the antagonist, but instead seeks to transform or "purify" it to a higher level. A euphemism sometimes used for Satyagraha is that it is a "silent force" or a "soul force" (a term also used by Martin Luther King Jr. during his famous "I Have a Dream" speech). It arms the individual with moral power rather than physical power. Satyagraha is also termed a "universal force," as it essentially "makes no distinction between kinsmen and strangers, young and old, man and woman, friend and foe."

Gandhi contrasted satyagraha (holding on to truth) with "duragraha" (holding on by force), as in protest meant more to harass than enlighten opponents. He wrote: "There must be no impatience, no barbarity, no insolence, no undue pressure. If we want to cultivate a true spirit of democracy, we cannot afford to be intolerant. Intolerance betrays want of faith in one's cause."

Civil disobedience and non-cooperation as practised under Satyagraha are based on the "law of suffering", a doctrine that the endurance of suffering is a means to an end. This end usually implies a moral upliftment or progress of an individual or society. Therefore, non-cooperation in Satyagraha is in fact a means to secure the cooperation of the opponent consistently with truth and justice.

Satyagraha in Large-scale Conflict

Main articles: Bardoli Satyagraha, Champaran and Kheda Satyagraha, Dharasana Satyagraha, Flag Satyagraha, Guruvayur Satyagraha, Non-cooperation movement, Quit India Movement, Salt Satyagraha, and Vaikom Satyagraha.

When using satyagraha in a large-scale political conflict involving civil disobedience, Gandhi believed that the satyagrahis must undergo training to ensure discipline. He wrote that it is "only when people have proved their active loyalty by obeying the many laws of the State that they acquire the right of Civil Disobedience."

He therefore made part of the discipline that satyagrahis:

1. appreciate the other laws of the State and obey them voluntarily
2. tolerate these laws, even when they are inconvenient
3. be willing to undergo suffering, loss of property, and to endure the suffering that might be inflicted on family and friends.

This obedience has to be not merely grudging, but extraordinary:

An honest, respectable man will not suddenly take to stealing whether there is a law against stealing or not, but this very man will not feel any remorse for failure to observe the rule about carrying headlights on bicycles after dark.... But he would observe any obligatory rule of this kind, if only to escape the inconvenience of facing a prosecution for a breach of the rule. Such compliance is not, however, the willing and spontaneous obedience that is required of a Satyagrahi.

Principles for Satyagrahis

Gandhi envisioned satyagraha as not only a tactic to be used in acute political struggle, but as a universal solvent for injustice and harm. He felt that it was equally applicable to large-scale political struggle and to one-on-one interpersonal conflicts and that it should be taught to everyone. He founded the Sabarmati Ashram to teach satyagraha. He asked satyagrahis to follow the following principles (Yamas described in Yoga Sutra):

1. Nonviolence (ahimsa)
2. Truth — this includes honesty, but goes beyond it to mean living fully in accord with and in devotion to that which is true
3. Non-stealing
4. Chastity (Brahmacharya) — this includes sexual chastity, but also the subordination of other sensual desires to the primary devotion to truth
5. Non-possession (not the same as poverty)
6. Body-labour or bread-labour
7. Control of the palate
8. Fearlessness
9. Equal respect for all religions
10. Economic strategy such as boycotts (swadeshi)
11. Freedom from untouchability.

On another occasion, he listed seven rules as "essential for every Satyagrahi in India":

1. must have a living faith in God
2. must believe in truth and non-violence and have faith in the inherent goodness of human nature which he expects to evoke by suffering in the satyagraha effort

3. must be leading a chaste life, and be willing to die or lose all his possessions
4. must be a habitual *khadi* wearer and spinner
5. must abstain from alcohol and other intoxicants
6. must willingly carry out all the rules of discipline that are issued
7. must obey the jail rules unless they are specially devised to hurt his self respect.

Rules for Satyagraha Campaigns

Gandhi proposed a series of rules for satyagrahis to follow in a resistance campaign:

1. harbour no anger
2. suffer the anger of the opponent
3. never retaliate to assaults or punishment; but do not submit, out of fear of punishment or assault, to an order given in anger
4. voluntarily submit to arrest or confiscation of your own property
5. if you are a trustee of property, defend that property (non-violently) from confiscation with your life
6. do not curse or swear
7. do not insult the opponent
8. neither salute nor insult the flag of your opponent or your opponent's leaders
9. if anyone attempts to insult or assault your opponent, defend your opponent (non-violently) with your life
10. as a prisoner, behave courteously and obey prison regulations (except any that are contrary to self-respect)
11. as a prisoner, do not ask for special favourable treatment
12. as a prisoner, do not fast in an attempt to gain conveniences whose deprivation does not involve any injury to your self-respect
13. joyfully obey the orders of the leaders of the civil disobedience action

14. do not pick and choose amongst the orders you obey; if you find the action as a whole improper or immoral, sever your connection with the action entirely
15. do not make your participation conditional on your comrades taking care of your dependents while you are engaging in the campaign or are in prison; do not expect them to provide such support
16. do not become a cause of communal quarrels
17. do not take sides in such quarrels, but assist only that party which is demonstrably in the right; in the case of inter-religious conflict, give your life to protect (non-violently) those in danger on either side
18. avoid occasions that may give rise to communal quarrels
19. do not take part in processions that would wound the religious sensibilities of any community.

Satyagraha and the Civil Rights Movement in the United States

Satyagraha theory also influenced Martin Luther King, Jr. during the campaigns he led during the civil rights movement in the United States:

Like most people, I had heard of Gandhi, but I had never studied him seriously. As I read I became deeply fascinated by his campaigns of nonviolent resistance. I was particularly moved by his Salt March to the Sea and his numerous fasts. The whole concept of *Satyagraha* (*Satya* is truth which equals love, and *agraha* is force; *Satyagraha*, therefore, means truth force or love force) was profoundly significant to me. As I delved deeper into the philosophy of Gandhi, my skepticism concerning the power of love gradually diminished, and I came to see for the first time its potency in the area of social reform.... It was in this Gandhian emphasis on love and nonviolence that I discovered the method for social reform that I had been seeking.

Satyagraha and the Holocaust

In view of the Nazi persecution of the Jews in Germany, Gandhi offered Satyagraha as a method of combating oppression and genocide, stating:

If I were a Jew and were born in Germany and earned my livelihood there, I would claim Germany as my home even as the tallest Gentile German might, and challenge him to shoot me or cast me in the dungeon; I would refuse to be expelled or to submit to discriminating treatment. And for doing this I should not wait for the fellow Jews to join me in civil resistance, but would have confidence that in the end the rest were bound to follow my example. If one Jew or all the Jews were to accept the prescription here offered, he or they cannot be worse off than now. And suffering voluntarily undergone will bring them an inner strength and joy [...] the calculated violence of Hitler may even result in a general massacre of the Jews by way of his first answer to the declaration of such hostilities. But if the Jewish mind could be prepared for voluntary suffering, even the massacre I have imagined could be turned into a day of thanksgiving and joy that Jehovah had wrought deliverance of the race even at the hands of the tyrant. For to the God-fearing, death has no terror.

When Gandhi was criticized for these statements, he responded in another article entitled "Some Questions Answered":

Friends have sent me two newspaper cuttings criticizing my appeal to the Jews. The two critics suggest that in presenting non-violence to the Jews as a remedy against the wrong done to them, I have suggested nothing new... What I have pleaded for is renunciation of violence of the heart and consequent active exercise of the force generated by the great renunciation."

In a similar vein, anticipating a possible attack on India by Japan during World War II, Gandhi recommended satyagraha as a defence.

What is Satyagraha?

Gandhi called his overall method of nonviolent action Satyagraha. This translates roughly as "Truth-force." A fuller rendering, though, would be "the force that is generated through adherence to Truth."

Nowadays, it's usually called nonviolence. But for Gandhi, nonviolence was the word for a different, broader concept-namely, "a way of life based on love and compassion." In Gandhi's terminology, Satyagraha-Truth-force-was an outgrowth of nonviolence. It may also help to keep in mind that the terms Satyagraha and nonviolent action, though often used one for the other, don't actually refer to the exact same thing. Satyagraha is really one special form of nonviolent action-Gandhi's own version of it. Much of what's called nonviolent action wouldn't qualify as Satyagraha. But we'll come back to that later.

Gandhi practiced two types of Satyagraha in his mass campaigns. The first was civil disobedience, which entailed breaking a law and courting arrest. When we today hear this term, our minds tend to stress the "disobedience" part of it. But for Gandhi, "civil" was just as important. He used "civil" here not just in its meaning of "relating to citizenship and government" but also in its meaning of "civilized" or "polite." And that's exactly what Gandhi strove for.

We also tend to lay stress differently than Gandhi on the phases of civil disobedience. We tend to think breaking the law is the core of it. But to Gandhi, the core of it was going to prison. Breaking the law was mostly just a way to get there.

Now, why was that? Was Gandhi trying to fill the jails? Overwhelm and embarrass his captors? Make them "give in" through force of numbers?

Not at all. He just wanted to make a statement. He wanted to say, "I care so deeply about this matter that I'm willing to take on the legal penalties, to sit in this prison cell, to sacrifice my freedom, in order to show you how deeply I care. Because when you see the depth of my concern, and how 'civil' I am in going about this, you're bound to change your mind about me, to abandon your rigid, unjust position, and to let me help you see the truth of my cause."

In other words, Gandhi's method aimed to win not by overwhelming but by converting his opponent-or as the Gandhian say, by bringing about a "change of heart."

Now, to many people, that sounds pretty naive. Well, I'll let you in on a secret. It was naive. The belief that civil disobedience succeeded by converting the opponent happened to be a myth held by Gandhi himself. And it's shared by most of his admirers, who take his word for it without bothering to check it out.

As far as I can tell, no civil disobedience campaign of Gandhi's ever succeeded chiefly through a change of heart in his opponents.

But this doesn't mean civil disobedience didn't work. As a matter of fact, it did work. The only thing off-kilter was Gandhi's explanation of how and why it worked.

Let me give a general description of what seems really to have happened when Gandhi and his followers committed civil disobedience:

Gandhi and followers break a law-politely. Public leader has them arrested, tried, put in prison. Gandhi and followers cheerfully accept it all. Members of the public are impressed by the protest, public sympathy is aroused for the protesters and their cause. Members of the public put pressure on public leader to negotiate with Gandhi. As cycles of civil disobedience recur, public pressure grows stronger. Finally, public leader gives in to pressure from his constituency, negotiates with Gandhi.

That's the general outline. Notice that there is a "change of heart," but it's more in the public than in the opponent. And notice too that there's an element of coercion, though it's indirect, coming from the public, rather than directly from Gandhi's camp.

Some campaigns of Gandhi's show a variation on this model. Sometimes Gandhi's opponents had superiors who wound up pressuring them or even ordering them to negotiate with Gandhi. These superiors might have been influenced by Gandhi's campaign, or by pressure from their own public-for instance, when British citizens pressured government leaders in Britain to intervene in affairs of their colonial government in India.

But the basic principle was the same: Gandhi's most decisive influence on his opponents was more indirect than direct.

Gandhi set out a number of rules for the practice of civil disobedience. These rules often baffle his critics, and often even his admirers set them aside as nonessential. But once you understand that civil disobedience, for Gandhi, was aimed at working a change of heart-whether in the opponent or the public-then it's easy to make sense of them.

One rule was that only specific, unjust laws were to be broken. Civil disobedience didn't mean flouting all law.

In fact, Gandhi said that only people with a high regard for the law were qualified for civil disobedience. Only action by such people could convey the depth of their concern and win respect. No one thinks much of it when the law is broken by those who care nothing for it anyway.

Other rules: Gandhi ruled out direct coercion, such as trying to physically block someone. Hostile language was banned. Destroying property was forbidden. Not even secrecy was allowed.

All these were ruled out because any of them would undercut the empathy and trust Gandhi was trying to build, and would hinder that "change of heart."

The second form of mass Satyagraha was non-co-operation.

This is just what it sounds like. non-co-operation meant refusing to co-operate with the opponent, refusing to submit to the injustice being fought. It took such forms as strikes, economic boycotts, and tax refusals.

Of course, non-co-operation and civil disobedience overlapped. Non-co-operation too was to be carried out in a "civil" manner. Here too, Gandhi's followers had to cheerfully face beating, imprisonment, confiscation of their property-and it was hoped that this willing suffering would cause a "change of heart."

But non-co-operation also had a dynamic of its own, a dynamic that didn't at all depend on converting the opponent or even molding public opinion. It was a dynamic based not on appeals but on the power of the people themselves.

Gandhi saw that the power of any tyrant depends entirely on people being willing to obey. The tyrant may get people to obey by threatening to throw them in prison, or by holding guns to their heads. But the power still resides in the obedience, not in the prison or the guns.

Now, what happens if those people begin to say, "We're not afraid of prison. We're even willing to die. But we're not willing to obey you any longer."

It's very simple. The tyrant has no power. He may rant and scream and hurt and destroy-but if the people hold to it, he's finished.

Gandhi said, "I believe that no government can exist for a single moment without the cooperation of the people, willing or forced, and if people suddenly withdraw their cooperation in every detail, the government will come to a standstill." That was Gandhi's concept of power-the one he's accused of not having. It's a hard one to grasp, for those used to seeing power in the barrel of a gun. Their filters do not pass it. And so they call Gandhi idealistic, impractical. Basic Concepts of Satyagraha: Gandhian Nonviolence: from the *APT Nonviolence Trainer's Manual.*

I. "Sat" – which implies openness, honesty, and fairness: Truth.

   A) Each person's opinions and beliefs represent part of the truth.

   B) In order to see more of the truth we must share our truths cooperatively.

   C) This implies a desire to communicate and a determination to do so, which in turn requires developing and refining relevant skills of communication.

   D) Commitment to seeing as much of the truth as possible means that we can not afford to categorize ourselves or others.

II. "Ahimsa" – refusal to inflict injury on others.

   A) Ahimsa is dictated by our commitment to communication and to sharing of our pieces of the truth. Violence shuts off channels of communication.

   B) The concept of ahimsa appears in most major religions, which suggests that while it may not be practiced by most people, it is respected as an ideal.

   C) Ahimsa is an expression of our concern that our own and other's humanity be manifested and respected.

   D) We must learn to genuinely love our opponents in order to practice ahimsa.

III. "Tapasya" – willingness for self-sacrifice.

   A) A satyagrahi (one who practices satyagraha) must be willing to shoulder any sacrifice which is occasioned by the struggle which they have initiated, rather than pushing such sacrifice or suffering onto their opponent, lest the opponent become alienated and access to their portion of the truth become lost.

B) The satyagrahi must always provide a face-saving "way out" for the opponents. The goal is to discover a wider vista of truth and justice, not to achieve victory over the opponent.

The Birth of 'Satyagraha'

Towards the end of 1907, the Government of South Africa tightened its laws against the Asian settlers in South Africa. It was called the 'Asiatic Act'. It lay down that all men and women of Asian origin above the age of eight years should get their names registered. In addition to this, the Government recognized only Christian marriages as legal. The result of this was that a Hindu couple or a Muslim couple who were married according to Hindu and Muslim religious rites were no longer considered as legally wedded husband and wife. Further, there was restriction on movement from one province to another.

Gandhi advised his men not to honour and obey the Registration Law. This led to a fierce struggle.Gandhi called it'Satyagraha'; it was the use of 'Soul-Force' or 'Love-Force' against 'Brute-Force' or violence. He trained men, women and children as volunteers to offer Satyagraha. He called his band a 'Peace Brigade'. It had to enter Transval from Natal. This was the civil dis-obedience that he planned. It continued for six months. All the Satyagrahisincluding Gandhi were arrested and put into prison. At last, the Government of South Africa came to an honourable settlement with Gandhi. The citizenship rights of Indians were recognized. Thus Gandhi was the champion of the self-respect of the Indians in South Africa.

Satyagraha, this new way of struggle in South Africa, began a new chapter in the political history of the world, Politics is generally understood to permit cheating, killing and violence. Its policy is that the end justifies the means. But Gandhi taught the principle that both the end and the means must be equally pure and moral. He himself put that principle into practice. He showed that if this is to be possible, love or nonviolence alone is the way to it.

Satyagraha: Introduction

Gandhi said he learned satyagraha from his wife — she practiced it on him. Hmmmm. Satyagraha is *not* just a technique for liberating colonies or achieving civil rights. It can be used at work, at home, and maybe even on the internet. Before you leave this website, I hope *you* realize satyagraha can be used whenever you are fighting for what is right.

To use satyagraha, especially in your own situation, you need to know the principles of satyagraha. Gandhi and King listed principles, but they weren't theoreticians. Before you leave this website, I hope you understand how and why satyagraha works.

Some people are attracted to the supposed nonviolence of satyagraha. That has its value. But before you leave this website, I hope you understand satyagraha can effectively achieve good goals.

Satyagraha is not a dead historical idea — it is an effective technique for fighting good fights. But I would not mind if you left this website with an;

"Oh Wow!" appreciation of Gandhi and King.

They were, in a nonviolent way, masters of battle technique.

Gandhi's Principles of Satyagraha

This is my best attempt to distil Gandhi's principles of Satyagraha. I have commented on each, based on my theory of satyagraha.

Love your enemy: I do not believe you need to love your enemy for satyagraha to succeed. However, you do need to act kindly and courteously towards your opponent, and you probably need to care about your opponent. Also, love would be a great way of naturally implementing the techniques of satyagraha (as long as your love for truth and morality is stronger). So loving your enemy is a good technique. Lacking that, you should try to understand your opponent well enough that you can be sympathatic to your opponent.

Always be truthful: The truth should be one of your strongest weapons. So if people find out you have not been truthful, your satyagraha is lost. You will not be believed. You will not be trusted. You will not win the hearts of your opponent or the spectators. And you cannot pretend to be working for an overarching goal of truth and morality. Even if your duplicity is never exposed, you will lose your own heart.

For the same reasons, you should always be moral.

Never use violence: By a strict criterion of violence, this is not true. In Vietnam, the monks burned themselves to death. This is violence on one's self. Gandhi made the British people feel badly about themselves. Does that count as violence?

Of course, gratuitous violence and unnecessary harm to the opponent are completely inappropriate. They undermine the basic principles of satyagraha. You win the hearts of spectators when you suffer and your opponent does not.

Try to win your enemy over to your side: This should be common to any battle. But you don't just argue your point of view, you also act virtuously, so as to make your opponent sympathetic to your efforts. Don't be angry; suffer the anger of your opponent: Anger leads to the desire to hurt your opponent, which is against the goals of winning hearts. So you don't want to respond to your opponents anger with your own anger. Actually suffering the anger of your opponent draws attention to your cause, shows the strength of your commitment, builds sympathy from the spectators, and weakens your opponent's heart.

Wean your opponents from error with patience and sympathy: You do not put your opponents in a position where they have to defend their wrong view. That would be like saying you want to avoid a battle and then not giving your enemy a chance to retreat. Establish the truth, not by infliction of suffering on your opponent, but by your own suffering.: Making your opponent suffer causes destruction, not awareness of the truth. Your own suffering signals your commitment to what you think is right, and it makes people think about what is right.

It appears to work slowly. In reality, there is no force in the world that is so direct or so swift in working. The 10 years between

Rosa Parks and the voting rights act probably went slowly for Martin Luther King. However, 10 years now seems remarkably quick.

The Term Satyagraha

Neither Gandhi nor King liked the phrase "passive resistance." They felt their actions were not passive. King apparently adopted (or created?) the term *nonviolent protest,* which of course assumes something to protest against.

The name *satyagraha* has problems too. According to Gandhi, it literally means "insistence upon truth". Truth is important, but just truth alone would not be satyagraha.

Gandhi combines satya with ahimsa, which I think is correct. Gandhi also translates ahimsa as meaning love. But ahimsa literally means harmlessness. Desikachar says that ahimsa implies concern and good will towards your enemy. I think the latter meanings better fit satyagraha.

So I have used Gandhi's term satyagraha, with the hopes that it has taken on a meaning of its own.

Gandhiji's Principles

Gandhi was to describe himself pre-eminently as a votary or seeker of *satya* (truth), which could not be attained other than through *ahimsa* (non-violence, love) and *Brahmacharya* (celibacy, striving towards God). Gandhi conceived of his own life as a series of experiments to forge the use of satyagraha in such a manner as to make the oppressor and the oppressed alike recognize their common bonding and humanity: as he recognized, freedom is only freedom when it is indivisible.

Truth

Gandhi dedicated his life to the wider purpose of discovering truth, or *Satya.* He tried to achieve this by learning from his own mistakes and conducting experiments on himself. He called his autobiography *The Story of My Experiments with Truth.*

Gandhi stated that the most important battle to fight was overcoming his own demons, fears, and insecurities. Gandhi summarized his beliefs first when he said "God is Truth". He would later change this statement to "Truth is God". Thus, *Satya* (Truth) in Gandhi's philosophy is "God".

Nonviolence

Mahatama Gandhi was in no way the originator of the principle of non-violence. But he was the first to apply it in political field on a huge scale. The concept of nonviolence (*ahimsa*) and nonresistance has a long history in Indian religious thought and has had many revivals in Hindu, Buddhist, Jain, Jewish and Christian contexts. Gandhi explains his philosophy and way of life in his autobiography *The Story of My Experiments with Truth*. He was quoted as saying:

"When I despair, I remember that all through history the way of truth and love has always won. There have been tyrants and murderers and for a time they seem invincible, but in the end, they always fall-think of it, always."

"What difference does it make to the dead, the orphans, and the homeless, whether the mad destruction is wrought under the name of totalitarianism or the holy name of liberty and democracy?"

"An eye for an eye makes the whole world blind."

"There are many causes that I am prepared to die for but no causes that I am prepared to kill for."

In applying these principles, Gandhi did not balk from taking them to their most logical extremes in envisioning a world where even government, police and armies were nonviolent.

In accordance with his views, in 1940, when invasion of the British Isles by Nazi Germany looked imminent, Gandhi offered the following advice to the British people (*Non-Violence in Peace and War*): "I would like you to lay down the arms you have as being useless for saving you or humanity. You will invite Herr Hitler and Signor Mussolini to take what they want of the countries you call your possessions.... If these gentlemen choose to occupy your homes, you will vacate them. If they do not give you free passage out, you will allow yourselves, man, woman, and child, to be slaughtered, but you will refuse to owe allegiance to them."

However, Gandhi was aware that this level of nonviolence required incredible faith and courage, which he realized not everyone possessed. He therefore advised that everyone need not keep to nonviolence, especially if it were used as a cover for cowardice.

Vegetarianism

As a young child, Gandhi experimented with meat-eating. This was due partially to his inherent curiosity as well as his rather persuasive peer and friend Sheikh Mehtab. The idea of vegetarianism is deeply ingrained in Hindu and Jain traditions in India, and, in his native land of Gujarat, most Hindus were vegetarian and so are all Jains. The Gandhi family was no exception. Before leaving for his studies in London, Gandhi made a promise to his mother, Putlibai and his uncle, Becharji Swami that he would abstain from eating meat, taking alcohol, and engaging in promiscuity. He held fast to his promise and gained more than a diet: he gained a basis for his life-long philosophies. As Gandhi grew into adulthood, he became a strict vegetarian. He wrote the book *The Moral Basis of Vegetarianism* and several articles on the subject, some of which were published in the London Vegetarian Society's publication, *The Vegetarian*. Gandhi, himself, became inspired by many great minds during this period and befriended the chairman of the London Vegetarian Society, Dr. Josiah Oldfield.

Having also read and admired the work of Henry Stephens Salt, the young Mohandas met and often corresponded with the vegetarian campaigner. Gandhi spent much time advocating vegetarianism during and after his time in London. To Gandhi, a vegetarian diet would not only satisfy the requirements of the body, it would also serve an economic purpose as meat was, and still is, generally more expensive than grains, vegetables, and fruits. Also, many Indians of the time struggled with low income, thus vegetarianism was seen not only as a spiritual practice but also a practical one. He abstained from eating for long periods, using fasting as a form of political protest. He refused to eat until his death or his demands were met. It was noted in his autobiography that vegetarianism was the beginning of his deep commitment to Brahmacharya; without total control of the palate, his success in Bramacharya would likely falter.

Bapu had been a frutarian, but started taking goat's milk on the advice of his doctor. He never took the dairy products (of cow) largely because of his philosophical views, partially because of disgust for phooka, and, specifically, because of a vow to his late mother.

Brahmacharya

Gandhi saw Brahmacharya as a means of becoming close with God and as a primary foundation for self realization. He followed Brahmacharya, so that he could learn to love, rather than lust. For Gandhi, Brahmacharya meant "control of the senses in thought, word and deed."

Simplicity

Gandhi earnestly believed that a person involved in social service should lead a simple life which he thought could lead to Brahmacharya. His simplicity began by renouncing the western lifestyle he was leading in South Africa. He called it "reducing himself to zero," which entailed giving up unnecessary expenditure, embracing a simple lifestyle and washing his own clothes. On one occasion he returned the gifts bestowed to him from the natals for his diligent service to the community.

Gandhi spent one day of each week in silence. He believed that abstaining from speaking brought him inner peace. This influence was drawn from the Hindu principles of *mauna* and *shanti*. On such days he communicated with others by writing on paper. For three and a half years, from the age of 37, Gandhi refused to read newspapers, claiming that the tumultuous state of world affairs caused him more confusion than his own inner unrest.

After reading John Ruskin's *Unto This Last*, he decided to change his lifestyle and create a commune called *Phoenix Settlement*.

Upon returning to India from South Africa, where he had enjoyed a successful legal practice, he gave up wearing Western-style clothing, which he associated with wealth and success. He dressed to be accepted by the poorest person in India, advocating the use of homespun cloth (*khadi*). Gandhi and his followers adopted the practice of weaving their own clothes from thread they themselves spun, and encouraged others to do so. While Indian workers were often idle due to unemployment, they had often bought their clothing from industrial manufacturers owned by

British interests. It was Gandhi's view that if Indians made their own clothes, it would deal an economic blow to the British establishment in India. Consequently, the spinning wheel was later incorporated into the flag of the Indian National Congress. He subsequently wore a dhoti for the rest of his life to express the simplicity of his life.

Faith

Gandhi was born a Hindu and practised Hinduism all his life, deriving most of his principles from Hinduism. As a common Hindu, he believed all religions to be equal, and rejected all efforts to convert him to a different faith. He was an avid theologian and read extensively about all major religions. He had the following to say about Hinduism:

"Hinduism as I know it entirely satisfies my soul, fills my whole being... When doubts haunt me, when disappointments stare me in the face, and when I see not one ray of light on the horizon, I turn to the *Bhagavad Gita,* and find a verse to comfort me; and I immediately begin to smile in the midst of overwhelming sorrow. My life has been full of tragedies and if they have not left any visible and indelible effect on me, I owe it to the teachings of the *Bhagavad Gita.*"

Gandhi believed that at the core of every religion was truth and love (compassion, nonviolence and the Golden Rule). He also questioned hypocrisy, malpractices and dogma in all religions and was a tireless social reformer. Later in his life when he was asked whether he was a Hindu, he replied:

"Yes I am. I am also a Christian, a Muslim, a Buddhist and a Jew."

Gandhi and Non-violence

In his trial speech made at Ahmadabad Sessions court in March 1922, Gandhi put forward his philosophy with great eloquence, when he stated non-violence to be the 'first article of (his) faith' and the 'last article of (his) creed'. Non-violence had always been the founding principle of Gandhian spirituality, and his bedrock of his political philosophy. Gandhi's distrust of violence as a mode to assume political power and as a tool of revolution was ingrained in his world-view from the very early days of his political career. It is impossible to look at Gandhi's political activism in isolation. Springing deeply from his belief in truth, Gandhi's political goals were ultimately specific correlatives of higher commitments to humanity and world peace. Non-violence preaches world peace and brotherhood, whereas political movements naturally revel in polemics of difference and anatagonism. Gandhi's greatness lies in bringing together these two apparently combative and incongruous ideas and putting them on a common platform, where they do not subtract, but support each other. Gandhi's significance in the world political scenario is two-fold. First, he retrieved non-violence as a powerful political tool, and secondly, he was the one of the chief promulgators of the theory that political goal is ultimately a manifestation of a higher spiritual and humanitarian goal, culminating in world peace. For Gandhi, the means were as important as the end, and there could be only one means-that of non-violence.

The Origins of Gandhi's Non-violence Philosophy

Gandhi's secularism and openness to all kinds of theological and philosophical schools is well-known. It was through an assimilation of various concepts and philosophical tenets that Gandhi arrived at his own understanding of non-violence. Jainism and Buddhism were the most important influences that lay behind the foundation of Gandhi's non-violence theory. Both Jainism and Buddhism preached non-violence as the basic principle of existence. All other thoughts and actions propagated by these two religious schools were based on this base of non-violence. Gandhi was deeply influenced by his readings of these scriptures.

The Acaranga Sutra of the Jains stated all life to be dear and precious, and Gandhi believed in it earnestly. The Bhagvadgita was another important influence, with its stress on non-attachment and selfless action. Christianity, along with its message of love and compassion, extended even to one's enemies, was another important influence on Gandhi's life. Bringing together all these theological schools, Gandhi was in search for a meaningful life, a life based on truth and honesty, a life that would boast of a moral courage to stand for the right and for justice, even at its own cost. It was this outlook that Gandhi employed as a tool to guide India's freedom struggle, which eventually succeeded to unite the length and breadth of the country like never before.

Gandhi and Nonviolence

Gandhi did not claim to be a prophet or even a philosopher. "There is no such thing as Gandhism," he warned, "and I do not want to leave any sect after me." There was only one Gandhian, he said, an imperfect one at that: himself.

The real significance of the Indian freedom movement in Gandhi's eyes was that it was waged nonviolently. He would have had no interest in it if the Indian National Congress had adopted Satyagraha and subscribed to nonviolence. He objected to violence not only because an unarmed people had little chance of success in an armed rebellion, but because he considered violence a clumsy weapon which created more problems than it solved, and left a trail of hatred and bitterness in which genuine reconciliation was almost impossible.

This emphasis on nonviolence jarred alike on Gandhi's British and Indian critics, though for different reasons. To the former, nonviolence was a camouflage; to the latter, it was sheer sentimentalism. To the British who tended to see the Indian struggle through the prism of European history, the professions of nonviolence rather than on the remarkably peaceful nature of Gandhi's campaigns. To the radical Indian politicians, who had browsed on the history of the French and Russian revolutions or the Italian and Irish nationalist struggles, it was patent that force would only yield to force, and that it was foolish to miss opportunities and sacrifice tactical gains for reasons more relevant to ethics than to politics.

Gandhi's total allegiance to nonviolence created a gulf between him and the educated elite in India which was temporarily bridged only during periods of intense political excitement. Even among his closest colleagues there were few who were prepared to follow his doctrine of nonviolence to its logical conclusion : the adoption of unilateral disarmament in a world armed to the teeth, the scrapping of the police and the armed forces, and the decentralization of administration to the point where the state would "wither away". Nehru, Patel and others on whom fell the task of organizing the administration of independent India did not question the superiority of the principle of nonviolence as enunciated by their leader, but they did not coperider it practical politics. The Indian Constituent Assembly include a majority of members owing allegiance to Gandhi or at least holding him in high esteem, but the constitution which emerged from their labours in 1949 was based more on the Western parliamentary than on he Gandhian model. The development of the Indian economy during the last four decades cannot be said to have conformed to Gandhi's conception of "self-reliant village republics". On the other hand, it bears the marks of a conscious effort to launch an Indian industrial revolution.

Jawaharlal Nehru—Gandhi's "political heir"—was thoroughly imbued with the humane values inculcated by the Mahatma. But the man who spoke Gandhi's language, after his death, was Vinoba Bhave, the "Walking Saint", who kept out of politics and government, Bhave's Bhoodan (land gift) Movement was designed as much as a measure of land reform as that of a spiritual renewal. Though more than five million acres of land were distributed to the landless, the movement, despite its early promise, never really spiraled into a social revolution by consent.

This was partly because Vinoba Bhave did not command Gandhi's extraordinary genius for organizing the masses for a national crusade, and partly because in independent India the tendency grew for the people to look up to the government rather than to rely on voluntary and cooperative effort for effecting reforms in society.

Soon after Gandhi's death in 1948, a delegate speaking at the United Nations predicted that "the greatest achievements of the Indian sage were yet to come" "Gandhi's times," said Vinoba Bhave, "were the first pale dawn of the sun of Satyagraha." Forty years after Gandhi's death, this optimism would seem to have been too high-pitched.

The manner in which Gandhi's techniques have sometimes been invoked even in the land of his birth in recent years would appear to be a travesty of his principles. And the world has been in the grip of a series of crises in Korea, the Congo, the Vietnam, the Middle East, and South Africa with a never-ending trail of blood and bitterness. The shadow of a thermo-nuclear war with its incalculable hazards continues to hang over mankind. From this predicament, Gandhi's ideas and techniques may suggest a way out. Unfortunately, his motives and methods are often misunderstood, and not only by mobs in the street, Not long ago, Arthur Koestler described Gandhi's attitude as one "of passive submission to bayonetting and raping, to villages without sewage, septic childhood's and trachoma."

Such a judgement is of course completely with the same tenacity with which he battled with the British Raj. He advocated nonviolence not because it offered an easy way out, but because he considered violence a crude and in the long run, an ineffective weapon. His rejection of violence stemmed from choice, not from necessity.

Horace Alexander, who knew Gandhi and saw him in action, graphically describes the attitude of the nonviolent resister to his opponent: "On your side you have all the mighty forces of the modern State, arms, money, a controlled press, and all the rest. On my side, I have nothing but my conviction of right and truth, the unquenchable spirit of man, who is prepared to die for his convictions than submit to your brute force. I have my comrades in armlessness. Here we stand; and here if need be, we fall." Far from being a craven retreat from difficulty and danger, nonviolent resistance demands courage of a high order, the courage to resist injustice without rancour, to unite the utmost firmness with the utmost gentleness, to invite suffering but not to inflict it, to die but not to kill.

Gandhi did not make the facile division of mankind into "good" and "bad" He was convinced that every human being—even the "enemy" –had a kernel of decency: there were only evil acts, no wholly evil men. His technique of Satyagraha was designed not to coerce the opponent, but to set into motion forces which could lead to his conversion.

Relying as it did on persuasion and compromise, Gandhi's method was not always quick in producing results, but the results were likely to be the more durable for having been brought about peacefully. "It is my firm conviction," Gandhi affirmed, "that nothing enduring can be built upon violence. " The rate of social change through the nonviolent technique was not in fact likely to be much slower than that achieved by violent methods; it was definitely faster than that expected from the normal functioning of institutions which tended to fossilize and preserve the status quo.

Gandhi did not think it possible to bring about radical changes in the structure of society overnight. Nor did he succumb to the illusion that the road to a new order could be paved merely with pious wishes and fine words. It was not enough to blame the opponent or bewail the times in which one's lot was cast.

However heavy the odds, it was the Satyagrahi's duty never to feel helpless. The least he could do was to make a beginning with himself. If he was crusading for a new deal for peasantry, he could go to a village and live there, If he wanted to bring peace to a disturbed district, he could walk through it, entering into the minds and hearts of those who were going through the ordeal, If an age-old evil like untouchability was to be fought, what could be a more effective symbol of defiance for a reformer than to adopt an untouchable child?

If the object was to challenge foreign rule, why not act on the assumption that the country was already free, ignore the alien government and build alternative institutions to harness the spontaneous, constructive and cooperative effort of the people? If the goal was world peace, why not begin today by acting peacefully6n towards the immediate neighbour, going more than half way to understand and win him over?

Though he may have appeared a starry-eyed idealist to so me, Gandhi's attitude to social and political problems was severely practical. There was a deep mystical streak in him, but even his mysticism seemed to have little of the ethereal about it. He did not dream heavenly dreams nor see things unutterable in trance; when "the still small voice" spoke to him, it was often to tell how he could fight a social evil or heal a rift between two warring communities. Far from distracting him from his role in public affairs, Gandhi's religious quest gave him the stamina to play it more effectively. To him true religion was not merely the reading of scriptures, the dissection of ancient texts, or even the practice of cloistered virtue: it had to be lived in the challenging context of political and social life.

Gandhi used his nonviolent technique on behalf of his fellow-countrymen in South Africa and India, but he did not conceive it only as a weapon in the armoury of Indian nationalism. On the other hand, he fashioned it as an instrument for righting wrongs and resolving conflicts between opposing groups, races and nations. It is a strange paradox that though the stoutest and perhaps the most successful champion of the revolt against colonialism in our time, Gandhi was frees from the taint of narrow nationalism. As early as 1924, he had declared that "the better mind of the world desires today, not absolutely independent states, warring one against another, but a federation of independent, of friendly interdependent states"

Gandhi's Prayer Ground at Sevagram Ashram, Wardha

Even before the First World War had revealed the disastrous results of the combination of industrialism and nationalism, he had become a convert to the idea that violence between nation-states must be completely abjured.

In 1931, during his visit to England, a cartoon in the Star depicted him in a loin cloth besides Mussolini, Hitler, de Valera and Stalin, who were clad in black, brown, green and red shirts respectively. The caption, "And he isn't wearing any blooming' shirt at all" was not only literally but figuratively true. For a man of nonviolence, who believed in the brotherhood of man, there was no superficial division of nations into good and bad, allies and adversaries. This did not, however, mean that Gandhi did not distinguish between the countries which inflicted and the countries which suffered violence. His own life had been one struggle against the forces of violence, and Satyagraha was designed at once to eschew violence and to fight injustice.

In the years immediately preceding the Second Word war, when the tide of Nazi and Fascist aggression was relentlessly rolling forward, Gandhi had reasserted his faith in nonviolence and commended it to the smaller nation which were living in daily dread of being overwhelmed by superior force. Through the pages of his weekly paper the Harijan, he expounded the nonviolent approach to military aggression and political tyranny. He advised the weaker nations to defend themselves not by increasing their fighting potential, but by nonviolent resistance to the aggressor. When Czechoslovakia was black-mailed into submission in September 1938, Gandhi suggested to the unfortunate Czechs: "There is no bravery greater than a resolute refusal.

To bend the knee to an earthly power, no matter how great, and that without bitterness of spirit, and in the fullness of faith that the spirit alone lives, nothing else does." Seven years later when the first atomic bombs exploded over Hiroshima and Nagasaki, Gandhi's reaction was characteristic: "I did not move a muscle.

On the contrary, I said to myself that unless now the adopts nonviolence, it will spell certain suicide for mankind." The irony of the very perfection of the weapons of war rendering them useless as arbiters between nations has become increasingly clear during the last forty years.

The atomic stockpiles which the major nuclear powers have already built up are capable of destroying civilization, as we know it several time over and peace has been precariously preserved by, what has been grimly termed, "the balance of atomic terror." The fact is that with the weapons of mass destruction, which are at hand now, to attack another nation is tantamount to attacking oneself. This is a bitter truth which old habits of thought have prevented from going home. "This splitting of the atoms has changed everything" bewailed Einstein, "save our modes of thinking and thus we drift towards unparalleled catastrophe."

Nonviolence, as Gandhi expounded it, has ceased to be a pious exhortation, and become a necessity. The advice he gave to the unfortunate Abyssinians and Czechs during the twilight years before the Second Word War, may have seemed utopian thirty years ago. Today, it sounds commonsense. Even some hardheaded military strategists such as Sir Stephen King-Hall have begun to see in Gandhi's method a possible alternative to suicidal violence.

Gandhi would have been the first to deny that his method offered an instant or universal panacea for world peace. His method is capable of almost infinite evolution to suit new situations in a changing world. It is possible that "applied nonviolence" is at present at the same.

Stage of development "as the invention of electricity was in the days of Edison and Marconi." The lives-and deaths-of Chief Lithuli and Dr. Martin Luther King have proved that there is nothing esoteric about nonviolence, limiting it to a particular country or a particular period. Indeed Tagore, the great contemporary and friend of Gandhi, prophesies that the West would accept Gandhi before the East "for the West has gone through the cycle of dependence on force and material things of life and has become disillusioned. They want a return to the spirit. The East has not yet gone through materialism and hence has not become so disillusioned."

Gandhi's Non-Violence

On April 6, 1930, after having marched 241 miles on foot from his village to the sea, Mohandas K. Gandhi arrived at the coastal village of Dandi, India, and gathered salt. It was a simple act, but one which was illegal under British colonial rule of India. Gandhi was openly defying the British Salt Law. Within a month, people all over India were making salt illegally, and more than 100,000 were sent to jail; many fell victim to police violence, but none retaliated or even defended themselves (Herman 99-101).

The Salt March of 1930 was a vital step toward India's independence from Britain. Gandhi, who was known to many as "Mahatma" (Great Soul), had led the masses of India into a programme of massive disobedience to British law; what was most important to Gandhi, however, was that Indians use neither violence nor hatred in their fight for freedom. What was Gandhi's philosophy? Was he successful?

Elements of Gandhi's philosophy were rooted in the Indian religions of Jainism and Buddhism. Both of these advocate ahimsa (non-violence), which is "absence of the desire to kill or harm". The Acaranga Sutra, a Jainist text, describes the fundamental need for non-violence: "All beings are fond of life; they like pleasure and hate pain, shun destruction and like to live, they long to live. To all, life is dear". Ahimsa is a way of living and thinking which respects this deeply.

Gandhi was both religious (he was Hindu) and open-minded, and saw the different religions as paths to the same goal. He was inspired by the teachings of Jesus, in particular the emphasis on love for everyone, even one's enemies, and the need to strive for justice. He also took from Hinduism the importance of action in one's life, without concern for success; the Hindu text Bhagavad-Gita says, "On action alone be thy interest,/Never on its fruits/ Abiding in discipline perform actions,/Abandoning attachment/ Being indifferent to success or failure".

For Gandhi, ahimsa was the expression of the deepest love for all humans, including one's opponents; this non-violence therefore included not only a lack of physical harm to them, but also a lack of hatred or ill-will towards them. Gandhi rejected the traditional dichotomy between one's own side and the "enemy;" he believed in the need to convince opponents of their injustice, not to punish them, and in this way one could win their friendship and one's own freedom. If need be, one might need to suffer or die in order that they may be converted to love.

Gandhi also firmly believed that if violence was used to achieve any end – even if it was employed in the name of justice – the result would be more violence. But such pragmatism in matters of non-violence was unimportant to Gandhi. Thomas Merton writes:

"In Gandhi's mind, non-violence was not simply a political tactic which was supremely useful and efficacious in liberating his people from foreign rule. [...] On the contrary, the spirit of non-violence sprang from an inner realization of spiritual unity in himself".

This way of thinking reflects the Hindu idea of "being indifferent to success or failure," which I described above.

Gandhi's main tactic in his fight against the British was what he called Satyagraha, which means "Soul-Force" or "The power of truth". Gandhi developed Satyagraha as the practical extension of ahimsa and love; it meant standing firmly behind one's ideals, but without hatred. Satyagraha took the form of civil disobedience and non-cooperation with evil. Civil disobedience involved breaking a specific law if it was believed to be unjust, and then facing the consequences. The Salt March of 1930, which I described above, was one of Gandhi's greatest successes in civil disobedience.

Salt was necessary to the life of Indian farmers' cattle, and the British monopoly on salt production had led to massive taxes on the vital substance.

The other element of Satyagraha, non-cooperation with evil, consisted of pulling out all support for an unjust system, such as the British rule of India. This tactic need not break any law, but might include boycotting British products, refusing to work for British employers, pulling one's children out of British schools, refusing to supply the British with services, and not paying taxes. In 1920, after the British army massacred 400 unarmed demonstrators, Gandhi organized a nation-wide Satyagraha which used non-cooperation techniques such as the ones above, as well as public demonstrations, in order to "withdraw Indian support from the vast, monstrous Machine of Empire until it ground to a halt".

Although this nation-wide strike hit the British hard, and led to thousands of Indians being jailed, in 1922 it erupted into violence. A mob of "Satyagrahis" lit fire to a police station, killing two dozen police officers trapped inside. Gandhi called off the entire Satyagraha and apologized for his "Himalayan blunder"; he had mistakenly believed that his followers truly understood non-violence.

To examine whether Gandhi's programme of Satyagraha was a success, we must first look at his objectives. I have already mentioned two of his aims — to earn Indian independence, and to do it non-violently. In these, Gandhi was successful. India became independent in 1947, with scarcely any violence toward the British, and Gandhi's leadership was crucial. The struggle had been difficult and long, but, in the end, Britain simply lowered its flag over India and left.

Sadly, however, Gandhi's dream was not fulfilled. Gandhi was dismayed by Hinduism's treatment of the Muslim minority in India, and by the resulting calls for the creation of a separate Muslim state of Pakistan. Widespread distrust and hatred was growing between Hindus and Muslims and, on the eve of India's independence, riots erupted all over India. The country became a bloodbath, in which it was estimated that a million lives were lost.

But had it? In these "months of chaos and terror," Gandhi spent his time in the most violent areas: "Each night he preached Peace and Love and prayed," writes Stanley Wolpert. "Gandhi walked from village to village through the heart of that violent madness, [...] preaching Ahimsa".

Mohandas K. Gandhi, the "Great Soul," was anything but a failure. In a world seemingly dominated by violence and hatred, Mahatma Gandhi reincarnated the ancient idea of Ahimsa, non-violence, as the only way of living in peace. His example influenced and inspired many later peaceful struggles, for example the civil rights movement of Martin Luther King, Jr. Despite India's shortcomings, Gandhi never lost faith in Ahimsa.

3

Role of Mahatma Gandhi in Freedom Struggle

One of the greatest men in the history of India is unarguably Mahatma Gandhi. The way he gave shape and character to India's freedom struggle is worthy of a standing ovation. He sacrificed his own life for the sake of his country. The respect that he earned for himself despite leading a simple lifestyle is much appreciable. Mahatma Gandhi played a pivotal role in the freedom struggle of India. His non violent ways and peaceful methods were the foundation for gaining independence from the British. Read about Mahatma Gandhi's role in freedom struggle of India.

Mahatma Gandhi was born Mohandas Karamchand Gandhi on 2nd October at Porbandar located in Gujarat. He went off to South Africa after marriage and worked as barrister there for twenty years. In South Africa, he had his first brush with apartheid. Once while he was travelling in a train, he was thrown out of the first class compartment despite having a ticket. This made him swear that he would do his best to erase apartheid from the face of his world. He went back to India only to find that his own country was being ruled by the British and his fellow citizens were being treated harshly by the British.

Like other great men in history, Gandhi took his time to grow and develop his techniques to ensure that his actions made an impact. His faith in different religions was commendable. His listened to the teachings of Christianity with the same belief and faith he read the Hindu scriptures with. He was brutally honest and truthful and this helped him throughout his life. Some of the major movements and freedom struggles led by him are discussed below.

Non Cooperation Movement

One of the first series of non violent protests nationwide was the non cooperation movement started by Mahatma Gandhi. This movement officially started the Gandhian era in India. In this freedom struggle, the non cooperation movement was basically aimed at making the Indians aware of the fact that the British government can be opposed and if done actively, it will keep a check on them.

Thus, educational institutions were boycotted, foreign goods were boycotted, and people let go off their nominated seats in government institutions. Though the movement failed, Indians awakened to the concept of going against the British.

Civil Disobedience Movement

Gandhi again took off with another non violent movement known as the civil disobedience movement. This movement was more active than the non cooperation movement and brought about a revolution of sorts. This movement aimed at bringing the British administration to a stop by withdrawing support from everything. There was agitation against land revenue, abolition of salt tax, cutting down military expenditure, levying duty on foreign cloth, etc. A very important movement was that of Salt Satyagraha where Gandhi undertook the Dandi march as a protest against the Salt tax.

Quit India Movement

The Quit India Movement was launched under the leadership of Mahatma Gandhi in August 1942. The main aim for launching this movement was to bring the British to negotiate with the Indian leaders. It was a call for immediate independence of India and the slogan of "Do or Die" was adopted for the same.

However the leaders were arrested soon after Gandhi's speech and were put in jail by British officials. Gandhi went on a fast for 21 days demanding the release of the leaders despite his failing health. The British had to secure the release of the leaders.

India Independence

After the Quit India Movement the freedom struggle got even more intense and passionate. Entire India was united together in the movement for freedom. Everyone contributed what they could in the freedom struggle. The cry of Purna Swaraj or complete independence was raised. After much sacrifices and efforts, India gained its independence on the 15th August, 1947.

Gandhiji's Popular Appeal

Indian political and spiritual leader, called Mahatma ("Great Soul"). Gandhi helped India's struggle for independence from Britain through a campaign based on nonviolence and civil disobedience. His doctrine of nonviolent action had a profound influence on Martin Luther King Jr., the leader of the civil rights movement in the U.S, and Nelson Mandela, the most prominent figure of the black opposition to apartheid in South Africa. However, Gandhi never received the Nobel Peace Prize.

"Nonviolence and truth (*Satya*) are inseparable and presupposes one another. There is no god higher than truth."

Mohandas Karamchand Gandhi was born in Poorbandar, Kathiawar, on the western coast of India. For several generations, the Gadhi's had been Prime Ministers in several Kathiawald States. Karamchand Gandhi, his father was the chief minister of Porbandar and a member of the Rajasthanik Court. He married four times. Putlibai, his last wife and Gandhi's mother, was a deeply religious Hindu. When Gandhi was sixteen, his father died-four years later he lost his mother. "The outstanding impression my mother has left on my memory is that of saintliness," Gandhi later wrote in his book of memoir, *An Autobiography: The Story of My Experiments With Truth* (1927-29).

Gandhi was married at the age of 13, as was not unusual by the custom. His bride, Kasturba, also was 13. She was the only daughter of rich merchants. Kastur Kapadian and Gandhi had four sons; their first child was born in 1885, but died after a few days. Kasturbai could not-read or write and Gandhi's attempts to teach her were fruitless. Although she often had to submit to her husband's decisions, she also had a will of her own. The marriage endured until her death in 1944..

In 1888 Gandhi went to London to study law, leaving his wife for three years. In the new surrounding he began experiments with diet that continued throughout his lifetime. After he was called to the bar at Inner Temple, he returned home to practice as a barrister in Bombay. Unable to find a suitable post, Gandhi moved to South Africa in 1893. During his journey to Pretoria he had a firsthand experience with racist degradation, a most crucial experience in his formative years. Gandhi worked for Dada Abdullah & Co and the Indian community. Kasturba had again waited with the children in India, but in 1897 she joined her husband in Durban. Gandhi gained fame as a tenacious political campaigner, who courageously opposed the Transvaal government's discriminatory legislation against Indian settlers. His ideological basis was much derived from the liberal-humanist values he had absorbed in England, exemplified in the works of Ruskin, Thoreau, and Emerson.

Gandhi remained in South Africa for 20 years and developed a system of nonviolent defiance. For his services during the Boer War (1899-1902) Gandhi was awarded the War Medal. After the birth of their fourth son, Gandhi suggested to his wife that they sleep in separate beds. Gandhi's one-sided decision and sexual abstinence caused Kasturba for a long time much stress. In search for spiritual development Gandhi studied the *Bible*, the *Koran*, and memorized the *Bhagavad Gita*. Also Leo Tolstoy influenced him deeply. Gandhi saw that his methods were in harmony with Hindu doctrines of *ahimsa* and that "the strongest physical force bends before moral force when it is used in the defence of truth." In his middle thirties, Gandhi took the vow of *bramahcharya*, which means not only complete chastity but the elimination of sexual desire. To test his self-control Gandhi slept naked with young women.

In 1914 Gandhi returned permanently to India. His most prominent adversary, Gen. Jan Smuts, wrote to a friend reliefed: "The saint has left our shores, I hope, forever." Gandhi became a highly influential figure in the National Congress, transforming it into an instrument of change. Following the massacre at Amritsar in 1919, in which British soldiers killed hundreds of Indians, Gandhi launched a policy of nonviolent non-co-operation to secure *swaraj* (independence) from Britain. This process made Gandhi a gurulike figure. Resistance methods included strikes, refusal to pay taxes, abandonment of western for Indian dress, and refusal to respect colonial law. "One step enough for me," Gandhi often said without planning his actions far ahead.

Gandhi himself adopted a simple, ascetic way of life, dressing only in a loincloth of handwoven cloth and sandals. He was jailed several times and went on hunger strikes to focus attention on his cause. When communal riots started on India's northwest frontier in 1924, Gandhi undertook a 21-day purificatory fast. After he had walked some 200 miles on foot to the sea to collect salt illegally, the Viceroy started to relieve the punitive salt taxes and the government monopoly.

Gandhi also strove to raise the status of untouchables, the caste whom everybody avoided. He gave them the name *harijan,* or "children of God", and founded the weekly paper *Harijan,* which was published in English and Hindi. In an attempt to persuade the orthodox Hindus to wipe out the "blight of untouchability", Gandhi undertook fast in the summer of 1933 for three weeks. In order to promote village self-sufficiency, Gandhi popularized handspinning and made know *khadi,* hand-spun cloth, the "livery of freedom." However, Gandhi's rejection of the Industrial Revolution wasn't supported by some his most close fiends, among them Jawaharlal Nehru.

"I am not built for academic writings. Action is my domain."

In 1936 Gandhi moved his headquarters from Sabarmati to Sevagram, a village near Wardha, which became a centre to test his ideas. His eldest son Harilal turned into Islam in 1936 and changed his name to Abdullah Gandhi. During World War II Gandhi's struggle for India's independence and *satyagraha* (defence of and by truth) became a threat to the war effort of the Allies. Gandhi argued that India should remain passive and neutral in the world conflict. On May 10, 1942, Gandhi wrote in his newspaper: "The presence of the British in India is an invitation to Japan to invade India. Their withdrawal would remove the bait. Assume however that it does not, Free India would be better able to cope with invasion. Unadulterated non-co-operation would then have full sway." Gandhi was arrested with Nehru and other Congress leaders, and interned in Aga Khan's Palace at Poona. At the age of 73, Gandhi began another fast. Winston Churchill,

Britain's prime minister, who had earlier called Gandhi a "seditious fakir", suspected that Gandhi was fed glucose whenever he drank water: "... and this, as well as his intense vitality and lifelong austerity, enabled this frail being to maintain his prolonged abstention from any visible form of food.

Nearly all the Indian members of the Viceroy's Executive Council demanded his release, and resigned in protest at our refusal. In the end, being quite convinced of our obduracy, he abandoned his fast and his health, though he was very weak, was not seriously affected." (from *The Second World War*, vol. 4., by Winston Churchill, 1951). Gandhi was released from custody unconditionally in the spring of 1944.

Kasturba died at the palace of Aga Khan in 1944. Before her death, Harilal, the eldest son, had appreared drunk in the palace, and was chased away. Gandhi saw India gain independence in 1947. However, he had to witness deploring the formation of two new nations-and savage fighting. His illusion that India would gain indepencence by nonviolent means was shattered. "Who listens to me today?" Gandhi said, and did not remain in New Delhi to celebrate India's freedom on the Fifteenth of August.

Gandhi's last months were shadowed by communal strife between Hindu and Muslim. When he walked barefoot through the scorched villages in East Bengal, locals strewed shattered glass on his path. Gandhi pleaded for amicable settlement between India and Pakistan, but on January 30, 1948, he was assassinated in Delhi on his way to an evening prayer. A young Hindu Brahmin, named Nathuram Godse, viewed Gandhi's acceptance of partition as a betrayal of the Hindu population, and fired three shots point-blank. Gandhi had not allowed police to search people near him. Godse believed that the prayer and the purity of the mind were signs of superstitions and without the "father of the nation" India would free to follow the course founded on reason.

"Even Gandhi, with all his charisma, did not melt the hearts of his oppressors, as he had hoped. After softening, hearts harden again. Asoka too was wrong to think that he was changing the course of history, and that his righteousness woul last 'as long as the sun and the moon'." (Theodore Zeldin in *An Intimate History of Humanity*, 1994).

Gandhi has been criticized for his nostalgia for ancient rural bliss and delaying the modernization and industrialization of his country. On the other hand, he has been regarded as the "true soul" of India. With other Hindu sages Gandhi shared a mistrust of worshipping followers, and he tried to avoid the title *mahatma*. In spite of this, his disciplines regarded him as a saint. Gandhi's denial of the pleasures of food, sex, family, and friendship, has made his way of life extremely demanding for ordinary people, who otherwise have found inspiration from his courage and teachings. This question troubled George Orwell in his essay 'Reflections on Gandhi' (1949). While admitting that Gandhi never made claims of sainthood, he did not hesitate to reject sainthood as an ideal : "The essence of being human is that one does not seek perfection, that one is sometimes willing to commit sins for the sake of loyalty, that one does not push asceticism to the point where it makes friendly intercourse impossible, and that one is prepared in the end to be defeated and broken up by life, which is the inevitable price of fastening one's love upon other human individuals.

Mohandas Karamchand Gandhi, the youngest son of Karamchand Gandhi and Putlibai, was born on October 2, 1869. His birthplace was Porbander, a small seaside town in the Kathiawar peninsula of western India. His mother was a devout and religious woman who attended temple services daily and never ate before she prayed.

At school in Porbander, Gandhiji was very shy and lacked the confidence and poise necessary to talk to strangers. But he was admirably punctual and obedient, and participated actively in school games.

In compliance with the prevailing custom of child marriage, Mohandas married at the age of thirteen. Kasturbai, his illiterate wife, was simple, persevering, bold and independent.

A Student of Law in England

Karamchand Gandhi died in the year 1885, leaving little property for his family. In 1887, Mohandas completed his matriculation and left for England to study law. He lived in London, where he found the life strange and difficult to adjust to. Although he adopted English dress and took dancing and violin lessons, he was nevertheless quite unsuccessful in conforming to the British mode of life. His friends tried to compel him to eat meat but he abstained, adhering very rigidly to a vegetarian diet. He joined vegetarian clubs and very soon became a champion of vegetarianism. It was in fact in England where Gandhiji's experiments in diet began.

A transformation in Gandhiji's life and character now began to take place. His heart ached deeply for religion. He was inspired by meetings with Madame Blavatsky and Annie Besant. He read their books on Theosophy and read the Bible. He was impressed by the similarity of the teachings of the *Sermon on the Mount* and the *Gita*. He began reading the *Gita* only during his second year in London, and in it found the comfort and solace he sought.

Gandhiji studied French, Latin and science. He was called to the Bar in 1891, after which he at once sailed for India. On his return to his native land he began to study Indian Law. At Rajkot he established a moderately successful practice. While there, he was insulted by a political agent, a British officer who was prejudiced against Gandhiji's brother. This insult changed the course of his life, inspiring him with the desire to learn something about the politics his of country.

Fight Against Racial Prejudice in S.A.

At this time, Gandhiji accepted an offer from the Meman firm of Porbander to go to South Africa as their legal representative. He arrived in Natal in 1893 and was immediately requested to go to Pretoria where his presence was required. He confronted difficulty when he entered a first-class compartment on a train to the Transvaal. At Pietermaritzburg he was ejected from the train with all his luggage. He now became resolved to fight colour prejudice.

The ill-treatment that the Indians received at the hands of colonialists was abhorrent to Gandhiji, and he was determined to champion their cause. This led him, in 1894, to found the Natal Indian Congress. In 1899, on the outbreak of the Anglo-Boer War, he led the Indian Ambulance Corps of one thousand members. They engaged in active service and on one occasion were under attack of heavy fire. In 1901, Gandhiji's health broke down and he returned to India.

After a year or two he was again summoned to South Africa. While there, in 1901, he founded the newspaper, *Indian Opinion.* Five years later, when a native rebellion broke out in Natal, Gandhiji offered a Stretcher-Bearer Corps. During the First World War he raised an Ambulance Corps and conducted a recruiting campaign in Karia.

It was in South Africa that Gandhiji first adopted Satyagraha, the method of non-violence, to fight the injustice to which Indians were subjected. The entire Indian community rallied around him magnificently, for he had readily identified himself with all.

His powerful Satyagraha campaign with which he confronted the unjust laws of the local government was overwhelmingly successful. He showed that this "soul force", as he called it, could be universally applied to bring peace and abolish despotism and ever-growing militarism.

Struggle for Independence

His mission accomplished, Gandhiji arrived in India in 1915. In 1918, he assumed leadership of the Indian National Congress and associated himself with the Khilafat movement. He used the peaceful method of non-co-operation and non-violence for achieving freedom for his country from the yoke of foreign rule.

The Gandhi movement spread like wild fire. He roused the masses to political consciousness and proved to them that they possessed immense soul-force. He was sentenced to six years imprisonment and was released in February, 1924. In that same year he became President of the Indian National Congress.

In April 1930, the Salt Satyagraha was started by Gandhiji. For his breach of the Salt Laws he was interned on the 5th May, 1930. He was released on the 25th January, 1931 in order to attend the Round Table Conference in London. He was again arrested in January, 1933 and released in May of the same year.

Gandhiji's intense love for his fellow men, his long fasts, his great sacrifices for his country's cause, indomitable will, moral force and deep spiritual life, won for him the hearts of his countrymen. In their excessive devotion, love and reverence for him they bestowed upon him the title of "Mahatma", meaning "Great Soul". They addressed him affectionately as Bapuji. It means "beloved father".

The tremendous soul-power of which Gandhiji spoke was essentially derived from the chanting of Ram-Nam and the study of the *Gita* and *Ramayana*. Not a day passed without a study of the second chapter of the *Gita*, in which, Gandhiji felt, was contained its entire philosophy.

On the 15th of August, 1947, Gandhiji won freedom for India. Soon after this he was shot at three times at point-blank range by Nathuram Vinayak Godse, a Hindu extremist. On Gandhiji's lips, just before he gave up his last breath, were the words "Hey Ram!"

Thus passed the life of a great soul.

The Pattern of a Perfect Life

Bharatavarsha, as India is known, has always been a land of eternal ideals and sublime idealism, and of supermen who converted these ideals into actuality in their everyday life. Gandhiji was such an ideal superman. His name has become synonymous with unbending moral rectitude, heroic allegiance to truth, and perfect righteousness both in private and public life.

Mahatma Gandhi's life is a monument to the triumph of spirit over flesh, a living witness to the victory of the divine over the base nature of man. A continuous exercise of self-restraint and discipline, along with deep prayer and an invincible faith in the Divine, enabled him to successfully resist all kinds of temptations, overcome all obstacles and gain full mastery over himself.

Gandhiji's firm and tenacious adherence to the cause of the poor, the downtrodden Harijans, and the common man of the Indian village, is indeed worthy of emulation.

Through all the vicissitudes of time and power and fame, he kept before the vision of the Indian Congress the fundamental purpose for which it came into being—the amelioration of the suffering of the poor. Uncrowned king of the land, he remained a friend of the poor; he lived for them, moved among them as one of them, and served them with all his heart. He saw God in them, and in their service wore out his body. As the Father of the Nation in every sense of the term, Gandhiji brought about a re-orientation in the outlook of the average Indian, and instilled into him the love of God, his religion and his motherland, all of which had been eclipsed for more than a century by the unhealthy influence of Western culture, manners and language.

Mahatmaji demonstrated how a life of complete detachment and renunciation may be led while remaining in the thick of battle. His was a supreme example of one who had completely annihilated the ego, the little "I", and led a divine life in the world. His life was like that of a lotus leaf in water.

Albert Einstein, the famous scientist who propounded the theory of relativity, said of Gandhiji: "Generations to come will scarcely believe that such a man in flesh and blood once trod upon this earth".

May the Mahatma's light of love illuminate the hearts of nations and individuals! May his dream of world unity materialise this very day! May his spirit bless us all with the vision and strength to realise in our everyday life all his lofty ideals of truth, purity, non-violence and faith in the Divine!

Mohandas Gandhi Biography

Mohandas Karamchand Gandhi (October 2, 1869-January 30, 1948), known popularly as Mahatma Gandhi (Mahatma-Sanskrit: "great soul"), was one of the founding fathers of the modern Indian state and an influential advocate of Satyagraha (nonviolent protest) as a means of revolution.

He helped bring about India's independence from British rule, inspiring other colonial peoples to work for their own independence and ultimately dismantle the British Empire and replace it with the Commonwealth.

Gandhi's principle of satyagraha, often roughly translated as "way of truth" or "pursuit of truth," has inspired generations of democratic and anti-racist activists including Martin Luther King, Jr. and Nelson Mandela. He often stated his values were simple, drawn from traditional Hindu beliefs: truth (satya), and non-violence (ahimsa).

Early life

Mohandas Gandhi was born on October 2, 1869, in Porbandar, Gujarat, India. He was the son of a Karamchand Gandhi, the dewan (Chief Minister) of Porbander, and Putliba, Karamchand's fourth wife. They were descendents of traders (The word "Gandhi" means grocer). At the age of 13 Gandhi married Kasturbai, who was of his same age. They had four children, all sons: Harilal Gandhi born in 1888, Manilal Gandhi born in 1892, Ramdas Gandhi born in 1897 and Devdas Gandhi born in 1900.

At the age of 19, Gandhi went to University College, in the University of London to train as a lawyer. He went to Durban, Scuth Africa to practice law in 1893 and began his political career by lobbying against laws discriminating against Indians in South Africa, inspired by an incident in which he was physically thrown off a train in Pietermaritzburg, after refusing to move to the third class coach, while travelling on a first class ticket. Gandhi was arrested on November 6, 1913 while leading a march of Indian miners in South Africa.

Gandhi drew inspiration from the Bhagavad Gita and the writings of Leo Tolstoy, who in the 1880s had undergone a profound conversion to a personal form of Christian anarchism. Gandhi translated Tolstoy's "Letter to a Hindu" [1] which was written in 1908 in response to aggressive Indian nationalists, and the two corresponded until Tolstoy's death in 1910. The letter by Tolstoy uses Hindu philosophy taken from the Vedas and sayings of the Hindu God Lord Krishna to present his view of that state of growing Indian nationalism.

During World War I, Gandhi returned to India, where he campaigned for Indians to join the British Indian Army.

Movement for Indian independence

After the war, he became involved with the Indian National Congress and the movement for independence. He gained worldwide publicity through his policy of civil disobedience and the use of fasting as a form of protest, and was repeatedly imprisoned by the British authorities (for example on March 18, 1922 he was sentenced to six years in prison for civil disobedience but served only 2 years).

His pro-independence stance hardened after the Amritsar Massacre in 1920.

One of his most striking actions was the salt march known as the Dandi March, that started on March 12, 1930 and ended on April 5, when he led thousands of people to the sea to collect their own salt rather than pay the salt tax. On May 8, 1933 Gandhi began a fast that would last 21 days to protest British 'oppression' in India. In Bombay, on March 3, 1939 Gandhi fasted again in protest of the autocratic rule in India.

World War II

Gandhi became even more vocal in his demand for independence during World War II, drafting a resolution calling for the British to Quit India, which soon sparked the largest movement for Indian independence ever, with mass arrests and violence on an unprecedented scale. Gandhi and his supporters made clear that they would not support the war effort unless India was granted immediate independence. During this time, he even hinted an end for his otherwise unwavering support of non-violence, saying that the 'ordered anarchy' around him was 'worse than real anarchy'. He was then arrested in Bombay by British forces on August 9, 1942 and was held for two years.

Partition of India

Gandhi had great influence among the Hindu and Muslim communities of India. It is said that he ended communal riots through his mere presence. Gandhi was vehemently opposed to any plan which partitioned India into two separate countries (the plan was eventually adopted, creating a Hindu-dominated India, and a Muslim-dominated Pakistan). On the day of the power transfer, Gandhi did not celebrate independence with the rest of India, but mourned partition alone in Calcutta instead. He was assassinated in New Delhi on January 30, 1948 by Naturam Godse, a Hindu radical who held him responsible for weakening the new government by insisting on a payment to Pakistan. Godse was later tried, convicted, and executed.

It is indicative of Gandhi's long struggle and search for God that his dying words was a popular two-word mantra to the Hindu conception of God as Rama: "Hey Ram!" Significantly though, in recent times there are many theories and ideas around his last words—some people even believe that that words must be a myth.

Principles

Gandhi's philosophies and his ideas of satya and ahimsa had been influenced by the Bhagavad Gita and Hindu beliefs as well as practiced Jain religion. The concept of 'nonviolence' (ahimsa) was a long-standing one in Indian religious thought and saw many revivals with Hindu, Buddhist and Jain contexts. Gandhi explains his philosophy and way of life in his autobiography The Story of my Experiments with Truth.

He was a strict vegetarian and had written books on the subject while studying law in London (where he met vegetarian campaigner Henry Salt at meetings of the Vegetarian Society). It might be added that the idea of vegetarianism was a deeply ingrained one in Hindu and Jain society in India, and that in his native land of Gujarat most Hindus were vegetarian. He experimented with different diets and believed that a diet should be enough to satisfy the minimum requirements of the body. He also abstained from taking food for periods of time, and he used this practice of fasting also as a political weapon.

Gandhi gave up sexual intercourse at the age of 36 and became totally celibate while still married, a course deeply influenced by the Hindu idea of Brahmacharya, or spiritual and practical purity, largely associated with celibacy.

Gandhi spent a day of the week in silence. He would abstain from speaking and he believed it brought him inner peace. These were drawn from such Hindu understandings of the power of 'mouna' and 'shanti'. On such days he communicated with others by writing on paper.

After returning to India from a successful lawyer career in South Africa, he gave up his clothing that represented wealth and success. His idea was to adopt a kind of clothing whereby he can be accepted by even the poorest person in India. He advocated use of home-spun cloth. Gandhi and his followers followed the practice of weaving their own cloth using a spinning-wheel and wearing a dress made of that. He also advocated others use spinning wheels to spin clothes. This was a threat to the British establishment-while Indian workers were often idle due to unemployment, they bought their clothing from foreign English industrial manufacturers-if Indians spun their own clothes, this would leave British industry idle. The spinning wheel was later incorporated into the flag of the Indian National Congress.

Gandhi was against conventional education as taught in schools and believed that children learn best from parents and from the society. While in South Africa, Gandhi along with other elders formed a group of teachers and directly imparted education to the children.

Artistic Depictions

The most famous artistic depiction of his life is the film Gandhi, directed by Richard Attenborough and starring Ben Kingsley (interestingly half-Gujarati) in the title role. Another film that deals with Gandhi's 21 years of life in South Africa is The Making of the Mahatma directed by Shyam Benegal and starring Rajit Kapur.

In the United States, there are statues of Gandhi outside the Ferry Building in San Francisco, in Union Square Park in New York City and near the Indian Embassy in the Dupont Circle neighbourhood of Washington, DC.

Nobel Peace Prize nominations

M.K.Gandhi never received the Nobel Peace Prize, though he was nominated five times for the same between 1937 and 1948. Decades later however, the omission was publicly regretted by the Nobel Committee. When the Dalai Lama was awarded the Peace Prize in 1989, the chairman of the committee said that this was "in part a tribute to the memory of Mahatma Gandhi".

Albert Einstein famously said of Gandhi, "Generations to come, it may be, will scarcely believe that such a one as this ever in flesh and blood walked upon this earth."

Mahatma Gandhi

Mohandas Karamchand Gandhi (October 2 1869 – January 30, 1948) was a major political and spiritual leader of India and the Indian independence movement. He is considered the father of

India. He was the pioneer resistance through mass civil disobedience strongly founded upon ahimsa (total non-violence) which came to be one of the strongest driving philosophies of the Indian Independence Movement, and has inspired movements for civil rights and freedom across the world. Gandhi is commonly known and addressed in India and worldwide as Mahatma Gandhi and as *Bapu* (in many Indian languages, *Father*).

An English-educated lawyer, Gandhi first employed his ideas of peaceful civil disobedience in the Indian community's struggle for civil rights in South Africa. Upon his return to India, Gandhi organised poor farmers and labourers to protest oppressive taxation and widespread discrimination. Leading the Indian National Congress, Gandhi led a nationwide campaign for the alleviation of poverty, for the liberation of Indian women, for brotherhood amongst communities of differing religions and ethnicity, for an end to untouchability and caste discrimination, and for the economic self-sufficiency of the nation, but above all for *Swaraj* the independence of India from foreign domination. Gandhi famously led Indians in the disobedience of the salt tax through the 400 kilometre (248 miles) Dandi Salt March in 1930, and in an open call for the British to *Quit India* in 1942. He spent his final years fighting for communal peace and harmony amongst Hindus, Muslims and Sikhs.

Throughout, Gandhi remained committed to non-violence and truth even in the most extreme situations. Gandhi was a student of Hindu philosophy and lived simply, organizing an ashram that was self-sufficient in its needs. He made his own clothes the traditional Indian dhoti and shawl, woven with a charkha and lived on a simple vegetarian diet. He used rigorous fasts abstaining from food and water for long periods for self-purification as well as a means of protest. Gandhi's life and teachings inspired Dr. Martin Luther King Jr., Steve Biko and Aung San Suu Kyi and, respectively, the American civil rights movement, civil rights struggles in South Africa and Myanmar. His criticism of many aspects of western modernity (such as modern technology and industrialization) in that it harmed the poor and benefited the rich has also earned him the reputation of a development critic whose thinking has inspired many later political thinkers.

Gandhi is honoured as the *Father of the Nation* in India, a title first given him by Subhash Chandra Bose "Father of Our Nation" (Address to Mahatma Gandhi over the Rangoon Radio on 6th July 1944) The Essential Writings of Netaji Subhas Chandra Bose Edited by Sisir K Bose & Sugata Bose (Delhi: Oxford University Press) 1997 pp301-2. Gandhi's birthday on October 2 is annually commemorated as Gandhi Jayanti, and is a national holiday.

Early Life

Mohandas Karamchand Gandhi was born into a Hindu Modh Vanik family in Porbandar, Gujarat, India, in 1869. He was the son of Karamchand Gandhi, the *diwan* (Prime Minister) of Porbandar, and Putlibai, Karamchand's fourth wife, a Hindu of the Pranami Vaishnava order. Karamchand's first two wives, who each bore him a daughter, died from unknown reasons (rumoured to be in childbirth). His third wife was deemed incapacitated and gave her permission to Karamchand for him to marry again. Growing up with a devout mother and surrounded by the Jain influences of Gujarat, Gandhi learned from an early age the tenets of non-injury to living beings, vegetarianism, fasting for self-purification, and mutual tolerance between members of various creeds and sects. He was born into the *vaishya*, or business, caste.

In May 1883, at the age of 13, Gandhi was married through his parents' arrangement to Kasturba Makhanji (also spelled "Kasturbai" or known as "Ba"), who was his age. They had four sons: Harilal Gandhi, born in 1888; Manilal Gandhi, born in 1892; Ramdas Gandhi, born in 1897; and Devdas Gandhi, born in 1900. Gandhi was a mediocre student in his youth at Porbandar and later Rajkot. He barely passed the matriculation exam for the University of Bombay in 1887, where he joined Samaldas College. He was also unhappy at the college, because his family wanted him to become a barrister. He leapt at the opportunity to study in England, which he viewed as "a land of philosophers and poets, the very centre of civilization."

At the age of 18 on September 4 1888, Gandhi went to University College London to train as a barrister. His time in London, the Imperial capital, was influenced by a vow he had made to his mother in the presence of a Jain monk Becharji, upon leaving India to observe the Hindu precepts of abstinence from meat, alcohol, and promiscuity. Although Gandhi experimented with adopting "English" customs taking dancing lessons for example he could not stomach his landlady's mutton and cabbage. She pointed him towards one of London's few vegetarian restaurants. Rather than simply go along with his mother's wishes, he read about, and intellectually embraced vegetarianism. He joined the Vegetarian Society, was elected to its executive committee, and founded a local chapter. He later credited this with giving him valuable experience in organizing institutions. Some of the vegetarians he met were members of the Theosophical Society, which had been founded in 1875 to further universal brotherhood and devoted to the study of Buddhist and Hindu Brahmanistic literature. They encouraged Gandhi to read the *Bhagavad Gita.* Not having shown a particular interest in religion before, he read works of and about Hinduism, Christianity, Buddhism, Islam and other religions. He returned to India after being admitted to the bar of England and Wales, but had limited success establishing a law practice in Bombay, later applying and being turned down for a part-time job as a high school teacher. He ended up returning to Rajkot to make a modest living drafting petitions for litigants but was forced to close down that business as well when he ran afoul of a British officer. In his autobiography, he describes this incident as a kind of unsuccessful lobbying attempt on behalf of his older brother. It was in this climate that (in 1893) he accepted a year-long contract from an Indian firm to a post in Natal, South Africa.

Gandhiji and the Struggle for Liberation in South Africa

As important as the fortieth anniversary of the assassination of Gandhiji which is observed on January 30, 1988, is the eightieth anniversary of his first imprisonment in South Africa in January 1908, which was a turning point in his life.

Gandhiji always considered himself an Indian and a South African. Not only had he spent twenty-one years of his adult life in South Africa, but he had served four of his ten terms of imprisonment in that country-in the prisons of Johannesburg, Volksrust and Dundee. It was in South Africa that he developed his philosophy of *satyagraha.*

In a sense, his last *satyagraha* was also in South Africa. Though he could not be physically present, he guided and inspired the great Indian passive resistance movement of 1946-48 and lent it enormous support.

Birth of Satyagraha

The small Indian community in the Transvaal had launched, in July 1907, a passive resistance campaign against the Asiatic Registration Act (the Black Act) designed to humiliate, harass and eventually expel them from the territory. Volunteers picketed registration offices and most of the Indians refused to take out permits under the Black Act.

Gandhiji found that "passive resistance" was seen even by European friends as a "weapon of the weak." He sought a term which could be understood by Indians and make it clear that the resistance was out of moral strength rather than any weakness. He invited suggestions and, in November 1907, invented the term "*satyagraha*" (firmness in truth). The choice of the term itself appears to have helped crystallise his thinking.

On December 28, 1907, Gandhiji and several of his colleagues were taken to court for refusing to register and were ordered to leave the Transvaal within two weeks. They defied the order and were sentenced on January 10, 1908, to two to three months' imprisonment.

General Smuts, however, was obliged soon to negotiate a settlement with Gandhiji and the prisoners were released on January 30th-the very day that Gandhiji was to be assassinated forty years later.

The brief imprisonment was not only the "baptism of fire" for Gandhiji but transformed him from a public servant and adviser to the Indian community into the leader of resistance.

In the many years that the struggle lasted with its ups and downs-jailings, beatings, torture and deportations of resisters, as well as the intervals when they were obliged to while away their time on the Tolstoy Farm-Gandhiji developed the concept of *satyagraha* which was later to inspire the national movement in India.

There was little discussion at the time of non-violence, for no one had contemplated an armed struggle which was, in any case, unthinkable for an unarmed and vulnerable community of a mere

12,000 Indians in the Transvaal. Gandhiji had not yet become an uncompromising devotee of non-violence: he had in fact favoured the enlistment of Indians in the armed forces. The emphasis was on the duty to defy an unjust law and to defend the honour of India.

Satyagraha-the common heritage of India and South Africa

The *satyagraha* in South Africa was not only a struggle for the rights of the Indians or the redress of their grievances, but a part of the struggle of India for freedom and dignity. It was influenced by the upsurge in India in protest against the partition of Bengal and the mass boycott of British goods in the *swadeshi* movement.

The experience of Gandhiji in the struggle in South Africa had, in its turn, a great influence on the Indian national movement.

Out of his close association with the Muslims in South Africa, and their great contribution to the passive resistance campaign, came his stress on Hindu-Muslim unity as a tenet of the Indian national movement.

Out of his outrage at the treatment of Indians in South Africa by the Europeans as virtual untouchables came his determination to eliminate untouchability in India.

Out of his experience in trying to unify the Indian people in South Africa, speaking many languages, came his advocacy of a *lingua franca* for India. It was in *Indian Opinion* in Durban on August 18, 1906, that he first called for the adoption of Hindustani as the common language for India.

As the national movement developed in India under Gandhiji's leadership-from non-cooperation to civil disobedience and then to the "do or die" struggle in 1942-it became radicalised. It stopped seeking a compromise settlement with the oppressors and became committed to the complete independence of India. It also became strongly internationalist under the influence of Pandit Jawaharlal Nehru, and by 1946 Gandhiji began advocating the unity of all the oppressed peoples of the world for the elimination of colonialism.

Gandhiji, meanwhile, kept in contact with developments in South Africa. He encouraged the Indian passive resistance movement of 1946, under the leadership of Dr. Yusuf M. Dadoo and Dr. G.M. Naicker, and lent it great support. While he had confined the first *satyagraha* in South Africa to the Indian and Chinese settlers whose security was threatened, he gave his blessings to the efforts of the Dadoo-Naicker leadership to build a united democratic front.

He was, in a sense, a patron of the movements both in India and among Indians in South Africa. In the last year of his life, when he felt anguish at the eruption of violence between Hindus and Muslims in India, he seemed to find some solace in the *satyagraha* in South Africa. One of his last speeches-at the prayer meeting in Delhi on January 28, 1948-was devoted to the struggle in South Africa. He said:

"Today we are also a free country as South Africa and are members of the same Commonwealth, which implies that we should all live like brothers and equals... Why should they look down on the Coloured people? Is it because they are industrious and thrifty? I shall tell the Government of South Africa through this meeting that it should mend its ways."

The Indian people in South Africa benefited from the lessons of their own *satyagraha* of 1907-14, as well as the experience of the Indian national movement. The concept of *satyagraha* was enriched by their passive resistance of 1946-48 which was joined by several Africans, Coloured people and whites out of solidarity.

The Indian *satyagraha* was the precursor of the great nonviolent resistance under African leadership in 1952, aptly named the "Campaign of Defiance against Unjust Laws" and, indeed, the beginning of mass resistance in South Africa.

The heritage of Gandhiji and of *satyagraha* is thus a common heritage South Africa and India.

Continuing Inspiration of Gandhiji

One does not need to be a Gandhian to recognise that the philosophy and example of Gandhiji remain a powerful force in the world, spreading wider and adapting to the traditions and circumstances in different countries.

The leaders of the freedom movements in many colonial countries acknowledge the inspiration of Gandhiji. The civil rights movement in the United States, led by the Reverend Dr. Martin Luther King, Jr., was inspired by his example, as was much of the movement against the Vietnam war. The mass movement for disarmament and against nuclear war, and the environmentalist movement, have been influenced, among others, by Gandhiji.

Nonviolent resisters in the Philippines played a significant role in the struggle to overthrow the Marcos dictatorship. The mobilisation of hundreds of thousands of unarmed people to surround and protect the armed forces which turned against Marcos was a crucial event in the struggle and added a new dimension to the history of nonviolent resistance.

Liberation theology, which has spread in Latin America, Africa and Asia, draws some of its inspiration from Gandhiji.

A dramatic affirmation of the vitality of the heritage of Gandhiji was the Delhi Declaration of Mikhail Gorbachev and Rajiv Gandhi in November 1986-calling for a non-nuclear and nonviolent world-the reference to non-violence reportedly included at the suggestion of Gorbachev.

None of the recent nonviolent movements perhaps strictly follows the tenets of Gandhiji, as understood by his disciples in India, but he has been an inspiration as people tried to choose the most peaceful and effective means of struggle against injustice and oppression in the light of the relevant conditions. The philosophy of Gandhiji cannot be codified into immutable rules, but must always be creative. It evolved with his experience in forty years of struggle. He kept his windows open to receive inspiration from all sources. He learnt from the humblest in the resistance campaigns. He welcomed discussion and debate. He changed his views many times and never hesitated to admit errors.

It is a pity that Indian thinkers and public leaders have not followed the spread and development of Gandhian ideology and have made little contribution to the movements inspired by it.

Is Nonviolent Resistance Relevant to South Africa?

Has *satyagraha* lost all relevance in South Africa as a means of resistance, especially after the Sharpeville massacre?

The answer is not simple.

I believe that patient suffering with love has hardly ever melted the hearts of oppressive rulers. *Satyagraha* has succeeded to the extent that it aroused public opinion in the camp of the adversaries and beyond so as to restrain and exert pressure on the oppressors. That is why Gandhiji always devoted great attention to publicity.

Given the possibility to reach and arouse public conscience, nonviolent resistance makes it difficult for the oppressors to resort to extreme savagery and thereby saves lives. It helps the oppressed people to overcome fear of prison and torture and steels them in the struggle. It makes it possible to reach settlements without bitterness.

In South Africa, however, the movement faced not only an enemy which became ever more brutal, refusing to recognise the humanity of the black people, but powerful international forces of greed and prejudice hindered effective pressure against the racist regime.

Regrettably, many people in the Western world are not outraged by violence against people with a black skin and such violence gets little press and public attention. As powerful vested interests from abroad became involved in South Africa, they tended to exert their influence to protect the racist structures which ensure them exorbitant profit. Perhaps even more important, mass resistance in South Africa began at a time when the world was divided by the "cold war" and cold war calculations began to influence the policies of powerful nations much more than justice. The And was branded by Western intelligence services as pro-Communist, because like most national movements it tried to encompass all the people and had not excluded Communists or followers of other ideologies. This has largely determined the actions of Western Governments, particularly that of the United States, whatever the public pronouncements of their leaders.

As a result, even on occasions when some of the white rulers in South Africa contemplated a change of course, powerful influences from abroad reinforced those who advocated reliance on ever greater violence to perpetuate racist domination.

It is, therefore, understandable, to say the least, that the leaders of the liberation movement felt that they had to undertake violent resistance. But that does not necessarily mean that nonviolent resistance has become totally irrelevant nor that the spirit of *satyagraha* had disappeared.

In many countries, nonviolent resistance took place at the same time as violent resistance, or threat of such resistance. There was, for instance, violent resistance in India on many occasions and a threat of violence by others in the United States when Dr. King was leading the civil rights movement. The oppressors are often obliged to choose between compromise with the mainstream of the movement pursuing nonviolent resistance and confrontation with the growing trend toward violent resistance. In South Africa, the movement has used peaceful means whenever possible and hardly any other country has seen such persistent nonviolent resistance, even alongside armed struggle, as South Africa.

There are also situations in which effective nonviolent resistance by the oppressed people is not practicable, but nonviolent action can be carried on by those abroad outraged by the injustice. For instance, the Vietnamese peasants could not non-violently resist unseen persons throwing bombs from high up in the sky, but the American people could carry on such resistance against involvement in the Vietnam war. In the case of South Africa, too, there have been times when *satyagraha* abroad in solidarity with the oppressed people was more feasible and effective than nonviolent resistance inside the country.

Mass *satyagraha* against apartheid and all its protectors and accomplices all over the world may well be the most effective means to put an end to the continuing tragedy in South Africa.

The answer to the question of relevance is then that even though the oppressed people and their leaders are convinced that clandestine activity, sabotage and armed struggle have become essential or indispensable, the spirit of Gandhiji has not lost all its relevance.

I would like briefly to trace the course of the liberation struggle, in the context of violence and non-violence, to underline this conclusion.

Unconcern for African Lives

One of the first mass actions of the And was the 1919 campaign against the pass laws, reminiscent of the Indian *satyagraha* in South

Africa a few years earlier. Thousands of men and women threw away their passes and were sentenced to imprisonment with hard labour; those who were sentenced to fines refused to pay fines and chose to go to prison.

The regime reacted with savagery. Many Africans, including even children, were trampled under horses' hoofs as mounted policemen charged on a peaceful demonstration outside a Johannesburg court and shot at by white vigilantes. Several were killed. But there was hardly a murmur of protest in the world-though that was the time when leaders of Allied Powers were waxing eloquent about human rights-as the victims were Africans.

When the Indian people launched passive resistance on June 13, 1946, the police in Durban stood by without arresting the resisters and let white ruffians attack them with bicycle chains. At least two resisters fell unconscious, and one bystander died.

Fortunately, a white priest, the Reverend Michael Scott, felt compelled to join the resisters. Gandhiji expressed his outrage and sent a personal appeal to General Smuts so that the violence was curbed.

The great Campaign of Defiance against Unjust Laws in 1952 attracted attention and sympathy around the world as 8,000 people of all racial origins courted imprisonment. The regime responded with inhuman laws for whipping passive resisters. There was hardly a protest from the governments of the great Western democracies.

The And, however, managed to carry on nonviolent resistance-bus boycotts, school boycott, potato boycott and resistance against the removal of African communities-over the next few years. Its leaders were subjected to arbitrary restrictions and even a four-year trial for "High Treason". But there was not even verbal condemnation of apartheid violence by the major Western Powers until the Sharpeville massacre of 1960.

Instead, they called for sympathy and understanding for white fears for the future rather than for the suffering of the black majority. They invited the Pretoria regime to discussions of Western military strategy and alliances in Africa and the Middle East. Britain signed the Simonstown military alliance with the Pretoria regime in 1955. When some National Party leaders advocated a change of course in the wake of the flight of capital after the Sharpeville massacre, Western financial interests bailed out the regime and thereby strengthened the position of Prime Minister Hendrik Verwoerd and other advocates of greater repression.

Combination of Armed Struggle and Nonviolent Resistance

As a result, the And leaders felt obliged, in 1961, to abandon strict adherence to non-violence and prepare for armed resistance. As Nelson Mandela explained in his statement to the court in April 1964, members of the And had begun to lose confidence in the And policy, as fifty years of non-violence seemed to have achieved nothing, and were developing ideas of terrorism. Scattered incidents of violence had broken out in the country and there was a danger of uncontrolled violence. The And leaders felt that a properly controlled violent resistance, under the guidance of the And, was essential to avert the danger of terrorism and make any progress.

The *Umkhonto we Sizwe*, the military wing of the And, said in its first manifesto on December 16, 1961: "We of *Umkhonto we Sizwe* have always sought to achieve liberation without bloodshed and civil clash. We hope, even at this late hour, that our first actions will awaken everyone to a realisation of the dangerous situation to which the Nationalist policy is leading. We hope we will bring the government and its supporters to their senses before it is too late, so that both the government and its policies can be changed before matters reach the desperate stage of civil war."

The *Umkhonto* carried on some three hundred acts of sabotage between 1961 and 1963 against symbols of apartheid and some economic installations in order to warn the regime and its supporters, give hope to the people and promote international action. Every care was taken to avoid loss of human life. Only one person-a police informer in the eastern Cape-was killed by the And underground while the regime tortured several leaders of the people to death. Vuyisile Mini, the respected composer of freedom songs, and his colleagues were executed.

Until today, the total number of persons killed in numerous And armed actions is perhaps less than two hundred. Several of the casualties were possibly unintended and resulted from malfunction of the timing mechanisms of explosives.

Even after gruesome killings of refugees in Maputo and Maseru by South African raiders, and a series of tortures of detainees to death, the And was able to prevent retaliation in kind.

It was not beyond the capacity of And, or of the black people in spontaneous eruptions of anger, to kill thousands of whites. The absence of such terrorism was due to the enormous restraint of the And and its influence among the people, an influence which it would not have had if it had opposed all violence.

During all these years since 1961, the freedom movement has also utilised every opportunity for nonviolent defiance of unjust laws at great sacrifice.

The student upsurge in the 1970s was essentially nonviolent. The funeral processions defying laws prohibiting the display of the And flag and symbols-thereby making the laws virtually inoperative-were nonviolent resistance, as are the rent boycotts, the consumer boycotts and the "end conscription" campaign.

The United Democratic Front and allied organisations have contributed an impressive chapter to the history of nonviolent resistance.

The growth of nonviolent resistance in South Africa, and the development of international solidarity, encouraged and enabled Archbishop Desmond Tutu, the Reverend Alan Boesak and other churchmen to defy the laws on many occasions and force the regime to retreat.

Since 1985, the violence of the apartheid regime under its State of Emergency-the indiscriminate shootings and the mass torture of detainees-as well as the series of ghastly murders by vigilante groups, provoked counter-violence. Enraged youth groups resorted to killing suspected informers by "necklacing," and that was used by the regime and its friends to malign the liberation movement.

The And could perhaps have said-as even Mahatma Gandhi wrote from jail in 1942-that it could not condemn, without full information, people who were provoked to violence by the "leonine" violence of the regime when their leaders were confined and exiled.

But Oliver Tambo, the President of the And, declared last year that the And opposed "necklacing". He was reported to have advised African youth last September to try to win over informers and vigilante groups. I can think of none but a Mahatma Gandhi who could show such courage and humanism in the midst of a difficult battle and popular emotions.

Spirit of Gandhiji lives on in South Africa

The spirit of Gandhiji lives on in South Africa eighty years after he went to prison in the Transvaal defying unjust racist laws, forty years after his ashes were immersed in the ocean off the mouth of the Umgeni river in South Africa-not least in the hearts of the leaders of the liberation struggle.

They have stood firm on truth, despite constant provocation and bestiality by a racist regime, resisting all forms of racism and constantly upholding the objective of a non-racial democratic society. They have resisted unjust laws with exceptional courage and sacrifice. They have recognised that ends and means are inseparable, and have avoided the temptation to reply to the massive terrorism of the white racist regime with terrorism against white civilians. Even in the course of armed resistance, they have avoided the loss of innocent lives.

Gandhiji did not condemn Sant Bhagat Singh or those who resorted to sabotage when he was jailed along with other leaders of the national movement in 1942-but placed the blame squarely on the violence of the British Raj. Martin Luther King, Jr., did not condemn John Brown or Malcolm X, but only slavery and racism.

Chief Albert Lutuli did not condemn Nelson Mandela for founding and leading the military wing of the African National Congress, but declared when Mandela and his colleagues were sentenced in June 1964: "... in the face of the uncompromising white refusal to abandon a policy which denies the African and other oppressed South Africans their rightful heritage-freedom-no one can blame brave just men for seeking justice by the use of violent methods nor could they be blamed if they tried to create an organised force in order to ultimately establish peace and racial harmony... "They represent the highest in morality and ethics in the South African political struggle..."

The And is attacked by the Botha regime, which relies on violence and terrorism, as violent; and that charge is echoed by the friends of that regime who instigate and support violence and terrorism in many countries of the third world. But it has earned the understanding, sympathy and even active support of the greatest pacifists of our time, many of whom acknowledge the inspiration of Gandhiji.

Written in connection with the 80th anniversary of the imprisonment of Gandhiji in South Africa. Published in *Asian Times*, London, January 29, 1988, and in several papers in India.

Civil rights movement in South Africa (1893–1914)

Gandhi in South Africa (1895)

At this point in his life, Gandhi was a mild-mannered, diffident and politically indifferent individual. He had read his first newspaper at the age of 18, and was prone to stage fright while speaking in court. South Africa changed him dramatically, as he faced the discrimination that was commonly directed at blacks and Indians in that country. One day in court in the city of Durban, the magistrate asked him to remove his turban. Gandhi refused to do so and stormed out of the courtroom. In another incident, he was thrown off a train at Pietermaritzburg, after refusing to move from the first class coach to a third class compartment while holding a valid first class ticket. Later, travelling further on by stagecoach, he was beaten by a driver for refusing to travel on the footboard to make room for a European passenger. He suffered other hardships on the journey as well, including being barred from many hotels on account of his race. These incidents have been acknowledged by several biographers as a turning point in his life that would serve as the catalyst for his activism later in life. It was through witnessing first-hand the racism, prejudice and injustice against Indians in South Africa that Gandhi started to question his people's status, and his own place in society.

Gandhi in the uniform of a sergeant of the Indian Ambulance Corps. He served during the Boer War (1899).

At the end of his contract, Gandhi prepared to return to India. However, at a farewell party in his honour in Durban, he happened to glance at a newspaper and learned that a bill was being considered by the Natal Legislative Assembly to deny the right to vote to Indians. When he brought this up with his hosts, they lamented that they did not have the expertise necessary to oppose the bill, and implored Gandhi to stay and help them. He circulated several petitions to both the Natal Legislature and the British Government in opposition to the bill. Though unable to halt the bill's passage, his campaign was successful in drawing attention to the grievances of Indians in South Africa. Supporters convinced him to remain in Durban to continue fighting against the injustices levied against Indians in South Africa. He founded the Natal Indian Congress in 1894, with himself as the Secretary. Through this organization, he moulded the Indian community of South Africa into a homogeneous political force, publishing documents detailing Indian grievances and evidence of British discrimination in South Africa. Gandhi returned briefly to India in 1896 to bring his wife and children to live with him in South Africa. When he returned in January 1897, a white mob attacked and tried to lynch him. In an early indication of the personal values that would shape his later campaigns, he refused to press charges on any member of the mob, stating it was one of his principles not to seek redress for a personal wrong in a court of law.

At the onset of the South African War, Gandhi argued that Indians must support the war effort in order to legitimize their claims to full citizenship, organizing a volunteer ambulance corps of 300 free Indians and 800 indentured labourers called the Indian Ambulance Corps, one of the few medical units to serve wounded black South Africans. He himself was a stretcher-bearer at the Battle of Spion Kop, and was decorated. At the conclusion of the war, however, the situation for the Indians did not improve, but continued to deteriorate. In 1906, the Transvaal government promulgated a new Act compelling registration of the colony's Indian population. At a mass protest meeting held in Johannesburg that September, Gandhi adopted his methodology of *satyagraha* (devotion to the truth), or nonviolent protest, for the first time, calling on his fellow Indians to defy the new law and suffer the punishments for doing so, rather than resist through violent means. This plan was adopted, leading to a seven-year struggle in which thousands of Indians were jailed (including Gandhi himself on many occasions), flogged, or even shot, for striking, refusing to register, burning their registration cards, or engaging in other forms of nonviolent resistance. While the government was successful in repressing the Indian protesters, the public outcry stemming from the harsh methods employed by the South African government in the face of peaceful Indian protesters finally forced South African General Jan Christiaan Smuts to negotiate a compromise with Gandhi. In May 1915, Gandhi founded an ashram on the outskirts of Ahmedabad, India and called it Satyagrah Ashram (also known as Sabarmati Ashram). There lodged twenty five men and women who took vows of truth, celibacy, ahimsa, nonpossession, control of the palate, and service of the Indian people.

Mohandas Gandhi (1869-1948)

Mohandas Karamchand Gandhi was born on 2 October 1869 in Porbandar in Gujarat. After university, he went to London to train as a barrister. He returned to India in 1891 and in 1893 accepted a job at an Indian law firm in Durban, South Africa. Gandhi was appalled by the treatment of Indian immigrants there, and joined the struggle to obtain basic rights for them. During his 20 years in South Africa he was sent to prison many times. Influenced primarily by Hinduism, but also by elements of Jainism and Christianity as well as writers including Tolstoy and Thoreau, Gandhi developed the *satyagraha* ('devotion to truth'), a new nonviolent way to redress wrongs. In 1914, the South African government conceded to many of Gandhi's demands.

Gandhi returned to India shortly afterwards. In 1919, British plans to intern people suspected of sedition-the Rowlatt Acts-prompted Gandhi to announce a new *satyagraha* which attracted millions of followers. A demonstration against the acts resulted in the Amritsar Massacre by British troops. By 1920, Gandhi was a dominant figure in Indian politics. He transformed the Indian National Congress, and his programme of peaceful non-cooperation with the British included boycotts of British goods and institutions, leading to arrests of thousands.

In 1922, Gandhi himself was sentenced to six years' imprisonment. He was released after two years and withdrew from politics, devoting himself to trying to improve Hindu-Muslim relations, which had worsened. In 1930, Gandhi proclaimed a new campaign of civil disobedience in protest at a tax on salt, leading thousands on a 'March to the Sea' to symbolically make their own salt from seawater. In 1931, Gandhi attended the Round Table Conference in London, as the sole representative of the Indian National Congress, but resigned from the party in 1934 in protest at its use of non-violence as a political expedient. He was replaced as leader by Jawaharlal Nehru.

In 1945, the British government began negotiations which culminated in the Mountbatten Plan of June 1947, and the formation of the two new independent states of India and Pakistan, divided along religious lines. Massive inter-communal violence marred the months before and after independence. Gandhi was opposed to partition, and now fasted in an attempt to bring calm in Calcutta and Delhi. On 30 January 1948, he was assassinated in Delhi by a Hindu fanatic Mahatma Gandhi is one of the most fascinating personalities of the 20th century. The way in which he stood up against discrimination in South Africa and in India using non-violence combined with the theory he developed on his methods make him one of the most important examples in the history of humanity. He has been the inspiration for many people including Martin Luther King. Amazingly, Gandhi was never awarded the Nobel Peace Prize. The Nobel Committee was unable to reach a decision and have surely regretted this ever since. The following text deals with Gandhi's work in India. You will find a brief overview of the other things available in this section in the following table:

Gandhi's Work in India

India before the 15th of August 1947

Some statistical figures for British-India before the 15th August 1947 shed some stark light on the situation that faced Gandhi after his return to India: A population totaling 410 million, of whom 281 million were Hindus, 115 million Muslims, 7 million Christians, 6 million Sikhs, were faced by 150,000 Englishmen. Yet the Hindus were divided into 3,000 castes and sub-castes with 70 million people rated Untouchables and descendants of the original inhabitants. 310 million of the population lived under British administration and inhabited roughly two thirds of the territory. The remaining third held roughly 100 million people and was divided into 565 principalities speaking 15 different languages and 845 dialects. 85% illiteracy and indescribable poverty (...) hindered India in its struggle for independence.

Gradually Gandhi Found Strong Support Among India's Population

Following Gandhi's return to India he started presenting his ideas to the public. The concept of civil resistance against unrestricted British power was demonstrated by the Salt March in the year 1930, which ended the state's monopoly on salt and brought a degree of economic relief to India. To Gandhi however, it was essential that his fellow countrymen learned to overcome the British military supremacy by the means of stronger moral power. Initially nonviolent trials of strength failed again and again because of the undisciplined crowds, but gradually Gandhi found strong support among the population of India and strengthened their national self-confidence.

He praised the simple life and raised the spinning wheel as a symbol of this way of life.

Gandhi's path led him back to the power of religion. He bitterly fought against industrialisation and tried to shield himself and his fellow countrymen from western ideas and ways of life. He praised the simple life and set a personal example himself by his vegetarian life style, nature healing and hygiene. He chose the spinning wheel to be a symbol of this way of life, and beseeched the Indians to create a cottage industry by spinning and weaving their own cloth thereby taking on the struggle against the textile industry of England. For a while he commenced his public lectures by sitting at the spinning wheel in front of his audience in order to promote his idea.

To Gandhi conciliation of the higher-caste Hindus with the Untouchables was an obvious matter of concern, but it was one that he did not succeed in achieving. Maybe one reason was that he entreated the Untouchables to adopt a positive attitude to a life in contempt and insecurity. By 'fasting unto death', a method of making his demands expressive and compelling, he managed to gradually bring Hindus and Untouchables closer together, but he did not succeed in achieving the same between Hindus and Muslims. The members of his own religious community denied him their loyalty and so the bloody disputes between the rival groups increased. Finally, when the independence of India was proclaimed and then enacted on the 15th August 1947, it instantly resulted in partition into Pakistan and India.

He Looked on with Great Concern as the Individual Groups Fell into Disunity

Gandhi's attitude towards non-violence remains his legacy. However one must not fail to recognize that his one-sided life and 'return to the simple life' both missed the requirements of the times and hindered the political process of a modern state.

Gandhi's death was dramatic. On the 30th January 1948 the man whom the Indian poet Tragore had named Mahatma (Great Soul), was killed by shots from a pistol. His whole life he had preached a policy of non-violence.

With growing concern he saw how prior to and following the declaration of independence the different groups fell into disunity and fought each other for power. He tried to mediate and called for friendship among the religions. Ten days before his death a bomb had exploded on his property while he was holding a public prayer meeting.

Only a few days before the assassination, as if he had a premonition, Gandhi had said: "Should I die by the bullet of a madman, I have to do so with a smile. There must be no anger in me. God must be in my heart and on my lips and you must promise me one thing: Should such a thing happen, do not shed a tear. I have done my deeds for humanity not requested by any human and I cannot stop on request of anybody. I am like God wanted me and I do as he advises me to do. Let him do with me as he pleases. If he wants to he may kill me. I believe that I do as he orders." The news of his death left the whole world in mourning. The United Nations lowered their flags to half-mast. From the Vatican to the Kremlin sympathy was expressed. Gandhi remains a great example to the world.

Gandhi

A list of references are included in the Links and Book Lists, but I especially want to recognize Ved Mehta's book "Mahatma Gandhi & His Disciples", and Dennis Dalton's "Mahatma Gandhi:

Nonviolent Power in Action". Gandhi's own "Hind Swaraj" is also essential reading. The Leadership analysis and commentary is my own, faults and all. One of the greatest figures of the twentieth century, and perhaps of the millennium, Mohandas Karamchand Gandhi was born in Gujarat on October 2nd, 1869, and was assassinated January 30th, 1948.

He was both one of the most successful Leaders of the century, and, by his own standards, one of the least successful. He was charismatic, but he was also deliberate and analytical. Gandhi was very much a product of his times, yet one of his greatest sources of inspiration was the Bhagavad-Gita, written thousands of years ago. He was a politician, a writer, an intellectual and an orator. Without doubt he was a very complex man, but a man who believed in simple things.

So where do we start with an analysis of his Leadership style, ability and results?

Gandhi declared that "Action is my domain", so it is necessary to study the details of his life to begin to form a clear picture of his Leadership. The start point is also the end – he was called both "Mahatma", meaning great soul, and "Bapu", meaning Father. He was both of those things, not only to his native India, but also to millions of people around the world.

Family History

Gandhi was born into a minor Hindu political family, whose beliefs were influenced by Jainism (a nonviolent religious group), and who were vegetarian. Both his father and grandfather were at one time Prime Minister of nearby, small princely States. Of note, "Gandhi" means "grocer" in Gujarati.

Married at 13, his father died when he was 16. This greatly hurt him, not least as he was with his wife at the time rather than at his father's side when he died. Some commentators argue that this event was a root cause of Gandhi's later celibacy vows. I find this difficult to accept, as those vows were only made 16 years later, as part of a broader determination to focus his values. In fact, Gandhi had four sons. Gandhi was a lack-lustre scholar, later deciding to be trained as a lawyer in London, where he resided from 1888 to 1891. In so doing, he both broke convention and left behind his young, illiterate wife, Kasturbai. His London period was one of "avoiding temptation", and of learning new ideas. For example, he apparently liked the New Testament, but disliked the Old. After a brief stint unsuccessfully in an Indian law practice back home, he moved to South Africa in 1893, working as advisor to a well-to-do member of the Muslim Indian community. He went back to India to be with his wife in 1901, but returned in 1902 at the request of the South African Indian community.

Swaraj

Gandhi spent 21 years in South Africa. A critical event in his life was one week into his stay there, where he was asked to leave the First Class compartment of a train by a European. Despite having the right ticket, he was forcibly removed from the train. He suffered other racial indignities in those early months.

His two central ideas were born in South Africa. These were

- "Swaraj" (Independence for India, and personal spiritual renewal of all Indians),
- "Satyagraha" (truth, love and non-violence). Importantly, "Satyagraha" is more than just civil disobedience, as in Gandhi's view passive resistance could easily change into active resistance, and thus violence. Rather, in his conceptualization, respect for the other party was central, and all kinds of violence were forbidden absolutely.

Related to these two ideas was the "Constructive Programme"- Gandhi's Social Reform platform, consisting of three points:

1. Hindu/Muslim unity,
2. The abolition of Untouchability
3. "Swadeshi", the manufacture and use of indigenous products.

Gandhi's goal was none other than the complete transformation of India and its people. Whilst many of his later political colleagues shared some of these ideals, few shared all. We will return to these thoughts as we analyze Gandhi's Leadership.

Whilst in South Africa he learnt from Jewish and Christian friends, and developed respect for the ideas of Leo Tolstoy amongst others. Tolstoy's work "The Kingdom of God is within You" stated that all Government is based on war, and that one can only counter these evils through passive resistance. Gandhi also got involved in humanitarian activities. For example, he led a Red Cross unit in the Boer War, in 1899, and was decorated by the British authorities as a result.

When he was about to leave Durban in 1894 to return home to India, he was galvanized by newly written comments in the papers about the proposed Natal Franchise Amendment Bill. His friends and business acquaintances, hearing what he had to say about this, and how he said it, urged him to stay.

Thus, he drafted the first Indian Petition to the Government in 1894, against the Bill, which took away voting rights from Indians. In 1894 he also founded the Natal Indian Congress to build support for the Indian cause. He actually succeeded in reducing some of the harshness of the bill. However, his other campaigns against unjust laws and discrimination were not successful. Of note, British law overrode Natal law, and prohibited racial discrimination. But Natal had freedom on administrative matters, and loosely worded laws allowed much abuse. His activities and his support for the causes of the poor were rapidly building his reputation, in South Africa and in England.

South Africa

Another critical event was in 1906, when Gandhi organized an ambulance corps to go to Zululand. The Natal Government mounted a campaign to suppress the Zulu Rebellion, started when a chief killed a tax collector. The intense suffering of the Zulu's, and the lack of caring exhibited by the authorities for the wounded left him deeply moved. In his Autobiography, Gandhi had noted that nursing was one of his principal joys. In any event, in Zululand Gandhi made his famous vows:

- "Brahmacharya"-celibacy, an ancient Hindu vow
- "Satyagraha"-truth, love and non violence, Gandhi's own invention
- "Ahisma"-non violence to all creatures, and vegetarianism, a Jain vow

Gandhi later in his life slept naked with some of his women associates. These experiments in sexual self-control were often seen as controversial, but Gandhi's intent was to probe the limits of sexuality, and to show that it was possible to attain "absolute" and child-like innocence. It was in 1904 that he first started a weekly journal (the "Indian Opinion") and began living in communes, on the "Phoenix" Farm in Natal. In 1910 he started the Tolstoy Farm, near Johannesburg. This later was an 1,100 acre farm given to him by a close Jewish friend, saying a great deal about Gandhi's uncommonly wide and somewhat eclectic following, even in those early years.

"Satyagraha"

In 1906 in the Transvaal, the Government wanted Indians to register and be fingerprinted "like criminals". The law also meant that only existing Indian residents could be registered, Indians could not freely travel between Provinces, and future immigration was to be controlled.

At that time there were about 13,000 Indians in Transvaal, and about 100,000 in all of South Africa, so it was a large group affected. Gandhi even went to England to gain support for his view. But, despite reassurances he won there, and some concessions he received from the Transvaal Government, the law was passed in 1907 as the "Asiatic Registration Bill". Gandhi and his followers called it "The Black Act".

Gandhi at that moment galvanized his ideas into "Satyagraha", and founded the Passive Resistance Association. Importantly, "Satyagraha" combined both Political and religious goals in Gandhi's mind, for the first time, with a very clear focus an action.

Gandhi and others refused to register. He was involved in a mass burning of registration documents, he was tried and he went to jail. This was in Pretoria, in 1908, and it was his first time in jail. He served two weeks of his sentence.

After many Indians were jailed, Gandhi reached a compromise with General Jan Christian Smuts, the South African Leader. If Indians voluntarily registered, all Indian protesters in jail would be released. Gandhi agreed, although it led to his being attacked by extremist Indians and rescued by a white police officer. Smuts later reneged on the deal. Nevertheless, this left Gandhi relatively undeterred, and he believed totally in his nonviolent approach.

His second imprisonment was also in 1909 (his third was in 1910). On his way back from England later in 1909, where he was again soliciting support for the Indian cause, he wrote "Hind

Swaraj", his seminal work which set out his philosophy and action plan. It was published in December 1909, in Gujarati. In 1910, the Union of South Africa was created from the provinces, giving yet more legal autonomy to the Government.

In 1913, Judge Searle ruled that only marriages performed under Christian Rites were legal, instantly making Indian, Muslim and other marriages "irrelevant". Gandhi wanted to fill the jails with Indians. October of that year he led a march supporting mineworkers across the Transvaal border, and was arrested several times, including twice in one day.

Pressure was mounting on the Government to open an independent inquiry. However, at that time European railway workers went on strike, and the Government was in real jeopardy. So Gandhi called off the Indian actions, as he did not want to take advantage of his Government opponents weaknesses. In any event, in this case Gandhi won.

He reached agreement with Smuts in 1914, and the introduction of the Indian Relief Act of 1914 made Indian and other marriages fully legal. The head ("poll") tax was also abolished, which had been a long-standing source of discontent. He did not, however, succeed in reversing the Immigration restrictions.

Fasts

It was in South Africa that Gandhi first used fasting as a tool in "Satyagraha". Gandhi recognized that fasting could be misconstrued by others (he was, for example, accused of selfish egoism exhibited in his fasts!), so he developed very clear rules. In essence, fasts were an expression of "suffering love", in a deeply Christian sense.

According to Bhikhu Parekh, in his book in the Past Masters series, Gandhi's reasons for fasting were essentially fourfold:

- it was his way of expressing his own deep sense of sorrow at the way those he loved had disappointed him
- it was his way, as their Leader, for atoning for their misdeeds
- it was his last attempt to stir deep spiritual feelings in others and to appeal to their moral sense
- it was his way of bringing the quarreling parties together.

Gandhi also placed limits on when fasting was appropriate;

- Fasts could only be undertaken against those people he loved
- Fasts must have a concrete and specific goal, not abstract aims
- The fast must be morally defensible in the eyes of the target
- The fast must in no way serve his own interests
- The fast must not ask people to do something they were incapable of, or to cause great hardship.

Gandhi followed these principles on every fast. During his lifetime, he fasted 17 times.

To India

As a result of his activities, Gandhi became quite well known in India, and this gave a virtually instant platform for his activities when he returned.

Throughout the South African period he was never "anti-British", and was quite civil even towards General Smuts. He believed in his duties to the Empire, especially in time of war, as demonstrated by his organizing another (perhaps less successful) ambulance group for the British in World War 1, and recruiting troops for the British Army when back in India in 1918.

Rather, Gandhi was pro-Indian, pro-truth and pro-non-violence. In essence, he was pro-human rights (to steal a phrase he never actually used in its current Western meaning), but with a profound personal intensity and commitment. He carried this attitude with him as he returned to India.

He thus left South Africa with the basis of his life philosophy, a proven method of organizing people to get political results, a growing reputation, and massive personal self-confidence.

4

Gandhi and the Indian National Congress

Mahatma Gandhi's entry and meteoric rise in the Indian political scenario following his return from South Africa in 1918, has been variously equated with the emergence of a guiding light to a breath of fresh air. Indian national Congress was the single most popular party, spearheading India's war for independence when Gandhi returned, having led two successful revolutions in South Africa. They were conducted on the lines of Satyagraha, Gandhi's personal mode of nonviolent resistance. Indian National Congress (INC), at that point was dominated by the combative policies of the extremists. Bal Gangadhar Tilak, Lala Lajpat Rai and Bipin Chandra Pal were the chief propagators of these extremist tendencies within the ranks of the INC. Gandhi's modes and ideologies were markedly different, and were slow to gain acceptance. However, he soon became a member of the Indian National Congress, and then embarked in a nationwide journey under the command and wish of Sri Gopal Krishna Gokhale, his political mentor. What he saw reaffirmed in his mind his already firm faith in the ideals of satyagraha. The Home Rule movement under Tilak and Annie Besant were far from successful, and Gandhi knew that no mode of armed revolution could make India free from the clutches of the British rule.

Satyagraha at Champaran and Kheda

Gandhi's political career took a head start when he went to lead satyagraha against the indigo merchants at Champaran in

Bihar. He raised his voice against the unbearable exploitation of the indigo farmers of the region. His methods, as always, were based on non-violence, and he met with success. The British authorities were forced to accept to the demandes of the indigo workers. He repeated his success at Kheda in Gujarat against the increasing revenues and taxed imposed by the government on the farmers at rural Gujarat. Once again, the processes were nonviolent. With these successes, Gandhi was hailed as the new light in the Indian political scenario. He gained the appellation of the Mahatma (the great soul) and Bapu (father). Soon Rowlatt Act and the subsequent massacre at Jalianwallah Bagh at Amritsar in Punjab considerably heated up the scenario of Indian politics. Gandhiji assumed the responsibilities of the president of Indian National Congress in 1921, and unleashed a series of reforms in the party ranks, thereby giving impetus to the non-cooperation movement, that by that time took the entire nation in its grip.

Mahatma Gandhi as the President of Indian National Congress

Mahatma Gandhi was elected as the president of the Indian National Congress in 1921. He immediately introduced a number of reforms within the party ranks. The first responsibility that Gandhi undertook as the president of the Indian National Congress was to increase the reach of the party among the masses who reside in the remote corners in order to eradicate its elitist status. Gandhi famously stated that rural India was the very backbone of the country, both in economic and in logistical terms. Therefore no movement can be truly successful unless whole-heartedly supported by the inhabitants of the Indian villages. The first step that he took was to considerably reduce the membership fee of the party. Then he restructured the entire party hierarchy, and opened new party branches at various provinces and princely states of India. Soon congress took a national dimension with membership multiplied manifold. Gandhi became the new guiding star of Indian politics, operating under the umbrella of the Indian National Congress.

As the president of the Indian National Congress, Mahatma Gandhi introduced the tenets and the ideals of Satyagraha, and the party saw the emergence of many new and charismatic leaders with great public appeals, who were loyal followers of Gandhi. By then, Lala Lajpat Rai also became an admirer of Gandhi in spite of former differences. With such great following, non-cooperation movement against the Rowlatt Act and the Amritsar tragedy naturally took massive national dimension.

Gandhi's Contribution towards Unification of the Congress

Gandhi called off the non-cooperation movement abruptly following the unfortunate violence at Chauri Chaura. It was even condemned by many of his most loyal followers as a historic blunder, with the likes of Sri CR Das among them. Gandhi's arrest in 1922 was the beginning of a stormy period for the Indian National Congress. Two factions under CR Das and Chakraborty Rajagopalachari gathered force, and the entire coherent fabric of the INC was on the point of breaking down, thereby bringing down the impetus of the Indian nationalist movement and also tarnishing the image of the Congress in the public eye. Gandhi tried hard to bridge the differences. He undertook a fast in a bid to unite the warring factions. However, success was limited and Gandhi had to come back and hold the reins in order to guide Congress in the proper direction.

Gandhi returned from a brief hibernation following his imprisonment and in the Calcutta Conference of 1928, announced his arrival with aplomb, daring the British government with a one year deadline to free India. He was influenced by the enthusiasm of younger Congressmen like Jawaharlal Nehru and Subhash Chandra Bose. The government did not respond and the INC celebrated Indian independence on 26th January, 1930, following the proposals undertaken Lahore Congress the year before. The Civil Disobedience movement ensued with Gandhi at the helm, defying government orders.

Rowlatt Act

The Rowlatt Act was a law passed by the British in colonial India in March 1919, indefinitely extending "emergency measures" (of the Defence of India Regulations Act) enacted during the First World War in order to control public unrest and root out conspiracy. Passed on the recommendations of the Rowlatt commission, named for its chairman, British judge Sir Sidney Rowlatt, this act effectively authorized the government to imprison, without trial, any person suspected of terrorism living in the Raj. The Rowlatt Acts gave British imperial authorities power to deal with revolutionary activities.

Mahatma Gandhi, among other Indian leaders, was extremely critical of the Act and argued that not everyone should be punished in response to isolated political crimes. The Act led to indignation from Indian leaders and the public, which caused the government to implement repressive measures. Gandhi and others found that constitutional opposition to the measure was fruitless, so on April 6, a "hartal" was organized where Indians would suspend all business and fast as a sign of their hatred for the legislation. This event is known as the Rowlatt satyagraha.

However, the success of the hartal in Delhi, on 30 March, was overshadowed by tensions running high, which resulted in rioting in the Punjab and other provinces. Deciding that Indians were not ready to make a stand in consistence with the principle of ahimsa (non-violence), an integral part of satyagraha, Gandhi suspended the resistance.

The Rowlatt Act came into effect in March 1919. In the Punjab the protest movement was very strong, and on April 10, two outstanding leaders of the congress Dr. Satya Pal and Dr. Saifuddin Kitchlew, were arrested and taken to an unknown place.

Rowlatt Committee

The Rowlatt committee was a Sedition Committee appointed in 1918 by the British Indian Government with Mr. Justice Rowlatt, an English judge, as its president. The purpose of the committee was to evaluate political terrorism in India, especially Bengal and Punjab, its impact, and the links with the German government and the Bolsheviks in Russia. It was instituted towards the end of World War I when the Indian Revolutionary movement had been especially active and had achieved considerable success, potency and momentum and massive assistance was received from Germany which planned to destabilise British India.

These included supporting and financing Indian seditionist organisations in Germany and in United States as well as a destabilisation in the political situation in neighbouring

Afghanistan following a diplomatic mission that had attempted to rally the Amir of Afghanistan against British India. Attempts were also made by the Provisional Government of India established in Afghanistan following the mission to establish contacts with the Bosheviks. A further reason for institution of the committee was emerging civil and labour unrest in India around the post-war recession, e.g the Bombay mill worker's strikes and unrests in Punjab, and the Spanish Flu epidemic that killed nearly 13 million people in the country.

The evidence produced before the committee substantiated the German link, although no conclusive evidence was found for a significant contribution or threat from the Bolsheviks. On the recommendations of the committee, the Rowlatt Act, an extension of the Defence of India act of 1915, was enforced in response to the threat in Punjab and Bengal.

The Rowlatt Act, instituted on the Committee's recommendations, had a significant impact on the political situation of India, irrevocably placing her on a path of political movement headed by Gandhi that ultimately dominated the Indian Independence movement for the next 20 years. Also known as the Black Act, it vested the Viceroy's government with extraordinary powers to quell sedition by silencing the press, detaining the political activists without trial, and arresting without warrant any individuals suspected of sedition or treason. In protest, a nationwide cessation of work (*hartal*) was called, marking the beginning of widespread, although not nationwide, popular discontent.

The agitation unleashed by the acts culminated on 13 April 1919, in the Jallianwala Bagh massacre in Amritsar, Punjab when the British military commander, Brigadier-General Reginald Dyer, blocked the main entrance to the Jallianwallah Bagh, a walled in courtyard in Amritsar, and ordered his soldiers to fire into an unarmed and unsuspecting crowd of some 5,000 people who had assembled there in defiance of a ban. A total of 1,650 rounds were fired, killing 379 people (as according to an official British commission; Indian estimates ranged as high as 1,500) and wounding 1,137 in the episode, which dispelled wartime hopes of home rule and goodwill in a frenzy of post-war reaction.

The Rowlatt Act and its Aftermath

The positive impact of reform was seriously undermined in 1919 by the Rowlatt Act, named after the recommendations made the previous year to the Imperial Legislative Council by the Rowlatt Commission, which had been appointed to investigate "seditious conspiracy." The Rowlatt Act, also known as the Black Act, vested the Viceroy's government with extraordinary powers to quell sedition by silencing the press, detaining political activists without trial, and arresting any individuals suspected of sedition or treason without a warrant. In protest, a nationwide cessation of work (hartal) was called, marking the beginning of widespread, although not nationwide, popular discontent.

The agitation unleashed by the acts culminated on 13 April 1919, in the Amritsar Massacre in Amritsar, Punjab. The British military commander, Brigadier-General Reginald Dyer, ordered his soldiers to fire into an unarmed and unsuspecting crowd of some 10,000 people. They had assembled at Jallianwala Bagh, a walled garden, to celebrate Baisakhi, a Sikh festival, without prior knowledge of the imposition of martial law. A total of 1,650 rounds were fired, killing 379 people and wounding 1,137 in the episode, which dispelled wartime hopes of home rule and goodwill in a frenzy of postwar reaction

Jallianwalla Baug Massacre

India's History, Modern India : Rowlatt Act evokes protests, Jallianwalla Bagh massacre : 1919. The Protest as the Defence of India Act was to expire six months after the conclusion of the war, a new set of emergency measures for the detention and containment of 'terrorists' to meet what was termed the 'continuing threat' were planned by the Government of India. These measures were incorporated within the Anarchical and Revolutionary Crimes Act, known to Indians as the Rowlatt Act after the name of the chairman of the committee that recommended the institution of this legislation. The government could not have known that the Rowlatt Act would become the occasion for the most widespread movement of opposition to British rule since the Rebellion of 1857-58 and indeed the springboard from which the movement for independence would be launched until India was to become irretrievably lost to the British. The Rowlatt Act provided for the trial of seditious crime by benches of three judges; the accused were not to have the benefit of either preliminary commitment proceedings or the right of appeal, and the rules under which evidence could be obtained and used were relaxed. Other preventive measures included detention without the levying of charges and searches without warrants. As the Rowlatt committee noted in its report, "punishment or acquittal should be speedy both in order to secure the moral effect which punishment should produce and also to prevent the prolongation of the excitement which the proceedings may set up." The history of anti-terrorist legislation in colonial India by no means ends with the Rowlatt Act, but such of it as is here narrated suggests that much in the present legislation had already been anticipated. Jallianwala Bagh Massacre Jallianwalla Bagh massacre of April 13, 1919 was one of the most inhuman acts of the British rulers in India. The people of Punjab have gathered on the auspicious day of Baisakhi at Jallianwalla Bagh, adjacent to Golden Temple (Amritsar), to lodge their protest peacefully against persecution by the British Indian Government. General Dwyer apeared suddenly with his armed police force and fired indiscriminately at innocent empty handed people leaving hundreds of people dead, including women and children. General Dwyer, the butcher of Jallianwalla Bagh, was later murdered by Udham Singh to avenge this barbaric act.

The Rowlatt Act and its aftermath

The positive impact of reform was seriously undermined in *1919* by the *Rowlatt Act,* named after the recommendations made the previous year to the Imperial Legislative Council by the Rowlatt Commission, which had been appointed to investigate "seditious conspiracy." The *Rowlatt Act,* also known as the Black Act, vested the Viceroy's government with extraordinary powers to quell sedition by silencing the press, detaining political activists without trial, and arresting any individuals suspected of sedition or treason without a warrant. In protest, a nationwide cessation of work (*hartal*) was called, marking the beginning of widespread, although not nationwide, popular discontent.

The agitation unleashed by the acts culminated on *13 April, 1919,* in the *Amritsar Massacre* in *Amritsar,* Punjab. The British military commander, Brigadier-General *Reginald Dyer*, ordered his soldiers to fire into an unarmed and unsuspecting crowd of some 10,000 persons. They had assembled at Jallianwala Bagh, a walled garden, to celebrate *Baisakhi*, a *Sikh* festival, without prior knowledge of the imposition of martial law. A total of 1,650 rounds were fired, killing 379 persons and wounding 1,137 in the episode, which dispelled wartime hopes of home rule and goodwill in a frenzy of postwar

Rowlatt Act

The Rowlatt Act was passed in 1919, indefinitely extending wartime "emergency meaures" in order to control public unrest and root out conspiracy. This act effectively authorised the government to imprison without trial, any person suspected of terrorism living in the Raj.

Mahatma Gandhi, among other Indian leaders, was extremely critical of the Act and argued that not everyone should be punished in response to isolated political crimes. The Act led to indignation from Indian leaders and the public, which caused the government to implement repressive measures. Some people who read the enactment found that constitutional opposition to the measure was fruitless so on April 6th, a "hartal" was organised where Indians would suspend all business and fast as a sign of their hatred for the legislation.

However, the hartal in Delhi was overshadowed by tensions running high which resulted in rioting in the Punjab and other provinces. Gandhi saw that the Indians were not ready for such a stand and suspended the hartal.

The Rowlatt Act came into effect in March 1919. In the Punjab the protest movement was very strong, and on April 10th, two outstanding leaders of the congress Dr. Satya Pal and Dr. Saifuddin Kithlew, were arrested and taken to an unknown place.

A protest was held in Amritsar, which led to the Amritsar Massacre of 1919.

Mahatma Gandhi was to spend much of 1917 in Champaran, seeking to obtain for the peasants security of tenure as well as the freedom to cultivate the crops of their choice. The following year, 1918, Gandhiji was involved in two campaigns in his home state of Gujarat. First, he intervened in a labour dispute in Ahmedabad, demanding better working conditions for the textile mill workers. Then he joined peasants in Kheda in asking the state for the remission of taxes following the failure of their harvest.

These initiatives in Champaran, Ahmedabad and Kheda marked Gandhiji out as a nationalist with a deep sympathy for the poor. At the same time, these were all localised struggles. Then, in 1919, the colonial rulers delivered into Gandhiji's lap an issue from which he could construct a much wider movement. During the Great War of 1914-18, the British had instituted censorship of the press and permitted detention without trial. Now, on the recommendation of a committee chaired by Sir Sidney Rowlatt, these tough measures were continued. In response, Gandhiji called for a countrywide campaign against the "Rowlatt Act".

In towns across North and West India, life came to a standstill, as shops shut down and schools closed in response to the *bandh* call. The protests were particularly intense in the Punjab, where many men had served on the British side in the War – expecting to be rewarded for their service. Instead they were given the Rowlatt Act. Gandhiji was detained while proceeding to the Punjab, even as prominent local Congressmen were arrested.

The situation in the province grew progressively more tense, reaching a bloody climax in Amritsar in April 1919, when a British Brigadier ordered his troops to open fire on a nationalist meeting. More than four hundred people were killed in what is known as the Jallianwala Bagh massacre. It was the Rowlatt satyagraha that made Gandhiji a truly *national* leader. Emboldened by its success, Gandhiji called for a campaign of "non-cooperation" with British rule. Indians who wished colonialism to end were asked to stop attending schools, colleges and law courts, and not pay taxes. In sum, they were asked to adhere to a "renunciation of (all) voluntary association with the (British) Government". If noncooperation was effectively carried out, said Gandhiji, India would win swaraj within a year. To further broaden the struggle he had joined hands with the Khilafat Movement that sought to restore the Caliphate, a symbol of Pan-Islamism which had recently been abolished by the Turkish ruler Kemal Attaturk.

Champaran and Kheda Satyagraha

The first Satyagraha revolutions inspired by Mahatma Gandhi in the Indian Independence Movement occurred in Kheda district of Gujarat and the Champaran district of Bihar between the years of 1918 and 1919. Champaran Satyagraha was the first to be started but the word Satyagraha was used for the first time in Anti Rowlatt agitation.

Champaran, Bihar

In Champaran, a district in state of Bihar, tens of thousands of landless serfs, indentured labourers and poor farmers were forced to grow indigo and other cash crops instead of the food crops necessary for their survival. These goods were bought from them at a very low price. Suppressed by the ruthless militias of the landlords (mostly British), they were given measly compensation, leaving them mired in extreme poverty. The villages were kept extremely dirty and unhygienic, and alcoholism, untouchability and purdah were rampant. Now in the throes of a devastating famine, the British levied an oppressive tax which they insisted on increasing in rate. Without food and without money, the situation was growing progressively unlivable and the Bhumihar Brahmins in Champaran revolted against indigo cultivation in 1914 (at Pipra) and 1916 (Turkaulia) and Pandit Raj Kumar Shukla took Mahatma Gandhi to Champaran and the Champaran Satyagraha began.

Kheda, Gujarat

In Kheda, a district of villages and small towns in Gujarat, the peasants mostly owned their own lands, and were economically better-off than their compatriots in Bihar, although on the whole, the district was plagued by poverty, scant resources, the social evils of alcoholism and untouchability, and overall British indifference and hegemony.

However, a terrible famine had struck the district and a large part of Gujarat, and virtually destroyed the agrarian economy. The poor peasants had barely enough to feed themselves, but the British government of the Bombay Presidency insisted that the farmers not only pay full taxes, but also pay the 23% increase stated to take effect that very year.

Gandhi's Solution

While many civic groups sent petitions and published editorials, Gandhi proposed *satyagraha*-non-violence, mass civil disobedience. While it was strictly nonviolent, Gandhi was proposing real action, a real revolt that the oppressed peoples of India were dying to undertake.

Gandhi also insisted that neither the protestors in Bihar nor in Gujarat allude to or try to propagate the concept of *Swaraj*, or *Independence*. This was not about political freedom, but a revolt against abject tyranny amidst a terrible humanitarian disaster. While accepting participants and help from other parts of India, Gandhi insisted that no other district or province revolt against the Government, and that the Indian National Congress not get involved apart from issuing resolutions of support, to prevent the British from giving it cause to use extensive suppressive measures and brand the revolts as treason.

In Champaran

Gandhiji established an ashram in Champaran, organizing scores of his veteran supporters and fresh volunteers from the region. He organized a detailed study and survey of the villages, accounting the atrocities and terrible episodes of suffering, including the general state of degenerate living.

Building on the confidence of villagers, he began leading the clean-up of villages, building of schools and hospitals and encouraging the village leadership to undo purdah, untouchability and the suppression of women. He was joined by many young nationalists from all over India, including Dr. Sri Krishna Sinha, Ramarshi Deo Trivedi "Rishi Ji", Brajkishore Prasad, Dr. Rajendra Prasad, Dr. Anugrah Narayan Sinha and Jawaharlal Nehru.

But his main assault came as he was arrested by police on the charge of creating unrest and was ordered to leave the province. Hundreds of thousands of people protested and rallied outside the jail, police stations and courts demanding his release, which the court unwillingly did. Gandhi led organized protests and strike against the landlords, who with the guidance of the British government, signed an agreement granting more compensation and control over farming for the poor farmers of the region, and cancellation of revenue hikes and collection until the famine ended. It was during this agitation, that Gandhi was addressed by the people as *Bapu* (*Father*) and *Mahatma* (*Great Soul*).

In Kheda

In Gujarat, Gandhi was only the spiritual head of the struggle. His chief lieutenant, Sardar Vallabhbhai Patel and a close coterie of devoted Gandhians, namely Narhari Parikh, Mohanlal Pandya and Ravi Shankar Vyas toured the countryside, organized the villagers and gave them political leadership and direction. Many aroused Gujaratis from the cities of Ahmedabad and Vadodara joined the organizers of the revolt, but Gandhi and Patel resisted the involvement of Indians from other provinces, seeking to keep it a purely Gujarati struggle.

Patel and his colleagues organized a major tax revolt, and all the different ethnic and caste communities of Kheda rallied around it. The peasants of Kheda signed a petition calling for the tax for this year to be scrapped in wake of the famine. The government in Bombay rejected the charter. They warned that if the peasants did not pay, the lands and property would be confiscated and many arrested. And once confiscated, they would not be returned even if most complied. None of the villages flinched.

The tax withheld, the government's collectors and inspectors sent in thugs to seize property and cattle, while the police forfeited the lands and all agrarian property. The farmers did not resist arrest, nor retaliate to the force employed with violence. Instead, they used their cash and valuables to donate to the *Gujarat Sabha* which was officially organizing the protest.

The revolt was astounding in terms of discipline and unity. Even when all their personal property, land and livelihood were seized, a vast majority of Kheda's farmers remained firmly united in the support of Patel. Gujaratis sympathetic to the revolt in other parts resisted the government machinery, and helped the shelter the relatives and property of the protesting peasants. Those Indians who sought to buy the confiscated lands were ostracized from society. Although nationalists like Sardul Singh Caveeshar called for sympathetic revolts in other parts, Gandhi and Patel firmly rejected the idea.

The Government finally sought to foster an honourable agreement for both parties. The tax for the year in question, and the next would be suspended, and the increase in rate reduced, while all confiscated property would be returned.

Gujaratis also worked in cohesion to return the confiscated lands to their rightful owners. The ones who had bought the lands seized were influenced to return them, even though the British had officially said it would stand by the buyers.

Success and Legacy

Gandhi's resulting fame spread like fire all over the nation. He had become a defining influence on Indian Nationalism. People in Gujarat still revere Gandhi and Sardar Patel, and their role in the freedom struggle. Gujarat is the most industrialized and progressive state in India today. In Bihar, poverty and social conflict pervades what was the founding of the Satyagraha movement. The Naxalite insurgency is centred around the same age-old problem of class struggle between poor farmers and rich landlords, now involving.

Champaran

Champaran is a notable place in Bihar that has got an immense importance in the history of the freedom movement of India. This was the place where Mahatma Gandhi took his first attempt towards the structuring of the nationalist movement in India.

The place is renowned for the great Champaran movement which was started as a protest against the tortures and the exploitations of the indigo planters in Bihar as well as other parts of the country. This movement had quite a long lasting effect.

Mahatma Gandhi was firm in his efforts to bring good days in Champaran of Bihar. The British Government was at last compelled to establish a Committee of Inquiry. The committee was entrusted with the responsibility of examination and submission of report on the conditions of the farmers in Champaran.

Mahatma Gandhi was himself a member of that Committee. It signed the report on the 3rd of October 1917. This was forwarded to the Government of Bihar. It was then that the Champaran Agrarian Act was passed in March 1918. This brought an end to the exploitation of the indigo planters. While in Champaran, Mahatma Gandhi went to almost all of the villages there and did a lot of social work. Special mention should be made of some of those places in the Champaran district:

- Motihari in the East Champaran
- Hazarimal Dharmshala,Betia in the West Champaran
- Bhitiharwa Ashram in the West Champaran
- Brindaban in the West Champaran
- Shri Rampur in the West Champaran
- Koeldih in the West Champaran
- Amolwa in the West Champaran
- Sariswain the West Champaran
- Hardiya Kothi in the West Champa.

West Champaran District was carved out of the old Champaran District in the year 1972 as a result of re-organization of the District in the state. It was formerly a subdivision of Saran District and then Champaran District with its Head quarters as Bettiah. It is said that Bettiah got its name from Baint (Cane) plants commonly found in this district. The name Champaran is a degenerate form of Champaka aranya, a name which dates back to the time when the district was a tract of the forest of Champa (Magnolia) trees & was the abode of solitary asectics.

As per District Gazetteer, it seems probable that Champaran was occupied at an early period by races of Aryan descent and formed part of the country in which the Videha empire ruled. After the fall of Videhan empire the district formed part of the Vrijjain oligarchical republic with its capital at Vaishali of which Lichhavis were the most powerful and prominent. Ajatshatru the emperor of Magadh, by tact and force annexed Lichhavis and occupied its capital, Vaishali. He extended his sovereignty over Paschim Champaran which continued under the Mauryan rule for the next hundred years. After the Mauryas, the Sungas and Kanvas ruled over the Magadh territories. The district thereafter formed part of the Kushan empire and then came under Gupta empire. Along with Tirhut, Champaran was possibly annexed by Harsha during whose reign Huen-Tsang, the famous Chinese pilgrim, visited India. During 750 to 1155 AD, the Palas of Bengal were in the possession of Eastern India and Champaran formed the part of their territory. Towards the close of the 10th century Gangaya Deva of the Kalacheeri dynasty conquered Champaran.He was succeeded by Vikramaditya of the Chalukya dynasty.

During 1213 and 1227, the first Muslim influence was experienced when Ghyasuddin Iwaz the Muslim governor of Bengal extended his influence over Tribhukti or Tirhut. It was however, not a complete conquest and he was only able to have Tirhut from Narsinghdeva, a Simraon king. In about 1320, Ghyasuddin Tughlaq annexed Tirhut to the Tughlaq Empire and placed it under Kameshwar Thakur, who established Sugaon or Thakur dynasty. This dynasty continued to rule the area till Nasrat Shah, son of Allauddin Shah attacked Tirhut in 1530, annexed the territory, and killed the Raja and thus put an end to the Thakur dynasty. Nasrat Shah appointed his son-in-law as viceroy of Tirhut and thence forward the country continued to be ruled by the Muslim rulers. After the fall of Mughal Empire the British rulers came to power in India.

The history of the district during the late medieval period and the British period is linked with the history of Bettiah Raj. Bettiah Raj has been mentioned as a great estate. It traces its descent from one Ujjain Singh and his son, Gaj Singh, who received the title of Raja from the Emperor Shah Jahan (1628-58). The family came into prominence as independent chief in the 18th century during the downfall of the Mughal Empire. At the time when Sarkar Champaran passed under British rule, is was in the possession of Raja Jugal Kishore Singh, who succeeded Raja Dhurup Singh in 1763. The Raj was succeeded by the descendents of Raja Jugal kishore Singh. Harendra Kishore Singh, the last Maharaja of Bettiah, died in 1893, issueless and was succeeded by his first wife, who died in 1896. The estate came under the management of Court of Wards since 1897 and was held by the Maharaja's junior widow, Maharani Janki Kuar.

The British Raj palace occupies a large area in the centre of the town. In 1910 at the request of Maharani, the palace was built after the plan of Graham's palace in Calcutta. The Court Of Wards is at present holding the property of Bettiah Raj.

The rise of nationalism in Bettiah in early 20th century is intimately connected with indigo plantation. Raj Kumar Shukla, an ordinary raiyat and indigo cultivator of Champaran met Gandhijii and explained the plight of the cultivators and the atrocities of the planters on the raiyats.

Gandhijii came to Champaran in 1917 and listened to the problems of the cultivators and the started the movement known as Champaran Satyagraha Movement to end the oppression of the British indigo planters. By 1918 the long standing misery of the indigo cultivators came to an end and Champaran became the hub of Indian National Freedom Movement and the launch pad of Gandhi's Satyagraha.

Champaran and Kheda Satyagraha

The first Satyagraha revolutions inspired by Mahatma Gandhi in the Indian Independence Movement occurred in Kheda district of Gujarat and the Champaran district of Bihar between the years of 1918 and 1919. Champaran Satyagraha was the first to be started but the word Satyagraha was used for the first time in Anti Rowlatt agitation.

Champaran, Bihar

In Champaran, a district in state of Bihar, tens of thousands of landless serfs, indentured labourers and poor farmers were forced to grow indigo and other cash crops instead of the food crops necessary for their survival. These goods were bought from them at a very low price. Suppressed by the ruthless militias of the landlords (mostly British), they were given measly compensation, leaving them mired in extreme poverty.

The villages were kept extremely dirty and unhygienic, and alcoholism, untouchability and purdah were rampant. Now in the throes of a devastating famine, the British levied an oppressive tax which they insisted on increasing in rate. Without food and without money, the situation was growing progressively unlivable and the Bhumihar Brahmins in Champaran revolted against indigo cultivation in 1914 (at Pipra) and 1916 (Turkaulia) and Pandit Raj Kumar Shukla took Mahatma Gandhi to Champaran and the Champaran Satyagraha began.

Kheda, Gujarat

In Kheda, a district of villages and small towns in Gujarat, the peasants mostly owned their own lands, and were economically better-off than their compatriots in Bihar, although on the whole, the district was plagued by poverty, scant resources, the social evils of alcoholism and untouchability, and overall British indifference and hegemony.

However, a terrible famine had struck the district and a large part of Gujarat, and virtually destroyed the agrarian economy. The poor peasants had barely enough to feed themselves, but the British government of the Bombay Presidency insisted that the farmers not only pay full taxes, but also pay the 23% increase stated to take effect that very year.

Gandhi's Solution

While many civic groups sent petitions and published editorials, Gandhi proposed *satyagraha*-non-violence, mass civil disobedience. While it was strictly nonviolent, Gandhi was proposing real action, a real revolt that the oppressed peoples of India were dying to undertake.

Gandhi also insisted that neither the protestors in Bihar nor in Gujarat allude to or try to propagate the concept of *Swaraj*, or *Independence*. This was not about political freedom, but a revolt against abject tyranny amidst a terrible humanitarian disaster. While accepting participants and help from other parts of India, Gandhi insisted that no other district or province revolt against the Government, and that the Indian National Congress not get involved apart from issuing resolutions of support, to prevent the British from giving it cause to use extensive suppressive measures and brand the revolts as treason.

In Champaran

Gandhiji established an ashram in Champaran, organizing scores of his veteran supporters and fresh volunteers from the region. He organized a detailed study and survey of the villages, accounting the atrocities and terrible episodes of suffering, including the general state of degenerate living. Building on the confidence of villagers, he began leading the clean-up of villages, building of schools and hospitals and encouraging the village leadership to undo purdah, untouchability and the suppression of women. He was joined by many young nationalists from all over India, including Dr. Sri Krishna Sinha, Ramarshi Deo Trivedi "Rishi Ji", Brajkishore Prasad, Dr. Rajendra Prasad, Dr. Anugrah Narayan Sinha and Jawaharlal Nehru.

But his main assault came as he was arrested by police on the charge of creating unrest and was ordered to leave the province. Hundreds of thousands of people protested and rallied outside the jail, police stations and courts demanding his release, which the court unwillingly did. Gandhi led organized protests and strike against the landlords, who with the guidance of the British government, signed an agreement granting more compensation and control over farming for the poor farmers of the region, and cancellation of revenue hikes and collection until the famine ended. It was during this agitation, that Gandhi was addressed by the people as *Bapu* (*Father*) and *Mahatma* (*Great Soul*).

In Kheda

In Gujarat, Gandhi was only the spiritual head of the struggle. His chief lieutenant, Sardar Vallabhbhai Patel and a close coterie of devoted Gandhians, namely Narhari Parikh, Mohanlal Pandya and Ravi Shankar Vyas toured the countryside, organized the villagers and gave them political leadership and direction. Many aroused Gujaratis from the cities of Ahmedabad and Vadodara joined the organizers of the revolt, but Gandhi and Patel resisted the involvement of Indians from other provinces, seeking to keep it a purely Gujarati struggle.

Patel and his colleagues organized a major tax revolt, and all the different ethnic and caste communities of Kheda rallied around it. The peasants of Kheda signed a petition calling for the tax for this year to be scrapped in wake of the famine. The government in Bombay rejected the charter. They warned that if the peasants did not pay, the lands and property would be confiscated and many arrested. And once confiscated, they would not be returned even if most complied. None of the villages flinched.

The tax withheld, the government's collectors and inspectors sent in thugs to seize property and cattle, while the police forfeited the lands and all agrarian property. The farmers did not resist arrest, nor retaliate to the force employed with violence. Instead, they used their cash and valuables to donate to the *Gujarat Sabha* which was officially organizing the protest.

The revolt was astounding in terms of discipline and unity. Even when all their personal property, land and livelihood were seized, a vast majority of Kheda's farmers remained firmly united in the support of Patel. Gujaratis sympathetic to the revolt in other parts resisted the government machinery, and helped the shelter the relatives and property of the protesting peasants. Those Indians who sought to buy the confiscated lands were ostracized from society. Although nationalists like Sardul Singh Caveeshar called for sympathetic revolts in other parts, Gandhi and Patel firmly rejected the idea.

The Government finally sought to foster an honourable agreement for both parties. The tax for the year in question, and the next would be suspended, and the increase in rate reduced, while all confiscated property would be returned.

Gujaratis also worked in cohesion to return the confiscated lands to their rightful owners. The ones who had bought the lands seized were influenced to return them, even though the British had officially said it would stand by the buyers.

Success and Legacy

Gandhi's resulting fame spread like fire all over the nation. He had become a defining influence on Indian Nationalism. People in Gujarat still revere Gandhi and Sardar Patel, and their role in the freedom struggle. Gujarat is the most industrialized and progressive state in India today. In Bihar, poverty and social conflict pervades what was the founding of the Satyagraha movement. The Naxalite insurgency is centred around the same age-old problem of class struggle between poor farmers and rich landlords, now involving terrorism.

Champaran, Bihar

In Champaran, a district in state of Bihar, tens of thousands of landless serfs, indentured labourers and poor farmers were forced to grow indigo and other cash crops instead of the food crops necessary for their survival. These goods were bought from them at a very low price. Suppressed by the ruthless militias of the landlords (mostly British), they were given measly compensation, leaving them mired in extreme poverty. The villages were kept extremely dirty and unhygienic, and alcoholism, untouchability and purdah were rampant. Now in the throes of a devastating famine, the British levied an oppressive tax which they insisted on increasing in rate. Without food and without money, the situation was growing progressively unlivable and the Bhumihar Brahmins in Champaran revolted against indigo cultivation in 1914 (at Pipra) and 1916(Turkaulia) and Pandit Raj Kumar Shukla took Mahatma Gandhi to Champaran and the Champaran Satyagraha began.

Kheda, Gujarat

In Kheda, a district of villages and small towns in Gujarat, the peasants mostly owned their own lands, and were economically better-off than their compatriots in Bihar, although on the whole, the district was plagued by poverty, scant resources, the social evils of alcoholism and untouchability, and overall British indifference and hegemony.

However, a terrible famine had struck the district and a large part of Gujarat, and virtually destroyed the agrarian economy. The poor peasants had barely enough to feed themselves, but the British government of the Bombay Presidency insisted that the farmers not only pay full taxes, but also pay the 23% increase stated to take effect that very year.

Gandhi's Solution

While many civic groups sent petitions and published editorials, Gandhi proposed *satyagraha*-non-violence, mass civil disobedience. While it was strictly nonviolent, Gandhi was proposing real action, a real revolt that the oppressed peoples of India were dying to undertake.

Gandhi also insisted that neither the protestors in Bihar nor in Gujarat allude to or try to propagate the concept of *Swaraj*, or *Independence*. This was not about political freedom, but a revolt against abject tyranny amidst a terrible humanitarian disaster. While accepting participants and help from other parts of India,

Gandhi insisted that no other district or province revolt against the Government, and that the Indian National Congress not get involved apart from issuing resolutions of support, to prevent the British from giving it cause to use extensive suppressive measures and brand the revolts as treason.

In Champaran

Gandhiji established an ashram in Champaran, organizing scores of his veteran supporters and fresh volunteers from the region. He organized a detailed study and survey of the villages, accounting the atrocities and terrible episodes of suffering, including the general state of degenerate living.

Building on the confidence of villagers, he began leading the clean-up of villages, building of schools and hospitals and encouraging the village leadership to undo purdah, untouchability and the suppression of women. He was joined by many young nationalists from all over India, including Dr. Sri Krishna Sinha, Ramarshi Deo Trivedi "Rishi Ji", Brajkishore Prasad, Dr. Rajendra Prasad, Dr. Anugrah Narayan Sinha and Jawaharlal Nehru.

But his main assault came as he was arrested by police on the charge of creating unrest and was ordered to leave the province. Hundreds of thousands of people protested and rallied outside the jail, police stations and courts demanding his release, which the court unwillingly did. Gandhi led organized protests and strike against the landlords, who with the guidance of the British government, signed an agreement granting more compensation and control over farming for the poor farmers of the region, and cancellation of revenue hikes and collection until the famine ended. It was during this agitation, that Gandhi was addressed by the people as *Bapu* (*Father*) and *Mahatma* (*Great Soul*).

In Kheda

In Gujarat, Gandhi was only the spiritual head of the struggle. His chief lieutenant, Sardar Vallabhbhai Patel and a close coterie of devoted Gandhians, namely Narhari Parikh, Mohanlal Pandya and Ravi Shankar Vyas toured the countryside, organized the villagers and gave them political leadership and direction. Many aroused Gujaratis from the cities of Ahmedabad and Vadodara joined the organizers of the revolt, but Gandhi and Patel resisted the involvement of Indians from other provinces, seeking to keep it a purely Gujarati struggle.

Patel and his colleagues organized a major tax revolt, and all the different ethnic and caste communities of Kheda rallied around it. The peasants of Kheda signed a petition calling for the tax for this year to be scrapped in wake of the famine. The government in Bombay rejected the charter. They warned that if the peasants did not pay, the lands and property would be confiscated and many arrested. And once confiscated, they would not be returned even if most complied. None of the villages flinched.

The tax withheld, the government's collectors and inspectors sent in thugs to seize property and cattle, while the police forfeited the lands and all agrarian property. The farmers did not resist arrest, nor retaliate to the force employed with violence. Instead, they used their cash and valuables to donate to the *Gujarat Sabha* which was officially organizing the protest.

The revolt was astounding in terms of discipline and unity. Even when all their personal property, land and livelihood were seized, a vast majority of Kheda's farmers remained firmly united in the support of Patel. Gujaratis sympathetic to the revolt in other parts resisted the government machinery, and helped the shelter the relatives and property of the protesting peasants. Those Indians who sought to buy the confiscated lands were ostracized from society. Although nationalists like Sardul Singh Caveeshar called for sympathetic revolts in other parts, Gandhi and Patel firmly rejected the idea.

The Government finally sought to foster an honourable agreement for both parties. The tax for the year in question, and the next would be suspended, and the increase in rate reduced, while all confiscated property would be returned.

Gujaratis also worked in cohesion to return the confiscated lands to their rightful owners. The ones who had bought the lands seized were influenced to return them, even though the British had officially said it would stand by the buyers.

Success and Legacy

Gandhi's resulting fame spread like fire all over the nation. He had become a defining influence on Indian Nationalism. People in Gujarat still revere Gandhi and Sardar Patel, and their role in the freedom struggle. Gujarat is the most industrialized and progressive state in India today. In Bihar, poverty and social conflict pervades what was the founding of the Satyagraha movement. The Naxalite insurgency is centred around the same age-old problem of class struggle between poor farmers and rich landlords, now involving terrorism.

Movement of Ahamadabad Mill Worker

There exists in India a powerfully organised Labour movement. The secretary of the Indian Labour Federation, or "Standing Committee of the All-India Trade Union Congress," as it is called, is Mr. Chiman Lal, who claimed that under this federation are combined 97 unions, with 1,500,000 members. These unions embrace nearly all the industries of the country. The leading organisation is the Railwaymen's Union, which has organised 50 per cent of those employed, which is about 325,000 workers. The second in importance is the Textile Workers' Union, and the third is the Miners' Union.

Trade Unionism is a new thing in India. Before 1918 it did not exist except for a few unions for white workers. It was out of the strike movement of 1918 that the unions came into existence. The first one was organised at Madras by Mr. B. P. Wadia. Since then the progress of the movement has been both rapid and successful. The amount of success can be determined from the huge number of organised members, representing about 25 per cent of the total number of the factory-going workers. This growth indicates that the Indian labourers are speedily realising the need for their own organisations.

It is important to observe that the Indian Labour movement is rapidly becoming revolutionary. To illustrate this, take, for example, the number of strikes that have taken place in India since 1918, the history of which are written in blood. Strikes were common in the Indian factories, but they were never of a country-wide nature, and did not demonstrate any solidarity among the workers. The first instance of such a strike took place in Bombay, known as the General Strike, in which 120,000 workers, mostly textile operators, took part. The solidarity of the masses on that occasion was shown by sympathetic strikes in other parts of the country. The strike was practically lost. About 200 workers were shot down by the soldiers. There were no proletarian leaders at that time, and the Nationalist middle-class politicians who took the lead utilised the strike for demonstration purposes. Similarly, another strike of several hundred thousand plantation workers took place in Assam, about 2,000 miles from Bombay, three years after the general strike, and it, too, was lost, due to the Nationalist leaders exploiting it for political purposes. Once again strikers were killed. According to the report of the Government Commission appointed to inquire into the reason for labour unrest in India it was shown that in nine months, from July, 1920, to March, 1921, in the province of Bengal, 137 strikes took place, reacting on all branches of industry. 244,180 workers took part in these strikes, and 2,631,488 working days were lost. Of these strikes 110 were for higher wages and 13 were for the continuation of former strikes. A note issued by the labour officer of Bombay states that in three months, from April to June, 1921, 33 strikes took place in that town alone, involving 240,000 workers, with a loss of 500,000 working days. About the middle of the same year a strike of 20,000 workers took place in the town of Madras. To suppress the labour movement in Madras, the Government, with the help of the capitalists, tried by all means to subdue the labourers. They imprisoned strikers, burnt their houses, and fined the unions, but the labourers were very determined in their demands. The strike ended in a compromise due to the reformist character of the leaders. This strike movement was country wide. In the north, in 1920, a strike of over 60,000 railway workers took place; the printers struck work to show their sympathy with their railroad comrades. Out of this strike was organised the Punjab Labour Union. The strike of the Cawnpore leather and textile workers, altogether about 30,000 men, is also noteworthy. They organised themselves and put forward 21 demands, including increased wages, unemployment insurance, and a share in profits. In short, in the year 1920, altogether 2,500,000 workers were involved in the strike movement, and in many cases it ended in bloodshed. It is estimated that altogether there were 1,000 workers wounded and killed.

An important fact is that this strike agitation was not a class-conscious revolutionary movement, but it does mark the beginning of the class struggle in India. To illustrate the growth of capitalism in India I quote the following figures from the 15 volumes of official statistics for the year 1917. In the year 1917 there were 8,000 mills and workshops, of which 67 per cent. were driven by mechanical power. The railway and tramways amount to 38,000 miles. The total industrial production was valued at £261,000,000. This is excluding handicraft work and including railways. The persons taking part in this production numbered 3,500,000; thus the production per person employed was £74 for the year. In the United Kingdom in 1907 the production per person amounted to £100. Of these workers 327,000 formed the bureaucracy, both native and Europeans; the rest were wage earners.

The sum paid as wages amounted only to £27,000,000, or little over 10 per cent. of the production, as against 53 per cent. in the United Kingdom and 50 per cent. in the United States in 1907. The salaries paid amounted to £33,000,000, or £6,000,000 more than the wages of the proletarians. These salaries are due to the existence of about 28,000 European workers, whom the capitalists have to bribe with high wages in order to keep them on their side and to keep them out of the Labour movement and away from the Indian native workers. Deducting 33 per cent. of the total production as cost of material and 23 per cent. from wages and salary, we can fix the profit at 44 per cent. on an average. To support this the following figures from the Labour Review of November last may prove interesting. In one year the Indian cotton textile mills profited 100 per cent. of its outlayed capital. One factory in 1920 declared a dividend of 160 per cent. on an inflated capital of £300,000, while the dividend declared becomes 500 per cent. when the original capital invested by the shareholders is taken into account, which was only £100,000. Another mill, the Ring Mills, declared a dividend of 365 per cent. in the same year. Over a dozen mills have given dividends between 100 per cent. and 300 per cent., and quite a number between 50 per cent. and 100 per cent.

The coal mining industry in that year produced £4,512,000. Deducting from this one and a half per cent. to cover the cost of material, which is the rate in the United Kingdom, Germany and France, we get the income of the mines at £3,902,880; of this 25 per cent. or £978,036 was paid as wages against 56 per cent. in France and 59 per cent. in Germany before the war. The salaries amounted to £350,000, and the rest was profit. The coal mines show dividends which rise to 120 per cent. In one case the average dividend for 15 years was 95 per cent. The cheapness of woman labour has already caused their wholesale introduction into all industrial spheres. In one year 43 per cent. of the coal mine workers were women. No less than 40,030 women and 665 children were employed underground, and 18,872 women and 2,283 children worked on the top. The earnings of the miners were £10 8s. per year as against £55 in France and £57 in Germany before the war. The average wages of the mine workers were £6 in 1917, which was raised to £7 5s. in 1918, or 6d. per working-day. The cheapness of labour in India has kept the modern improved machines out of the Indian mines; as a result of obsolete methods 30 per cent. of the labour is wasted.

Again, in the tea gardens, the output amounted to £12,400,000, and putting 20 per cent. aside as cost of material, we get £9,920,000 as the income. The workers numbered 703,585, of whom 640,267 are women. The wages paid amounted to £3,579,952, or 35 per cent. of the income. The salaries paid amounted to 60 per cent. of the amount paid in wages, and two-thirds of these salaries were drawn by a few European supervisors. The average wage of a woman worker in the tea plantations was £5 per year.

Eighty per cent. of the factory capital, 30 per cent. of the plantation capital, 40 per cent. of the mining capital, and 2 per cent. of the railway capital is Indian. Three-fourths of the rest is British and the rest international, mostly American. The following figures will show the increase of the Indian industry since 1917:— "The average total capital of the new companies registered in India year by year was approximately £12,000,000 per year for the years 1910-14. In the first three years of the war the average fell to £6,000,000 per year. After the war it rose to the enormous figure of £183,000,000, and in 1920, to March, 1921, owing to the extraordinary ordinary disturbances in the exchange rate, it went up to £100,000,000."

On the face of these figures it is needless to argue about the class struggle in India. These figures prove that the struggle between labour and capital in India is a struggle of a twofold character—it is both a class struggle against native capitalists and a fight against British imperialism. This explains why the class war sometimes appears in a national form. There is an idea that the Indian workers are semi-proletarian; and that they have connection with their native villages, where they can take refuge in case of long trouble. To disprove this I quote the following written by a Indian trade union secretary who inquired into the matter after the plantation workers' strike of last year. He writes:

"The nationalists repatriated the workers in their villages, with the result that all of them returned to the gardens and the strike was lost. I found that the repatriation of the coolies had practically resulted in sending them to death. Most of the returning emigrants had no homes, no lands. Many of them had been born in the gardens and did not even know the names of their villages. The village people absolutely refuse to have anything to do with them. The villagers find it difficult to keep themselves from starvation, and therefore feeding the returned coolies is an impossibility. In the villages there are no industries in which these men might be employed, nor any kind of work can be found for the day labourers. It is futile to bring away the coolies from the gardens and send them to the villages, because 50 or 60 men are leaving daily for the gardens owing to the famine conditions prevailing there."

Indian labour can be divided into five groups: (1) The land labourers, who are the largest in number—about 30,000,000. Their chronic poverty, continual semi-starvation, are well known; it is bitterly illustrated by the fact that their earnings, including unemployed days, are between £4 and £6 per year. (2) The plantation workers, whom I have already described. The planters are organised, and consequently their misery is not growing. (3) The mine workers. In the mining districts rice is the main food of the miners. The price of clothing has gone up three times, but the wages have remained the same since 1918; the average wage is 6d. per day, and 300 working days a year. (4) The handicraft workers, numbering about 2,500,000 hand weavers and 8,700,000 metal wood, ceramic, and other hand labourers. Their income, according to the calculation of the India Industrial Commission of 1916-18, was, weavers £2 7s. per year, and others £4 a year. (5) The factory going workers, who stand as the advance guard of the labour movement. To a certain extent the second and third groups are still the mainstay of the Nationalist leaders, whose opportunism is forcing the workers towards class-consciousness, as was proven during the plantation strikes of last year.

The main principles of the Indian Trade Unions are as follow:—(1) The status of labour as a labourer, his relation to his employer, and effect on the economic and industrial life of the country. (2) The status of the labourer as a citizen, as related to the political movements and its result. (3) The status of the labourer in the industrial world, which has been rising ever since the Russian Revolution.

These extracts are from the Madras Labour Union's programme. It is said that the Union started with the first principle. "It was when the work of education was begun, when several questions were submitted by the Union men, that the second factor emerged.... In dealing with the second we were face to face with the necessity of recognising the third factor." It is further given out that in formulating these principles very little help was received from the educated class. "The workpeople themselves, with a culture of their own, vaguely felt, but were unable to express what was passing in their mind, and what was bound up in the three factors described above."

The value of solidarity has already been realised by the Indian workers. The president of the Madras Union, Mr. Wadia, writes "Indian labour understands that men working on the railway in Punjab, in the mills of Bombay, in the engineering shops of Bengal, are no better off than those working in the mills of Messrs. Binney & Co., Madras. The distance of a few hundred miles makes no difference in their solidarity, which alone will lead them to the final victory, the destruction of wage slavery." About the International he says: "The fate of the International is in the balance, what with the activities of the Second and Third, but as soon as a properly constituted International begins to work the Indian labourers will naturally ally themselves with the movement. The labourers, by themselves, are not sufficiently organised; they are not educated in the modern method of political struggle, and, therefore, if a long, weary fight between labour and capital, between landlordism and peasantry, is to be avoided, the Indian labourer must gain moral and other support from his comrades and brothers in other parts of the world."

The Unions in India were not recognised by the capitalists at the beginning, and the government backed their attitude. But the strength of the movement has forced recognition upon both of them. In November, when the Second Congress was to have taken place, the Mine Owners' Association opposed it and requested the Government to send the military to disperse it, but the Government refused. Consequently the conference went on unhampered, and the clever bourgeoisie, finding it not possible to fight labour face to face, adopted the diplomatic method and sent a deputation to make friendly relations with the workers, but not with the labour leaders. This capitalist deputation apologised for its former opposition and agreed to adopt 44 hours a week instead of 72, in addition to some other minor concessions.

The direction of this potential revolutionary labour movement in India is in the hands of people who can be classed into four groups (1) The Nationalists; (2) The Reformists; (3) The Government and capitalist agents; and (4) the leaders who have come out from the ranks of the labouring class. The foremost of the Nationalist politicians interested in labour is Mr. Lajpat Rai. He is the veteran centrist leader, a rich advocate, a journalist and landowner, but very orthodox. The same Mr. Rai in the year 1920 shamelessly condemned the printers' strike of Lahore because it touched his pocket. Despite this, in 1921, a year afterwards, he was elected as president of the First All-Indian Trade Union Congress.

The union leaders who elected him to preside, by this action alone, demonstrated their real character. Another Nationalist labour leader is Mr. B. K. Chakrabarty, an advocate, landowner, and multimillionaire. He was the president of the Calcutta Tramway Workers' Union, one of the most virile groups of Indian workers. Dr. R. K. Mukherji, a bourgeoisie economist and professor, is a leader of a small national centrist group.

He was delegated from the Bengal Unions to the First Congress of the Trade Unions. Some dozen other such advocates and professors can be shown to be interested in trade unionism; it is the fashion, at present, to become a labour leader in India. This is due to the fact that the nationalists understand the power of the industrial labour movement and want to control it; besides, it wants to frighten the Government with the organised force of the unions for political purpose.

Mr. Gandhi, the now imprisoned leader of the Indian nationalists, also tried his hand on the trade unions, but without much success. He left the labour field after the workers of the textile mills of Ahmedabad, Gandhi's native town, refused to break the strike on terms agreed between himself and the nationalist mill owners. He said: "We must not tamper with the labourers. It is dangerous to make political use of the factory proletariat" (*The Times*, May, 1921).

The most prominent leader of the labour movement is Mr. B. P. Wadia. It was he who first started the labour unions in India. Wadia is an ex-member of the Indian Home Rule League (a moderate political organisation with a programme to achieve self-government by gradual concessional process) and a well-known theosophist. He is president of five virile unions in Madras. He says that the economic aim of the Indian labour movement is not only to get higher wages, etc., but the ultimate destruction of wage slavery. In his opinion the international labour movement is too materialistic, and lacks a soul. This spiritual task, he contends, is a special one left for the Indian workers to develop. His reformist attitude became most marked in his evidence on labour reform, given before the Joint Parliamentary Committee, which collected material to find the best means of introducing political reforms into India. He said: "It is my considered opinion that Indian Ministers are better fitted to carry out adequate factory reforms than the Official Executive."

The next leader in importance is the reformist Indian Labour leader, Mr. Joseph Baptista. He was president of the Second Congress of the Indian Trade Union Congress. Four months before the Congress, on the 29th July, he addressed a mass meeting requesting them to follow the pacificism preached by Gandhi. He was met with cries of "Shame." The chairman of this meeting was Mr. Jamnadas Dwarkadas, a well known member of the Bombay Mill Owners' Association, and among those present on the platform was Mr. R. Williams, chief Publicity Bureau officer of the Government of Bombay. This bureau was specially created to fight the revolutionary tendency of the masses. Mr. Baptista came to the forefront after Colonel Wedgewood's visit to India, and though we do not know of any relation or agreement between them we know that Mr. Baptista is following the policy of the very moderate I.L.P.

Labour M.P., and is introducing Fabian Socialism to India. In his presidential speech he declared that: "The political policy of the Congress must steer clear of extreme Individualism and Bolshevism and follow the golden path of Fabian Socialism."

The Government and capitalist agent types of labour leaders are Mr. Lokhande, of Bombay; Dr. Nair, of Madras, and Mr. Jones, of Calcutta. Jones was the general secretary of the All-Indian Railwaymen's union. He was the J. H. Thomas of India, and he had to resign because his treachery became too well known. The charges against the first two are so well known that Comrade Saklatvala had to warn everybody against them recently in the *Labour Monthly*. Regarding these types of labour leaders, there are very few Indians amongst them; they are mostly Europeans residing in India. We want European assistance, but we do not desire moderate Labourism of the I.L.P. brand. It is here that the British Communist Party can and ought to help us directly.

The labour leaders who have come from the masses themselves are not very well known. One who has become prominent is Comrade Viswanandda, leader of the miners of Bihar. At the Second Congress he declared that "If the present misery of the workers of India is allowed to continue nothing will stop Bolshevism. Let them take due warning, because the Indian workers are determined to become the rightful owners and rulers of the wealth produced by their labour."

These mass leaders lack a definite viewpoint. They have picked up, here and there, some news of the Russian revolution from the bourgeoisie newspapers, and a few Communist ideas have influenced them. But they are our men, and we ought to gather them together for the Indian Communist Party and then push them to take leadership of the unions. This is the immediate task of the Party.

But in India there is no strong Communist Party, and it will take some time to create an effective one. The Internationals are not yet in touch with India, and at the present rate no one knows how long it will take them to reach the native masses. On the other hand, as I have shown, the Indian Fabians and moderates are spending all their energy to capture the masses. That they are somewhat successful may be seen in the growing timidity of the strike movement. The Indian workers have been flattered by the moderate labour leaders, and have been urged to be contented with the little increases in wages, etc., which were won during the time of the great strikes.

The British Labour Party is also busy with the Indian workers and their unions. These British leaders must understand, however, that the industrial victories of the English workers can only be maintained by cooperation with the Indian masses. For their own interests, therefore, the British workers must stand on common ground with their coloured comrades of India. The tie of economic interests that binds them is very close. The British Labour Party, which expects to control the governing power very soon, must stop fooling the Indian masses by pushing the Baptista moderate type of labour leader. On the other hand the organising radical societies in England for helping the Indian workers must show the International comrades that the real driving force in Indian emancipation rests in the organised power of the native masses.

Khilafat Movement

The Khilafat movement (1919-1924) was a political campaign launched mainly by Muslims in British India to influence the British government and to protect the Ottoman Empire during the aftermath of World War I. The position of Caliph after the Armistice of Mudros of October 1918 with the military occupation of Istanbul and Treaty of Versailles (1919) fell into a disambiguation along with the Ottoman Empire's existence. The movement gained force after the Treaty of Sèvres (August 1920) which solidified the partitioning of the Ottoman Empire.

In India, although mainly a Muslim religious movement, the movement became a part of the wider Indian independence movement. The movement was a topic in Conference of London (February 1920).

History

The Caliphate is an Islamic system of governance in which the state rules under Islamic law. Caliph literally means "successor" or "representative" and emphasizes religious authority for the head of state. It was adopted as a title by the Ummayad Caliphs and then by the Abbasid Caliphs, as well as by the Fatimid Caliphs of North Africa, the Almohad Caliphs of North Africa and Spain and the Ottoman Dynasty. Most historical Muslim rulers were sultans or amirs, and gave token obedience to a caliph who often had very little real authority. Moreover, the Muslim clergy, the ulema and the various Sufi orders, exercised more religious influence than the Caliph.

Ottoman Caliphate

Ottoman emperor Abdul Hamid II (1876-1909) had launched his Pan-Islamic program in a bid to protect the Ottoman empire from Western attack and dismemberment, and to crush the Westernizing democratic opposition in Turkey. He sent an emissary, Jamaluddin Afghani, to India in the late 19th century. The cause of the Ottoman monarch evoked religious passion and sympathy amongst Indian Muslims. Being a Caliph, the Ottoman emperor was the supreme religious and political leader of all Sunni Muslims across the world (although this authority was titular in practice).

A large number of Muslim religious leaders began working to spread awareness and develop Muslim participation on behalf of the Caliphate. Muslim religious leader Maulana Mehmud Hasan attempted to organise a national war of independence against the British with support from the Ottoman Empire. He was overthrown by a secretive nationalist group called the 'Young Turks.' Abdulhamid was succeeded by his brother Mehmed VI (1844-1918) but real power lay with the nationalists.

Partitioning

The Ottoman empire, having sided with the Central Powers during World War I, suffered a major military defeat. The Treaty of Versailles (1919) reduced its territorial extent and diminished its political influence but the victorious European powers promised to protect the Ottoman emperor's status as the Caliph. However, under the Treaty of Sèvres (1920), territories such as Palestine, Syria, Lebanon, Iraq, Egypt severed from the empire.

Within Turkey, a pro-Western nationalist movement arose, Turkish national movement. During the Turkish War of Independence (1919-1924) led by one of the Turkish revolutionaries, Mustafa Kemal Atatürk, abolished the Treaty of Sèvres with the Treaty of Lausanne (1923). Pursuant to Atatürk's Reforms, the

Republic of Turkey abolished the position of Caliphate in 1924 and transferred its powers within Turkey to the Grand National Assembly of Turkey.

Khilafat in South Asia

Although political activities and popular outcry on behalf of the caliphate emerged across the Muslim world, the most prominent activities took place in India. A prominent Muslim cleric and journalist, Maulana Mohammad Ali Jouhar had spent four years in prison for preaching resistance to the British and support for the caliphate. At the onset of the Turkish war of independence, Muslim religious leaders feared for the caliphate, which the European powers were reluctant to protect.

Ali and his brother Maulana Shaukat Ali joined with other Muslim leaders such as Sheikh Shaukat Ali Siddiqui, Dr. Mukhtar Ahmed Ansari, Raees-Ul-Muhajireen Barrister Jan Muhammad Junejo, Hasrat Mohani, Maulana Abul Kalam Azad and Dr. Hakim Ajmal Khan to form the All India Khilafat Committee. The organization was based in Lucknow, India at Hathe Shaukat Ali, the compound of Landlord Shaukat Ali Siddiqui. They aimed to build political unity amongst Muslims and use their influence to protect the caliphate. In 1920, they published the Khilafat Manifesto, which called upon the British to protect the caliphate and for Indian Muslims to unite and hold the British accountable for this purpose.

In 1920 an alliance was made between Khilafat leaders and the Indian National Congress, the largest political party in India and of the nationalist movement. Congress leader Mohandas Gandhi and the Khilafat leaders promised to work and fight together for the causes of Khilafat and *Swaraj*.

Seeking to increase pressure on the British, the Khilafatists became a major part of the Non-cooperation movement – a nationwide campaign of mass, peaceful civil disobedience. The support of the Khilafatists helped Gandhi and the Congress ensure Hindu-Muslim unity during the struggle. Khilafat leaders such as Dr. Ansari, Maulana Azad and Hakim Ajmal Khan also grew personally close to Gandhi. These leaders founded the Jamia Millia Islamia in 1920 to promote independent education and social rejuvenation for Muslims.

The non-cooperation campaign was at first successful. Massive protests, strikes and acts of civil disobedience spread across India. Hindus and Muslims collectively offered resistance, which was largely peaceful. Gandhi, the Ali brothers and others were imprisoned by the British. However, the Congress-Khilafat alliance began withering soon. The Khilafat campaign had been opposed by other political parties such as the Muslim League and the Hindu Mahasabha. Many Hindu religious and political leaders identified the Khilafat cause as Islamic fundamentalism based on a pan-Islamic agenda.

Collapse

In wake of these disturbances, the Ali brothers began distancing themselves from Gandhi and the Congress. The Ali brothers criticised Gandhi's commitment to non-violence and severed their ties with them after he suspended all non-cooperation movement after the killing of 22 policemen at Chauri Chaura in 1922. Although holding talks with the British and continuing their activities, the Khilafat struggle weakened as Muslims were divided between working for the Congress, the Khilafat cause and the Muslim League.

The final blow came with the victory of Mustafa Kemal's forces, who overthrew the Ottoman rule to establish a pro-Western, secular republic in independent Turkey. The Khilafat leadership fragmented on different political lines. Leaders such as Dr. Ansari, Maulana Azad and Hakim Ajmal Khan remained strong supporters of Gandhi and the Congress. The Ali brothers joined the Muslim League. They would play a major role in the growth of the League's popular appeal and the subsequent Pakistan movement. There was, however, a Caliphate Conference in Jerusalem in 1931 following Turkey's abolition of the Khilafat, to determine what should be done about the caliphate.

Legacy

The Khilafat struggle evokes controversy and strong opinions. It is regarded as a political agitation based on a pan-Islamic, fundamentalist platform and being largely indifferent to the cause of Indian independence. Critics of the Khilafat see its alliance with the Congress as a marriage of convenience. Proponents of the

Khilafat see it as a major milestone in improving Hindu-Muslim relations, while advocates of Pakistan and Muslim separatism see it as a major step towards establishing the separate Muslim state. The Ali brothers are regarded as founding-fathers of Pakistan, while Azad, Dr. Ansari and Hakim Ajmal Khan are widely celebrated as national heroes in India.

The cause of establishing an Islamic State by reviving the caliphate system has been adopted by organisations such as the Muslim Brotherhood, Jamaat-e-Islami umbrella groups in South Asia, founded in 1941 by Maulana Maududi and most of all Hizb ut Tahrir.

Maulana Shaukat Ali

Maulana Shaukat Ali was an Indian Muslim nationalist and leader of the Khilafat movement. He was the brother of Maulana Mohammad Ali.

Early life

Shaukat Ali was born in 1873-in Rampur state in what is today Uttar Pradesh or known as Lucknow. He was of Azeri Turkish descent, Turks that settled in modern day Iran, Afghanistan, and Northern India. He was educated at the Aligarh Muslim University. He was extremely fond of playing cricket, captaining the university team.

Ali served in the civil service of United Provinces of Oudh and Agra from 1896 to 1913.

Khilafat

Shaukat Ali helped his brother Mohammed Ali publish the Urdu weekly *Hamdard* and the English weekly *Comrade*. In 1919, while jailed for publishing what the British charged as seditious materials and organizing protests, he was elected as the first president of the Khilafat conference.

He was re-arrested and imprisoned from 1921 to 1923 for his support to Mahatma Gandhi and the Indian National Congress during the Non-Cooperation Movement (1919-1922). His fans accorded him and his brother the title of *Maulana*. In March 1922, he was in Rajkot jail.

Muslim League

Along with his brother, Shaukat Ali grew disilliusioned with the Congress and Gandhi's leadership. He opposed the 1928 Nehru Report, demanding separate electorates for Muslims, and attended the first and second Round Table Conferences in London. His brother died in 1931, and Ali continued on and organized the World Muslim Conference in Jerusalem.

In 1936, Ali joined the All India Muslim League and became a close political ally of and campaigner for Muhammad Ali Jinnah, the future founder of Pakistan. He served as member of the Central Assembly from 1934 to 1938. He travelled over the Middle East, building support for India's Muslims and the struggle for independence.

Shaukat Ali died in 1938.

Mukhtar Ahmed Ansari

Dr. Mukhtar Ahmed Ansari was an Indian nationalist and political leader, and former president of the Indian National Congress and the Muslim League during the Indian Independence Movement.

Early Life and Medical Career

Mukhtar Ahmed Ansari was born on December 25, 1880 in Yusufpur-Mohammadabad town, district of Ghazipur, North-Western Provinces (now part of Uttar Pradesh). Educated at the Victoria High School, Ansari and his family moved to Hyderabad. Ansari obtained a medical degree from the Madras Medical College and went to England on scholarship studies. He achieved the M.D. and M.S. degrees. He was a top-class student and worked at the Lock Hospital and the *Charing Cross Hospital* in London. He was an Indian pioneer in surgery, and today there is an *Ansari Ward* in the Charing Cross Hospital in honour of his work.

Nationalist Activities

Dr. Ansari became involved in the Indian Independence Movement during his stay in England. He moved back to Delhi and joined both the Indian National Congress and the Muslim League. He played an important role in the negotiation of the 1916

Lucknow Pact and served as the League's president in 1918 and 1920. He was an outspoken supporter of the Khilafat movement, and worked to bring the official Khilafat body, the League and the Congress Party together on the issue against the Mustafa Kemal's decision to oust the Sultan of Turkey, who was the Caliph of Islam, and to protest the recognition of Turkey's independence by the British Empire.

Dr. Ansari served several terms as the AICC General Secretary, as well as the President of the Indian National Congress during its 1927 session. As a result of in-fighting and political divisions within the League in the 1920s, and later the rise of Muhammad Ali Jinnah and Muslim separatism, Dr. Ansari drew closer to Mahatma Gandhi and the Congress Party. Dr. Ansari was one of the (Foundation Committee of Jamia Millia Islamia) founders and also served as the chancellor of the Jamia Millia Islamia university in Delhi soon after the death of its primary founder, Dr. Hakim Ajmal Khan.

Personal Life and Beliefs

Dr. Ansari's wife was a deeply religious woman, who worked with him for the uplift of Delhi's Muslim women. The Ansaris lived in a palatial house, called the *Darus Salaam* or *Abode of Peace* in Urdu. The Ansaris would often host Mahatma Gandhi when he visited Delhi, and the house was a regular base for Congress political activities. However, he never stopped practising medicine, and often came to the aid of Indian political leaders and the Indian princely order. Dr. Ansari was amongst a new generation of Indian Muslim nationalists, which included Maulana Azad, Muhammad Ali Jinnah and others. He was very passionate about the issues of common Indian Muslims, but unlike Jinnah, was resolutely against separate electorates and opposed Jinnah's viewpoint that the Muslim League could be the only representative of India's Muslim communities.

Dr. Ansari was very close to Mahatma Gandhi and an adherent of Gandhism, with his core teachings of ahimsa and nonviolent civil resistance. He enjoyed an intimate friendship with the Mahatma. Dr. Ansari died in 1936 en route from Mussoorie to Delhi on a train due to a heart attack, and is buried in the premises of the Jamia Millia Islamia in Delhi.

Hakim Ajmal Khan

Ajmal Khan or Hakim Ajmal Khan (1863-1927) was a physician and Indian Muslim nationalist politician and political leader.

Early Life

Hakim Ajmal Khan sahib was born in 1863. Ajmal Khan's ancestors, a distinguished line of physicians, had come to India during the reign of Babar, the founder of the Mughal Empire in India. All members of the family of Hakim Ajmal Khan were Unani doctors.

The family had been practicing this ancient form of medicine from the time of the Mughal rulers. They were then known as the Rais of Delhi. He learnt Quran by heart and studied traditional Islamic knowledge including Arabic and Persian in his childhood, before turning his energy to the study of medicine under the wise guidance of his senior relatives, all of whom were well-known physicians.

His grandfather Hakim Sharif Khan sought to promote the practice of Tibb-i-unani or Unani medicine and for this purpose, had setup the Sharif Manzil hospital-cum-college that was known throughout the subcontinent as one of the finest philanthropic Unani hospitals that charged no fees from poor patients.

Once qualified, Hakim Ajmal Khan was appointed chief physician to the Nawab of Rampur. No praise is too high for Hakim Sahib, hailed as "Massiha-e-Hind" (Messiah of India) and "a king without a crown". He could effect miraculous cures, like his father, and is said to have possessed "magical" medicine chest, the secrets of which were known to him alone. Such was his medical acumen that it is said that he could diagnose any illness by just looking at a person's face.. Hakim Ajmal Khan charged Rs.1000 for a visit. That was his daily fee if he went out of town, but if the patient came to Delhi he was treated free, even if he was a Maharaja.

Hakim Mohammed Ajmal Khan proved to be the most outstanding and multifaceted personality of his era. His contribution to the cause of India's freedom, National integration and communal harmony is matchless. A sound and far cited statesman and an educationist of highest calibre.

Hakim Ajmal Khan took much interest in the expansion and development of the native system of Unani medicine. Hakim Ajmal Khan built three great institutions-the Central College in Delhi, Hindustani Dawakhana and the Ayurvedic and Unani Tibbia College, in order to expand the research and practice hence saved Unani System of Medicine from extinction in India. His untiring efforts in the field of Unani medicine infused a new force and life into an otherwise decaying Indian Unani medical system under the British regime.

Nationalism

The life history of Ajmal Khan changed its course from medicine towards politics after he started writing for an Urdu weekly 'Akmal-ul-Akhbar' that was launched by his family. Khan was also heading the Muslim team, who met the Viceroy of India in Shimla in the year 1906 to give him a memorandum made by them. The following year, he was present at Dhaka when the All India Muslim League was formulated. At a time when many Muslim leaders were arrested, Dr. Ajmal Khan approached Mahatma Gandhi for help. As such, Gandhiji united with him and other Muslim leaders like Maulana Azad, Maulana Mohammad Ali and Maulana Shaukat Ali in the famous Khilafat movement. Ajmal Khan is also the sole person who has had the honour to be elected the President of the Indian National Congress, the Muslim League and the All India Khilafat Committee.

Legacy

Hakim Ajmal Khan's whole life was a portrayal of altruistic service and sacrifice. Hakim Ajmal Khan died of heart problems on 29 December 1927. Hakim Ajmal Khan had renounced his government title, and many of his Indian fans awarded him the title of Masih-ul-Mulk (Healer of the Nation). He was succeeded in the position of JMI Chancellor by Dr. Mukhtar Ahmed Ansari.

Dawakhana Hakim Ajmal Khan Private Ltd

After Partition

After the partition of India Hakim Khan's grandson Hakim Muhammad Nabi Khan migrated to Pakistan. Hakim Nabi learnt Tibb (medicine) from Hakim Ajmal Khan and opened 'Dawakhana

Hakim Ajmal Khan' in Lahore which has its branches throughout Pakistan. The motto of Ajmal Khan family has been Azal-ul-Allah-Khudatulmal, which when translated means that the best way to keep oneself busy is by serving humanity, which his descendants are following since ages.

Hasrat Mohani

Maulana Hasrat Mohani (1875–1951) was a romantic poet of Urdu language, journalist, politician, parliamentarian and a fearless freedom fighter of Indo-Pak Subcontinent. His real name was Syed Fazl ul Hasan. He was born in 1875 at Mohan in Unnao district of U.P. India.

He was a brilliant student as well as a topper in his first state level exams. Later, he studied in Aligarh Muslim University, where some of his colleagues were Molana Mohammad Ali Johar, Molana Shaukat Ali, etc. His teachers in poetry were Tasleem Lucknawi and Naseem Dehlvi. A few of his books are Kulliyat-e-Hasrat Mohani (Collection of Hasrat Mohani's poetry), Sharh-e-Kalam-e-Ghalib (Explanation of Ghalib's poetry), Nukaat-e-Sukhan (Important aspects of poetry), Mushahidaat-e-Zindaan (Observations in Prison), etc. A very popular ghazal sung by Ghulam Ali, *Chupke Chupke raat din...* was penned by Hasrat Mohani.

Hasrat Mohani participated in the struggle for Indian Independence (end of British Raj); and was jailed for many years by British authorities. He was the first person in Indian History who demanded 'Complete Independence' (Azadi-e-Kaamil) in 1921 as he presided over an annual seesion of All India Muslim League. He was not only a practising Muslim but also a strong supporter of the communist philosophy, as he could see that British could be possibly defeated by following its principles. Therefore, he was among the founders of The Communist Party of India. He was also imprisoned for promoting anti-British ideas especially for publishing an article against British policies in Egypt, in his magazine 'Urdu-e-Mualla'. Afterwards, unlike some Urdu poets, notably Josh Malihabadi and Nasir Kazmi, and many Muslim leaders, he chose to live in India rather than move to Pakistan after independence (1947) in order to represent left over Indian Muslims on various platforms. In recognition for his efforts, he was made a member of the constituent assembly which drafted the Indian constitution. But unlike other members, he never signed it since he saw hypocrisy towards Muslim minorities in it (he was a Muslim himself). According to Akhtar Payami: Hasrat's poetic genius has been acclaimed by many writers and critics. In the not too distant past (beginning and the first half of the 20th century), Hasrat, Jigar and Asghar formed a constellation of emerging poets in a crucial period of India's history. Major political developments were taking place in the subcontinent and the sun was about to set on the British Empire. As conscious members of society, poets and writers do not remain indifferent to the changes in their socio-political milieu. Not only India but the whole world was in a state of flux.

Maulana died on 13 May, 1951 in Lucknow, India.

Hasrat Mohani Memorial Society was founded by Maulana Nusrat Mohani in 1951. In Karachi, Pakistan, a Memorial Hall and Library have been established by Hasrat Mohani Memorial Society (Regd.) Every year, on his death anniversary, a memorial meeting is conducted by this Trust as well as many other organisations in India and Pakistan. Also Hasrat Mohani Colony, at Korangi Town in Karachi, Pakistan, was named after Maulana Hasrat Mohani.

Abul Kalam Azad

Maulana Abul Kalam Muhiyuddin Ahmed (11 November 1888 – 22 February 1958) was a Muslim scholar and a senior political leader of the Indian independence movement. He was one of the most prominent Muslim leaders to support Hindu-Muslim unity, opposing the partition of India on communal lines. Following India's independence, he became the first Minister of Education in the Indian government. He is commonly remembered as Maulana Azad; he had adopted *Azad* (*Free*) as his pen name.

As a young man, Azad composed poetry in Urdu as well as treatises on religion and philosophy. He rose to prominence through his work as a journalist, publishing works critical of the British Raj and espousing the causes of Indian nationalism. Azad became a leader of the Khilafat Movement during which he came into close contact with Indian leader Mahatma Gandhi. Azad became an enthusiastic supporter of Gandhi's ideas of nonviolent civil disobedience, and worked actively to organise the Non-cooperation movement in protest of the 1919 Rowlatt Acts. Azad committed himself to Gandhi's ideals, including promoting *Swadeshi* (*Indigenous*) products and the cause of *Swaraj* (*Self-rule*) for India. He would become the youngest person to serve as the President of the Indian National Congress in 1923.

Azad was one of the main organisers of the Dharasana Satyagraha in 1931, and emerged as one of the most important national leaders of the time, prominently leading the causes of Hindu-Muslim unity as well as espousing secularism and socialism. He served as Congress President from 1940 to 1945, during which the *Quit India* rebellion was launched and Azad was imprisoned with the entire Congress leadership for three years. Azad became the most prominent Muslim opponent of the demand for a separate Muslim state of Pakistan and served in the interim national government. Amidst communal turmoil following the partition of India, he worked for religious harmony. As India's Education Minister, Azad oversaw the establishment of a national education system with free primary education and modern institutions of higher education. He is also credited with the establishment of the Indian Institutes of Technology and the foundation of the University Grants Commission, an important institution to supervise and advance the higher education in the nation.

Early Life

Azad's family descended from a line of eminent *Ulama* or scholars of Islam, hailing from Herat, Afghanistan, and had settled in India during the reign of the Mughal emperor Babur. His mother was of Arab descent, the daughter of Shaikh Muhammad Zahir Watri, and his father, Maulana Khairuddin was, then living in Bengal, was from Herat. The family lived in the Bengal region until Maulana Khairuddin left India during the Indian rebellion of 1857 and settled in Mecca, the holiest city in Islam, where he met his wife. Azad mastered several languages, including Urdu, Arabic, Hindko, Persian, and Hindi. He was also trained in the subjects of Hanafi fiqh, shariat, mathematics, philosophy, world history and science by reputed tutors hired by his family. An avid and determined student, the precocious Azad was running a library, a reading room, a debating society before he was twelve, wanted to write on the life of Ghazali at twelve, was contributing learned articles to *Makhzan* (the best known literary magazine of the day) at fourteen, was teaching a class of students, most of whom were twice his age, when he was merely fifteen and succeeded in completing the traditional course of study at the young age of sixteen, nine years ahead of his contemporaries, and brought out a magazine at the same age.

In fact, in the field of journalism, he was publishing a poetical journal (*Nairang-e-Aalam*) and was already an editor of a weekly (*Al-Misbah*), in 1900, at the age of twelve and, in 1903, brought out a monthly journal, *Lissan-us-Sidq*, which soon gained popularity. At the age of thirteen, he was married to a young Muslim girl, Zuleikha Begum. Azad was, more closer, a follower of the Ahl-i-Hadith school and compiled many treatises reinterpreting the Qur'an, the *Hadith*, and the principles of *Fiqh* and *Kalam*.

A young man, Azad was also exposed to the modern intellectual life of Kolkata, the then capital of British-ruled India and the centre of cultural and political life.

He began to doubt the traditional ways of his father and secretly diversified his studies. Azad learned English through intensive personal study and began learning Western philosophy, history and contemporary politics by reading advanced books and modern periodicals. Azad grew disillusioned with Islamic teachings and was inspired by the modern views of Muslim educationalist Sir Syed Ahmed Khan, who had promoted rationalism. Increasingly doubtful of religious dogma, Azad entered a period of self-described "atheism" and "sinfulness" that lasted for almost a decade.

Revolutionary and Journalist

Azad developed political views considered radical for most Muslims of the time and became a full-fledged Indian nationalist. He fiercely criticised the British for racial discrimination and ignoring the needs of common people across India. He also criticised Muslim politicians for focusing on communal issues before the national interest and rejected the All India Muslim League's communal separatism. Azad developed curiosity and interest in the pan-Islamic doctrines of Jamal al-Din al-Afghani and visited Afghanistan, Iraq, Egypt, Syria and Turkey. But his views changed considerably when he met revolutionary activists in Iraq and was influence by their fervent anti-imperialism and nationalism. Against common Muslim opinion of the time, Azad opposed the partition of Bengal in 1905 and became increasingly active in revolutionary activities, to which he was introduced by the prominent Hindu revolutionaries Sri Aurobindo and Shyam Sundar Chakravarthy. Azad initially evoked surprise from other revolutionaries, but Azad won their praise and confidence by working secretly to organise revolutionaries activities and meetings in Bengal, Bihar and Mumbai (then Bombay).

Azad's education had been shaped for him to become a cleric, but his rebellious nature and affinity for politics turned him towards journalism. He established an Urdu weekly newspaper in 1912 called *Al-Hilal* and openly attacked British policies while exploring the challenges facing common people. Espousing the ideals of Indian nationalism, Azad's publications were aimed at encouraging young Muslims into fighting for independence and Hindu-Muslim unity. His work helped improve the relationship between Hindus and Muslims in Bengal, which had been soured by the controversy surrounding the partition of Bengal and the issue of separate communal electorates.

With the onset of World War I, the British stiffened censorship and restrictions on political activity. Azad's *Al-Hilal* was consequently banned in 1914 under the *Press Act*. Azad started a new journal, the *Al-Balagh*, which increased its active support for nationalist causes and communal unity. In this period Azad also became active in his support for the Khilafat agitation to protect the position of the Sultan of Ottoman Turkey, who was the caliph for Muslims worldwide. The Sultan had sided against the British in the war and the continuity of his rule came under serious threat, causing distress amongst Muslim conservatives. Azad saw an opportunity to energise Indian Muslims and achieve major political and social reform through the struggle. With his popularity increasing across India, the government outlawed Azad's second publication under the *Defence of India Regulations Act* and arrested him. The governments of the Bombay Presidency, United Provinces, Punjab and Delhi prohibited his entry into the provinces and Azad was moved to a jail in Ranchi, where he was incarcerated until 1 January 1920.

Non-cooperation

Upon his release, Azad returned to a political atmosphere charged with sentiments of outrage and rebellion against British rule. The Indian public had been angered by the passage of the Rowlatt Acts in 1919, which severely restricted civil liberties and individual rights. Consequently, thousands of political activists had been arrested and many publications banned. The killing of unarmed civilians at Jallianwala Bagh in Amritsar on 13 April 1919 had provoked intense outrage all over India, alienating most Indians, including long-time British supporters from the authorities. The Khilafat struggle had also peaked with the defeat of the Ottoman Empire in World War I and the raging Turkish War of Independence, which had made the caliphate's position precarious. India's main political party, the Indian National Congress came under the leadership of Mahatma Gandhi, who had aroused excitement all over India when he led the farmers of Champaran and Kheda in a successful revolt against British authorities in 1918. Gandhi organised the people of the region and pioneered the art of *Satyagraha* – combining mass civil disobedience with complete non-violence and self-reliance.

Taking charge of the Congress, Gandhi also reached out to support the Khilafat struggle, helping to bridge Hindu-Muslim political divides. Azad and the Ali brothers warmly welcomed Congress support and began working together on a programme of *non-cooperation* by asking all Indians to boycott British-run schools, colleges, courts, public services, the civil service, police and military. Non-violence and Hindu-Muslim unity were universally emphasized, while the boycott of foreign goods, especially clothes were organised. Azad joined the Congress and was also elected president of the All India Khilafat Committee. Although Azad and other leaders were soon arrested, the movement drew out millions of people in peaceful processions, strikes and protests.

This period marked a transformation in Azad's own life. Along with fellow Khilafat leaders Dr. Mukhtar Ahmad Ansari, Hakim Ajmal Khan and others, Azad grew personally close to Gandhi and his philosophy. The three men founded the Jamia Millia Islamia in Delhi as an institution of higher education managed entirely by Indians without any British support or control. Both Azad and Gandhi shared a deep passion for religion and Azad developed a close friendship with him. He adopted the Prophet Muhammad's ideas by living simply, rejecting material possessions and pleasures. He began to spin his own clothes using *khadi* on the *charkha,* and began frequently living and participating in the ashrams organised by Gandhi. Becoming deeply committed to *ahimsa* (*non-violence*) himself, Azad grew close to fellow nationalists like Jawaharlal Nehru, Chittaranjan Das and Subhash Chandra Bose. He strongly criticised the continuing suspicion of the Congress amongst the Muslim intellectuals from the Aligarh Muslim University and the Muslim League.

The rebellion began a sudden decline when with rising incidences of violence; a nationalist mob killed 22 policemen in Chauri Chaura in 1922. Fearing degeneration into violence, Gandhi asked Indians to suspend the revolt and undertook a five day fast to repent and encourage others to stop the rebellion. Although the movement stopped all over India, several Congress leaders and activists were disillusioned with Gandhi. The following year, the caliphate was overthrown by Mustafa Kemal Atatürk and the Ali brothers grew distant and critical of Gandhi and the Congress. Azad's close friend Chittaranjan Das co-founded the Swaraj Party, breaking from Gandhi's leadership. Despite the circumstances, Azad remained firmly committed to Gandhi's ideals and leadership. In 1923, he became the youngest man to be elected Congress President. Azad led efforts to organise the Flag Satyagraha in Nagpur. Azad served as president of the 1924 Unity Conference in Delhi, using his position to work to re-unite the Swarajists and the Khilafat leaders under the common banner of the Congress. In the years following the movement, Azad travelled across India, working extensively to promote Gandhi's vision, education and social reform.

Congress Leader

Azad became an important national leader, and served on the Congress Working Committee and in the offices of general secretary and president many times. The political environment in India re-energised in 1928 with nationalist outrage against the Simon Commission appointed to propose constitutional reforms. The commission included no Indian members and did not even consult Indian leaders and experts. In response, the Congress and other political parties appointed a commission under Motilal Nehru to propose constitutional reforms from Indian opinions. In 1928, Azad endorsed the Nehru Report, which was criticised by the Ali brothers and Muslim League politician Muhammad Ali Jinnah. Azad endorsed the ending of separate electorates based on religion, and called for an independent India to be committed to secularism. At the 1928 Congress session in Guwahati, Azad endorsed Gandhi's call for dominion status for India within a year. If not granted, the Congress would adopt the goal of complete political independence for India. Despite his affinity for Gandhi, Azad also drew close to the young radical leaders Jawaharlal Nehru and Subhash Bose, who had criticised the delay in demanding full independence. Azad developed a close friendship with Nehru and began espousing socialism as the means to fight inequality, poverty and other national challenges.

When Gandhi embarked on the Dandi Salt March that inaugurated the Salt Satyagraha in 1930, Azad organised and led the nationalist raid, albeit nonviolent on the Dharasana salt works in order to protest the salt tax and restriction of its production and sale. The biggest nationalist upheaval in a decade, Azad was imprisoned along with millions of people, and would frequently be jailed from 1930 to 1934 for long periods of time. Following the Gandhi-Irwin Pact in 1934, Azad was amongst millions of political prisoners released. When elections were called under the Government of India Act 1935, Azad was appointed to organise the Congress election campaign, raising funds, selecting candidates and organising volunteers and rallies across India. Azad had criticised the Act for including a high proportion of un-elected members in the central legislature, and did not himself contest a seat. He again declined to contest elections in 1937, and helped head the party's efforts to organise elections and preserve coordination and unity amongst the Congress governments elected in different provinces.

At the 1936 Congress session in Lucknow, Azad was drawn into a dispute with right-wing Congressmen Sardar Vallabhbhai Patel, Dr. Rajendra Prasad and Chakravarthi Rajagopalachari regarding the espousal of socialism as the Congress goal. Azad had backed the election of Nehru as Congress President, and supported the resolution endorsing socialism. In doing so, he aligned with Congress socialists like Nehru, Subhash Bose and Jayaprakash Narayan. Azad also supported Nehru's re-election in 1937, at the consternation of many conservative Congressmen. Azad supported dialogue with Jinnah and the Muslim League between 1935 and 1937 over a Congress-League coalition and broader political cooperation. Less inclined to brand the League as obstructive, Azad nevertheless joined the Congress's vehement rejection of Jinnah's demand that the League be seen exclusively as the representative of Indian Muslims.

Quit India

In 1938, Azad served as an intermediary between the supporters of Gandhi and the Congress faction led by Congress President Subhash Bose, who criticised Gandhi for not launching another rebellion against the British and sought to move the Congress away from Gandhi's leadership. Azad stood by Gandhi with most other Congress leaders, but reluctantly endorsed the Congress's exit from the assemblies in 1939 following the inclusion of India in World War II. Nationalists were infuriated that the viceroy had entered India into the war without consulting national leaders. Although willing to support the British effort in return for independence, Azad sided with Gandhi when the British ignored the Congress overtures. Azad's criticism of Jinnah and the League intensified as Jinnah called Congress rule in the provinces as "Hindu Raj," calling the resignation of the Congress ministries as a "Day of Deliverance" for Muslims. Jinnah and the League's separatist agenda was gaining popular support amongst Muslims. Muslim religious and conservative leaders criticised Azad as being too close to the Congress and placing politics before faith. As the Muslim League adopted a resolution calling for a separate Muslim state in its session in Lahore in 1940, Azad was elected Congress President in its session in Ramgarh. Speaking vehemently against Jinnah's *Two-Nation Theory* — the notion that Hindus and Muslims were distinct nations — Azad lambasted religious separatism and exhorted all Muslims to preserve a united India, as all Hindus and Muslims were Indians who shared deep bonds of brotherhood and nationhood. In his presidential address, Azad said:

"...Full eleven centuries have passed by since then. Islam has now as great a claim on the soil of India as Hinduism. If Hinduism has been the religion of the people here for several thousands of years Islam also has been their religion for a thousand years. Just as a Hindu can say with pride that he is an Indian and follows Hinduism, so also we can say with equal pride that we are Indians and follow Islam. I shall enlarge this orbit still further. The Indian Christian is equally entitled to say with pride that he is an Indian and is following a religion of India, namely Christianity."

In face of increasing popular disenchantment with the British across India, Gandhi and Patel advocated an all-out rebellion demanding immediate independence. The situation had grown precarious as the Japanese conquered Burma and approached India's borders, which left Indians insecure but resentful of the British inability to protect India. Azad was wary and skeptical of the idea, aware that India's Muslims were increasingly looking to Jinnah and had supported the war. Feeling that a struggle would not force a British exit, Azad and Nehru warned that such a campaign would divide India and make the war situation even more precarious. Intensive and emotional debates took place between Azad, Nehru, Gandhi and Patel in the Congress Working Committee's meetings in May and June 1942. In the end, Azad became convinced that decisive action in one form or another had to be taken, as the Congress had to provide leadership to India's people and would lose its standing if it did not.

Supporting the call for the British to "*Quit India*," Azad began exhorting thousands of people in rallies across the nation to prepare for a definitive, all-out struggle. As Congress President, Azad travelled across India and met with local and provincial Congress leaders and grass-roots activists, delivering speeches and planning the rebellion. Despite their previous differences, Azad worked closely with Patel and Dr. Rajendra Prasad to make the rebellion as effective as possible. On 7 August 1942 at the Gowalia Tank in Mumbai, Congress President Azad inaugurated the struggle with a vociferous speech exhorting Indians into action. Just two days later, the British arrested Azad and the entire Congress leadership. While Gandhi was incarcerated at the Aga Khan Palace in Pune, Azad and the Congress Working Committee were imprisoned at a fort in Ahmednagar, where they would remain under isolation and intense security for nearly four years. Outside news and communication had been largely prohibited and completely censored. Although frustrated at their incarceration and isolation, Azad and his companions attested to feeling a deep satisfaction at having done their duty to their country and people.

Azad occupied the time playing bridge and acting as the referee in tennis matches played by his colleagues. In the afternoons, Azad began working on his classic Urdu work, the *Ghubhar-i-Khatir*. Sharing daily chores, Azad also taught the Persian and Urdu languages, as well as Indian and world history to several of his companions. The leaders would generally avoid talking of politics, unwilling to cause any arguments that could exacerbate the pain of their imprisonment. However, each year on 26 January, the leaders would gather to remember their cause and pray together. Azad, Nehru and Patel would briefly speak about the nation and the future. Azad and Nehru proposed an initiative to forge an agreement with the British in 1943. Arguing that the rebellion had been mis-timed, Azad attempted to convince his colleagues that the Congress should agree to negotiate with the British and call for the suspension of disobedience if the British agreed to transfer power. Although his proposal was overwhelmingly rejected, Azad and a few others agreed that Gandhi and the Congress had not done enough. When they learnt of Gandhi holding talks with Jinnah in Mumbai in 1944, Azad criticised Gandhi's move as counter-productive and ill-advised.

Partition of India

With the end of the war, the British agreed to transfer power to Indian hands. All political prisoners were released in 1946 and Azad led the Congress in the elections for the new Constituent Assembly of India, which would draft India's constitution. He headed the delegation to negotiate with the British Cabinet Mission, in his sixth year as Congress President. While attacking Jinnah's demand for Pakistan and the mission's proposal of 16 June 1946 that envisaged the partition of India, Azad became a strong proponent of the mission's earlier proposal of 16 May. The proposal advocated a federation with a weak central government and great autonomy for the provinces. Additionally, the proposal called for the "grouping" of provinces on religious lines, which would informally band together the Muslim-majority provinces. While Gandhi and others were suspicious of this clause, Azad argued that the Jinnah's demand for Pakistan would be buried and the concerns of the Muslim community would be assuaged. Under Azad and Patel's backing, the Working Committee approved the resolution against Gandhi's advice. Jawaharlal Nehru replaced Azad as Congress President and led the Congress into the interim government. Azad was appointed to head the Department of Education. However, Jinnah's *Direct Action Day* agitation for Pakistan, launched on 16 August sparked communal violence across India. Thousands of people were killed as Azad travelled across Bengal and Bihar to calm the tensions and heal relations between Muslims and Hindus. Despite Azad's call for Hindu-Muslim unity, Jinnah's popularity amongst Muslims soared and the League entered a coalition with the Congress in December, but continued to boycott the constituent assembly.

Azad had grown increasingly hostile to Jinnah, who had described him as the "Muslim Lord Haw-Haw" and a "Congress Showboy." Despite being a learned scholar of Islam and a *Maulana,* Azad had been assailed by Muslim religious leaders for his commitment to nationalism and secularism, which were deemed un-Islamic. Muslim League politicians accused Azad of allowing Muslims to be culturally and politically dominated by the Hindu community. Azad continued to proclaim his faith in Hindu-Muslim unity:

"I am proud of being an Indian. I am part of the indivisible unity that is Indian nationality. I am indispensable to this noble edifice and without me this splendid structure is incomplete. I am an essential element, which has gone to build India. I can never surrender this claim."

Amidst more incidences of violence in early 1947, the Congress-League coalition struggled to function. The provinces of Bengal and Punjab were to be partitioned on religious lines, and on 3 June 1947 the British announced a proposal to partition India on religious lines, with the princely states free to choose between either dominion. The proposal was hotly debated in the All India Congress Committee, with Muslim leaders Saifuddin Kitchlew and Khan Abdul Ghaffar Khan expressing fierce opposition. Azad privately discussed the proposal with Gandhi, Patel and Nehru, but despite his opposition was unable to deny the popularity of the League and the unworkability of any coalition with the League. Faced with the serious possibility of a civil war, Azad abstained from voting on the resolution, remaining silent and not speaking throughout the AICC session, which ultimately approved the plan.

Leading India

India's partition and independence on 15 August 1947 brought with it a scourge of violence that swept the Punjab, Bengal, Kolkata, Delhi and many other parts of India. Millions of Hindus and Sikhs fled the newly created Pakistan for India, and millions of Muslims fled for West Pakistan and East Pakistan, created out of East Bengal. Violence claimed the lives of an estimated one million people. Azad took up responsibility for the safety of Muslims in India, touring affected areas in Bengal, Bihar, Assam and the Punjab, guiding the organisation of refugee camps, supplies and security. Azad gave speeches to large crowds encouraging peace and calm in the border areas and encouraging Muslims across the country to remain in India and not fear for their safety and security. Focusing on bringing the capital of Delhi back to peace, Azad organised security and relief efforts, but was drawn into a dispute with the Deputy Prime Minister and Home Minister Sardar Vallabhbhai Patel when he demanded the dismissal of Delhi's police commissioner, who was a Sikh accused by Muslims of overlooking attacks and neglecting their safety. Patel argued that the commissioner was not biased, and if his dismissal was forced it would provoke anger amongst Hindus and Sikhs and divide the city police. In Cabinet meetings and discussions with Gandhi, Patel and Azad clashed over security issues in Delhi and Punjab, as well as the allocation of resources for relief and rehabilitation. Patel opposed Azad and Nehru's proposal to reserve the houses vacated by Muslims who had departed for Pakistan for Muslims in India displaced by the violence. Patel argued that a secular government could not offer preferential treatment for any religious community, while Azad remained anxious to assure the rehabilitation of Muslims in India.

Maulana Azad had been appointed India's first Minister for Education and served in the Constituent Assembly to draft India's constitution. Azad's persuasion was instrumental in obtaining the approval of Muslim representatives to end the communal electorates, and was a forceful advocate of enshrining the principle of secularism, religious freedom and equality for all Indians. He supported provisions for Muslim citizens to make avail of Muslim personal law in courts.

Azad remained a close confidante, supporter and advisor to Prime Minister Nehru, and played an important role in framing national policies. Azad masterminded the creation of national programmes of school and college construction and spreading the enrolment of children and young adults into schools, in order to promote universal primary education. Elected to the lower house of the Indian Parliament, the Lok Sabha in 1952 and again in 1957, Azad supported Nehru's socialist economic and industrial policies, as well as the advancing social rights and economic opportunities for women and underprivileged Indians. In 1956, he served as president of the UNESCO General Conference held in Delhi. Azad spent the final years of his life focusing on writing his book *India Wins Freedom*, an exhaustive account of India's freedom struggle and its leaders, which was published in 1957.

Criticism and Legacy

During his life and in contemporary times, Maulana Azad has been criticised for not doing enough to prevent the partition of India. He was condemned by the advocates of Pakistan and by religious Muslims, especially of the Deobandi order for his perceived affinity and proximity to Hindus. During and after partition, Azad was criticised for not doing enough for Muslim security and political rights in independent India. However, Azad is remembered as amongst the leading Indian nationalists of his time. His firm belief in Hindu-Muslim unity earned him the respect of the Hindu community and he still remains one of the most important symbols of communal harmony in modern India. His work for education and social upliftment in India made him an important influence in guiding India's economic and social development.

Maulana Azad is the namesake of many public institutions across India such as the Maulana Azad Medical College in New Delhi, the Maulana Azad National Institute of Technology in

Bhopal, the Maulana Azad National Urdu University and the Maulana Azad College in Kolkata. He is celebrated as the one of the founders and greatest patrons of the Jamia Millia Islamia. Azad's tomb is located next to the Jama Masjid in Delhi. In recent years great concern has been expressed by many in India over the poor maintenance of the tomb. On 16 November 2005 the Delhi High Court ordered that the tomb of Maulana Azad in New Delhi be renovated and restored as a major national monument. Azad's tomb is a major landmark and receives large numbers of visitors annually.

Azad was the "Mir-i-Karawan" (the caravan leader), said Nehru.

Khilafat Movement

Khilafat Movement (1919-1924) was a significant Islamic movement in India during the British rule. This was an attempt by the Indian Muslim community to unite together in support of the Turkish Empire ruled by the Khalifa, which was attacked by European powers. The Muslims considered the Khalifa as the custodian of Islam. They simply could not digest his dethronement. Under the leadership of prominent Muslim leaders, notable one being Maulana Abul Kalam Azad, they launched the Khilafat Movement in most parts of North India.

The Khilafat Movement, aimed against the British government, received the support of Mahatma Gandhi, who related his Non Cooperation Movement with it. The main objective behind this move was to enlist the support of the Muslim community into his movement, which addressed the issue of 'Swaraj' (Self-Government). By mid-1920 the Khilafat leaders assured full support to the nonviolent methods of Gandhi, which facilitated the establishment of a united front of Hindus and Muslims against the British government. This combined force formed a major threat to the British rule.

The Khilafat Movement however did not last long. Owing to some violent incidents in the country which resulted in the deaths of many Indian and British people, Mahatma Gandhi called off his Non Cooperation Movement. This was a major jolt to the Khilafat Movement.

Events in Turkey

An attempt was made towards inaugurating a Pan-Islamic movement i.e. the Aligarh movement during the last quarter of the 19th century. It did not succeed but the sentiment never died out altogether. It is proved by the active sympathy of the Indian Muslims (M) towards the Turks in their fight against Italy and the Balkhan powers. Turkey's entry into the war as an ally of Germany put the Indian M into a quandary. Their natural sympathy lie with the Sultan of Turkey as their Caliph or religious head but as British subjects they were to be loyal to the British throne. Realizing their predicament the British PM, Lloyd George declared on 05/01/1918, that the allies "were not fighting to deprive Turkey of the rich and renowned lands of Asia Minor and Thrace which are predominantly Turkish in race". These assurances led the Indian M to believe that whatever happened, the territorial integrity and independence of Turkey, so far as her Asiatic dominions would be maintained. However, what happened was different. Thrace was presented to Greece while the Asiatic portions of Turkey passed to England and France. Thus Turkey was dispossessed of her homelands and the Sultan deprived of all real authority. Indian M regarded this as a great betrayal and carried on agitations through out 1919 but to no effect.

At the same time, Mustufa Kemal Pasha a highly gifted leader rose in Turkey brushed aside the weak regime of the Caliph and resolved to make a new, powerful Turkey on modern nationalistic lines. Aware that the Caliph was the religious leader of the Arab world he decided to get rid his country of Arabism and liberate it from the stronghold of the maulvis and mullahs. (Something that Pakistan needs to do today). He was helped by Jamaluddin Afghani, an Arab born in Afghanistan in 1838.

The rise of a powerful state in Turkey did not suit the Brits. They prodded Aga Khan to join hands with the Caliph. Aga Khan and Amir Ali went to Kemal Pasha and begged him to save the Caliph, Abdul Majid. Kemal treated them with contempt and derided Aga Khan (a Shia) and Amir Ali (a Khoja) as heretics of Islam who had no business to advise the Sunni Turkish Muslims. Kemal said that it was ironical that two men who were the pillars of the Brit rule in India had come to advise Turkey on their national policy. He exposed these two men, dethroned Islam from the pedestal of the official state religion and transformed Turkey into a secular state.

But the Khilafat leaders in India would not give up. Under the leadership of the Ali brothers they approached King Abdul Azeez of Arabia to become the new Caliph. The King had the Indians in a corner by asking them "If it is Islam that you are zealous about, why do not you join hands with Gandhi and free India of the Brit rule. That's what Islam teaches. You come to me as a slave of the Brits and it seems to me that you have come to lead me into a Brit trap". Next the leaders approached Reza Shah, the ruler of Iran. But Shah proud of his Aryan tradition, evinced little interest.

In 1921, Muhammad Ali had written a letter to the Amir of Afghanistan inviting him to invade India. The Brits got scent of this and arrested the Ali brothers. On his written assurance that he was no opponent of the Brits he was released. In 1921, when the Khilafat agitation was at its peak, Ali again sent a wire to the Amir urging him not to enter into any agreement with the Brits. When Ali was taken to task by the Congress leaders he showed Swami Shraddananada (renowned Arya Samaj leader) a hand written draft of the wire. The Swami writes "What was my astonishment when I saw the draft of the same self-same telegram in the peculiar handwriting of the Father of the nonviolent non-cooperation movement". Writing in the Young India in May 1921 Gandhi said, "I would, in a sense, certainly assist the Amir of Afghanistan if he waged war against the British Govt.. It is no part of the duty of a nonviolent non-cooperator to assist the Govt. against war made upon it by others. I would rather see India perish at the hands of the Afghans than purchase freedom from Afghan invasion at the cost of her honour. To have India defended by an unrepentant Govt. that keeps the Khilafat and Punjab wounds still bleeding is to sell India's honour". Gandhi was criticized by Lala Lajpat Rai and B C Pal for his statements. Thus it is interesting to note that the Hindu Congress leaders took up the case of the Caliph when the Muslim world itself had refused to do so.

Khilafat Movement (1919-1924) was a Pan-Islamic movement influenced by Indian nationalism. The Ottoman Emperor Abdul

Hamid II (1876-1909) had launched a Pan-Islamic programme to use his position as the Sultan-Khalifa of the global Muslim community with a view to saving his disintegrating empire from foreign attacks and to crush the nationalistic democratic movement at home. The visit of his emissary, Jamaluddin Afghani, to India in the late nineteenth century to propagate Pan-Islamic ideas received a favourable response from some Indian Muslim leaders.

These sentiments intensified early in the twentieth century with the revocation in 1911 of the 1905 partition of bengal, the Italian (1911) and Balkan (1911-1912) attacks on Turkey, and Great Britain's participation in the First World War (1914-18) against Turkey.

The defeat of Turkey in the First World War and the division of its territories under the Treaty of Sevres (10 August 1920) among European powers caused apprehensions in India over the Khalifa's custodianship of the Holy places of Islam. Accordingly, the Khilafat Movement was launched in September 1919 as an orthodox communal movement to protect the Turkish Khalifa and save his empire from dismemberment by Great Britain and other European powers. The Movement was initiated by the Ali brothers, Muhammad Ali and Shawkat Ali, Maulana Abul Kalam Azad, Dr. MA Ansari, and Hasrat Mohani. Khilafat Conferences were organised in several cities in northern India. A Central Khilafat Committee, with provisions for provincial branches, was constituted at Bombay with Seth Chotani, a wealthy merchant, as its President, and Shawkat Ali as its Secretary. In 1920 the Ali Brothers produced the Khilafat Manifesto. The Central Khilafat Committee started a Fund to help the Nationalist Movement in Turkey and to organise the Khilafat Movement at home.

Contemporaneously, Mohandas Karamchand Gandhi led his nonviolent nationalist movement satyagraha, as a protest against government repression evidenced, for example, in the Rowlatt Act of 1919, and the Jalian Wallah Bagh Massacres of April 1919. To enlist Muslim support in his movement, Gandhi supported the Khilafat cause and became a member of the Central Khilafat Committee. At the Nagpur Session (1920) of the Indian national congress Gandhi linked the issue of Swaraj (Self-Government) with the Khilafat demands and adopted the non-cooperation plan to attain the twin objectives. By mid-1920 the Khilafat leaders had made common cause with Gandhi's non-cooperation movement promising non-violence in return for Gandhi's support of the Khilafat Movement whereby Hindus and Muslims formed a united front against British rule in India. Support was received also of Muslim theologians through the Jamiyat-al Ulama-i-Hind (The Indian Association of Muslim Theologians). Maulana Mohammed Akram Khan of Bengal was a member of its Central Executive and Constitution Committee.

However, the movement's objectives of communal harmony and nonviolence suffered a setback because of the *Hijrat* (Exodus) to Afghanistan in 1920 of about 18,000 Muslim peasants, mostly from Sindh and North Western Provinces, the excesses of Muslims who felt that India was *Dar-ul-Harb* (Apostate land), the Moplah rebellion in South India in August 1921, and the Chauri-Chaura incident in February 1922 in the United Provinces where a violent mob set fire to a police station killing twenty-two policemen. Soon after Gandhi called off the Non-cooperation movement, leaving Khilafat leaders with a feeling of betrayal.

The extra-territorial loyalty of Khilafat leaders received a final and deadly blow from the Turks themselves. The charismatic Turkish nationalist leader Mustafa Kemal's startling secular renaissance, his victories over invading Greek forces culminating in the abolition of the Sultanate in November 1922, and the transformation of Turkey into a Republic in October 1923, followed by the abolition of the Khilafat in March 1924, took the Khilafatists unaware. By 1924 the Khilafat Movement, had become devoid of any relevance and significance and met its end.

The first stirrings in favour of the Khilafat Movement in Bengal was seen on 30 December, 1918 at the 11th Session of the All India Muslim league held in Delhi. In his presidential address, AK Fazlul Huq voiced concern over the attitude of Britain and her allies engaged in dividing and distributing the territories of the defeated Ottoman Empire.

When the Paris Peace Conference (1919) confirmed these apprehensions, Bengali Khilafat leaders such as Maulana Akram Khan, Abul Kasem, and Mujibur Rahman Khan held a Public meeting in Calcutta on 9 February, 1919 to enlist public support in favour of preserving the integrity of the Ottoman Empire and saving the institution of Khilafat.

In Bengal, the Khilafat-Non-Cooperation Movement (1918 to 1924) became a mass movement in which both Muslims and Hindus participated. The Bengal movement benefited from coordinated action by and between the Central and Provincial Khilafat leaders. Maulana Abul Kalam Azad propagated Khilafat ideas in rural Bengal. In the initial stage, the movement was popularised by Bengali leaders such as Maulana Akram Khan, maniruzzaman islamabadi, Mujibur Rahman Khan, the brothers Maulana Abdullahil Kafi and Maulana Abdullahil Baqi, Ismail Hossain Shiraji, Abul Kasem and AK Fazlul Huq. Maulana Akram Khan and Maniruzzaman Islambadi toured Bengal and organised Khilafat meetings, particularly in Dhaka and Chittagong. In an article *Asahojogita-o-Amader Kartabya*, Maniruzzaman Islambadi declared that to protect Khilafat and to acquire Swaraj were the twin aims of the movement and that it was the sacred duty of every Indian to support these ideas.

During the observance of the first Khilafat Day on 17 October 1919, most Indian-owned shops remained closed in Calcutta, prayers were offered at different mosques, and public meetings were held all over Bengal. On 23-24 November 1919 the first All-India Khilafat Conference held in Delhi was presided over by AK Fazlul Huq from Bengal. It was resolved that pending a resolution of the Khilafat problem there would be no participation in the proposed peace celebrations, that British goods should be boycotted, and that a policy of non-cooperation with the government would be adopted. In early 1920 the Bengal Provincial Khilafat Committee was organised with Maulana Abdur Rauf as President, Maniruzzaman Islambadi as Vice President, Maulana Akram Khan as General Secretary, and Mujibur Rahman and Majid Baksh as Joint Secretaries respectively. The office of the organisation was located at Hiron Bari Lane of Kolutola Street in Calcutta.

The first Bengal Provincial Khilafat Conference was held at the Calcutta Town Hall on 28-29 February 1920. Several members of the Central Khilafat Committee attended. Prominent Bengali Khilafat leaders such as A K Fazlul Huq, Abul Kasem, Mujibur Rahman participated in the conference and reiterated the view that unless their demands on the Khilafat problem were met non-cooperation and boycott would continue. The conference decided to observe 19 March 1920 as the Second Khilafat Day.

In March 1920 a Khilafat delegation led by Maulana Muhammad Ali went to England to plead for the Khilafat cause. Abul Kasem represented Bengal in this delegation. Local Khilafat Committees were also constituted. Maulana Abul Kalam Azad and Maulvi Abdur Rahman became President and Secretary respectively of the Calcutta Khilafat Committee. On 20 December 1919 the Dhaka Committee was founded at the ahsan manzil with Nawab khwaja habibullah as President, Syed Abdul Hafez as alternate President, and Gholam Quddus as Secretary. In response to the demands of the citizens of Dhaka, a "Sadar Khilafat Committee" was formed; Khwaja Sulaiman Kadar was its President, Maulana Abdul Jabbar Ansari, Hafez Abdur Razzak, Hafez Abdul Hakim its Vice-Presidents, and Maulvi Shamsul Huda its Secretary.

On 19 March 1920 the Second Khilafat Day was observed in Bengal. In Calcutta life almost came to a standstill and numerous Khilafat meetings were held in Dhaka, Chittagong and Mymensingh. The largest meeting was held in Tangail and was presided over by Abdul Halim Ghaznavi, the liberal nationalist Muslim zamindar. At this meeting, Maniruzzaman Islambadi urged the public to adopt *Satyagraha* as the symbol of the Khilafat movement.

Most districts of Bengal witnessed a mushroom growth of Khilafat Committees alongside existing Congress Committees, often with common membership. This was the first significant anti-British mass movement in which Hindus and Muslims participated with equal conviction. The media, both Muslim and Hindu, played a vital role in popularising the movement. 'Mohammadi', 'Al-Eslam' and 'The Mussalman' were publications which deserve mention.

The Khilafat Movement engendered a Muslim political consciousness that reverberated throughout Bengal under the leadership of Maulana Azad, Akram Khan, Maniruzzaman Islambadi, Bipin Chandra Pal and Chitta Ranjan Das. Though the Khilafat movement was orthodox in origin, it did manage to generate liberal ideas among Muslims because of the interaction and close understanding between Hindus and Muslims. Following the example of Calcutta, volunteer organisations were set up in rural Bengal to train volunteers to enforce boycott of foreign goods, courts, and government offices. They were also engaged in spinning, popularising items of necessity, and raising contributions for the Khilafat cause. In some areas in Dhaka, Muslim zamindars extracted 'Khilafat Salami' from Muslim tenants by declaring themselves the representatives of the Sultan of Turkey. Ironically, due to the ignorance of these tenants this custom continued long after the Khilafat was abolished.

Visibly shaken by the popularity of the Movement, through a Notification on 19 November 1921 the Government of Bengal declared the activities of the Khilafat and Congress volunteers illegal. Government officers raided Khilafat offices, confiscated documents and papers, banned meetings, and arrested office bearers. About a hundred and fifty personalities including Maulana Azad, CR Das, Akram Khan, and Ambika Prashad Bajpai were arrested in Calcutta on 10 December 1921.

At this critical juncture, a rift arose among Khilafat and Non-cooperation leaders on the issue of boycotting educational institutions and legislative councils. Some Muslim leaders believed that such boycott would be suicidal for Muslims. They were in favour of participating in the elections under the India Act of 1919 that assured self-governing institutions in India.

Prominent among this group of Swarajist leaders were CR Das, Bipin Chandra Pal, Motilal Nehru, Surendranath Banerjea, Ashutosh Chowdhury, Asutosh Mookerjee and Sarat Chandra Bose. Notable Muslims subscribing to the same ideas were AK Fazlul Huq, Abul Kasem, Khwaja Muhammad Azam, Khwaja Afzal, Nawab Khwaja Habibullah, Hakim Habibur Rahman, Syed Nawab Ali Chowdhury, Sir Syed Shamsul Huda, Sir Abdullah Al-mamun Suhrawardi, Maulana Abu Bakr Siddiky (Pir of Furfura), Shah Ahsanullah, Kazem Ali and Huseyn Shaheed Suhrawardy. Indian National Congress and the Muslim nationalists were strongly opposed to the idea of joining the councils.

Eminent Hindu personalities in Bengal who supported the Khilafat movement were Bipin Chandra Pal, Shrish Chandra Chattopadhya, Kaminikumar Bandyopadhaya, Dr. Rai Kumar

Chakravarty, PC Ghosh, Basanta Kumar Majumdar, Aswini Kumar Dutta, Pyarilal Roy, Gurucharan Aich, Sarat Kumar Gupta, Poet Mukunda Das, Haranath Ghosh, Nagendra Bhattacharya, Satindra Sen, Dr. Tarini Gupta, Sarol Kumar Dutta, Nishi Kanta Ganguly, Monoranjan Gupta, Sarat Kumar Ghosh, Nagendra Bijoy Bhattacharya, Nalini Das, Sailendra Nath Das, Khitish Chandra Roy Chowdhury and many others.

Though the Khilafat movement ended abruptly, the political activities it gave rise to and the experience gained therefrom, proved invaluable to Bengali Muslims after the 1947 partition. Among the numerous participants in the Khilafat movement from Bengal the names of some representative notable personalities are mentioned below: Maulana Abdul Hamid Khan Bhasani originally from Pabna but later settled at Kagmari, in Tangail district, Zahiruddin Tarafdar (Mymensingh), Abul Mansur Ahmed (Mymensingh), Abul Kalam Shamsuddin (Mymensingh), Huseyn Shaheed Suhrawardy (Calcutta), Maulana Abdur Rashid Tarkabagish (Pabna), Habibur Rahman Chowdhury (Comilla), Ashrafuddin Ahmed Chowdhury (Comilla), Shah Badrul Alam (Chittagong), Maulvi Aman Ali (Chittagong), Nurul Huq Chowdhury (Chittagong), Muhammad Waliullah (Chittagong), Kazem Ali Miah (Chittagong) Tamizuddin Khan (Faridpur), Pir Badshah Miah (Faridpur), Moazzem Hossain Chowdhury alias Lal Miah (Faridpur), Justice Muhammad Ibrahim (Faridpur), Majid Baksh (Barisal), Abul Kashem (Barisal), Khan Bahadur Hemayetuddin Ahmed (Barisal), Poet Mozammel Huq (Bhola) Hashem Ali Khan (Barisal), Wahed Reza Chowdhury of Ulania (Barisal), Sultan Ahmed Chowdhury (Barisal), Majed Kazi of Kasbah (Barisal), Khan Sahib Hatem Ali Jamadar (Barisal), Syed Muhammad Afzal (Pirojpur), Ismail Khan Chowdhury (Barisal), Maulvi Muhammad Ibrahim (Noakhali), Abdul Jabbar Khaddar (Noakhali), Abdul Gofran (Noakhali), Syed Ahmed Khan (Noakhali), Nasir Ahmad Bhuiyan (Noakhali), Suren Chandra Das Gupta (Bogra), Hussein Ahmed (Gaibandha), Rajibuddin Tarafdar (Bogra), Kabiraj Sheikh Abdul Aziz (Bogra), Ishaq Gokuli (Bogra), Maulana Maniruddin Anwari (Dinajpur), Shomeshwar Prasad Chowdhury (Burdwan), Shah Abdul Hamid (Rangpur), Afsaruddin Ahmed (Khulna), Sukumar Bandyopadhaya (Kushtia), Maulvi Shamsuddin Ahmed (Kushtia), Syed Majid Baksh (Jessore) and Maulana Ahmed Ali (Khulna). In addition to the front-rank leaders of the Khilafat movement, a new class of Muslim leaders emerged during this period from urban as well as from distant parts of Bengal. They gained experience in organising and mobilising the public. The Khilafat movement provided an opportunity to throw up a new Mofassil based leadership which played a key role in introducing a coherent self-assertive political identity for Bengali Muslims. After the 1947 Partition, these personalities played effective roles in their respective areas of activity.

The Khilafat Movement

Khilafat Movement (1919-1924) was a Pan-Islamic movement influenced by Indian nationalism. The Ottoman Emperor Abdul Hamid II (1876-1909) had launched a Pan-Islamic programme to use his position as the Sultan-Khalifa of the global Muslim community with a view to saving his disintegrating empire from foreign attacks and to crush the nationalistic democratic movement at home. The visit of his emissary, Jamaluddin Afghani, to India in the late nineteenth century to propagate Pan-Islamic ideas received a favourable response from some Indian Muslim leaders. These sentiments intensified early in the twentieth century with the revocation in 1911 of the 1905 partition of Bengal, the Italian (1911) and Balkan (1911-1912) attacks on Turkey, and Great Britain's participation in the First World War (1914-18) against Turkey.

The defeat of Turkey in the First World War and the division of its territories under the Treaty of Sevres (10 August 1920) among European powers caused apprehensions in India over the Khalifa's custodianship of the Holy places of Islam. Accordingly, the Khilafat Movement was launched in September 1919 as an orthodox communal movement to protect the Turkish Khalifa and save his empire from dismemberment by Great Britain and other European powers. The Ali brothers, Muhammad Ali and Shawkat Ali, Maulana Abul Kalam Azad, Dr. MA Ansari, and Hasrat Mohani initiated the Movement. Khilafat Conferences were organised in several cities in northern India. A Central Khilafat Committee, with provisions for provincial branches, was constituted at Bombay with Seth Chotani, a wealthy merchant, as its President, and Shawkat Ali as its Secretary. In 1920 the Ali Brothers produced the

Khilafat Manifesto. The Central Khilafat Committee started a Fund to help the Nationalist Movement in Turkey and to organise the Khilafat Movement at home.

Mahathma Gandhi leads the Congress-Declaration of Non-Cooperation Movement

Contemporaneously, Mohandas Karamchand Gandhi led his nonviolent nationalist movement satyagraha, as a protest against government repression evidenced, for example, in the Rowlatt Act of 1919, and the Jallianwalla Bagh Massacres of April 1919. To enlist Muslim support in his movement, Gandhi supported the Khilafat cause and became a member of the Central Khilafat Committee. At the Nagpur Session (1920) of the Indiana national congress Gandhi linked the issue of Swaraj (Self-Government) with the Khilafat demands and adopted the non-cooperation plan to attain the twin objectives.

By mid-1920 the Khilafat leaders had made common cause with Gandhi's non-cooperation movement promising non-violence in return for Gandhi's support of the Khilafat Movement whereby Hindus and Muslims formed a united front against British rule in India. Support was received also of Muslim theologians through the Jamiyat-al Ulama-i-Hind (The Indian Association of Muslim Theologians). Maulana Mohammed Akram Khan of Bengal was a member of its Central Executive and Constitution Committee. However, the movement's objectives of communal harmony and nonviolence suffered a setback because of the Hijrat (Exodus) to Afghanistan in 1920 of about 18,000 Muslim peasants, mostly from Sindh and North Western Provinces, the excesses of Muslims who felt that India was Dar-ul-Harb (Apostate land), the Moplah rebellion in South India in August 1921, and the Chauri-Chaura incident in February 1922 in the United Provinces where a violent mob set fire to a police station killing twenty-two policemen. Soon after Gandhi called off the Non-cooperation movement, leaving Khilafat leaders with a feeling of betrayal.

The extra-territorial loyalty of Khilafat leaders received a final and deadly blow from the Turks themselves. The charismatic Turkish nationalist leader Mustafa Kemal's startling secular renaissance, his victories over invading Greek forces culminating in the abolition of the Sultanate in November 1922, and the transformation of Turkey into a Republic in October 1923, followed by the abolition of the Khilafat in March 1924, took the Khilafatists unaware. By 1924 the Khilafat Movement, had become devoid of any relevance and significance and met its end.

The first stirrings in favour of the Khilafat Movement in Bengal was seen on 30 December 1918 at the 11th Session of the All India Muslim league held in Delhi. In his presidential address, AK Fazlul Huq voiced concern over the attitude of Britain and her allies engaged in dividing and distributing the territories of the defeated Ottoman Empire. When the Paris Peace Conference (1919) confirmed these apprehensions, Bengali Khilafat leaders such as Maulana Akram Khan, Abul Kasem, and Mujibur Rahman Khan held a Public meeting in Calcutta on 9 February 1919 to enlist public support in favour of preserving the integrity of the Ottoman Empire and saving the institution of Khilafat.

In Bengal, the Khilafat-Non-Cooperation Movement (1918 to 1924) became a mass movement in which both Muslims and Hindus participated. The Bengal movement benefited from coordinated action by and between the Central and Provincial Khilafat leaders. Maulana Abul Kalam Azad propagated Khilafat ideas in rural Bengal. In the initial stage, the movement was popularised by Bengali leaders such as Maulana Akram Khan, maniruzzaman islamabadi, Mujibur Rahman Khan, the brothers Maulana Abdullahil Kafi and Maulana Abdullahil Baqi, Ismail Hossain Shiraji, Abul Kasem and AK Fazlul Huq. Maulana Akram Khan and Maniruzzaman Islambadi toured Bengal and organised Khilafat meetings, particularly in Dhaka and Chittagong. In an article Asahojogita-o-Amader Kartabya, Maniruzzaman Islambadi declared that to protect Khilafat and to acquire Swaraj were the twin aims of the movement and that it was the sacred duty of every Indian to support these ideas.

During the observance of the first Khilafat Day on 17 October 1919, most Indian-owned shops remained closed in Calcutta, prayers were offered at different mosques, and public meetings were held all over Bengal. On 23-24 November 1919 the first All-India Khilafat Conference held in Delhi was presided over by AK Fazlul Huq from Bengal. It was resolved that pending a resolution of the Khilafat problem there would be no participation in the proposed peace celebrations, that British goods should be boycotted, and that a policy of non-cooperation with the government would be adopted. In early 1920 the Bengal Provincial Khilafat Committee was organised with Maulana Abdur Rauf as President, Maniruzzaman Islambadi as Vice President, Maulana Akram Khan as General Secretary, and Mujibur Rahman and Majid Baksh as Joint Secretaries respectively. The office of the organisation was located at Hiron Bari Lane of Kolutola Street in Calcutta.

The first Bengal Provincial Khilafat Conference was held at the Calcutta Town Hall on 28-29 February 1920. Several members of the Central Khilafat Committee attended. Prominent Bengali Khilafat leaders such as A K Fazlul Huq, Abul Kasem, Mujibur Rahman participated in the conference and reiterated the view that unless their demands on the Khilafat problem were met non-cooperation and boycott would continue. The conference decided to observe 19 March 1920 as the Second Khilafat Day.

In March 1920 a Khilafat delegation led by Maulana Muhammad Ali went to England to plead for the Khilafat cause. Abul Kasem represented Bengal in this delegation. Local Khilafat Committees were also constituted. Maulana Abul Kalam Azad and Maulvi Abdur Rahman became President and Secretary respectively of the Calcutta Khilafat Committee. On 20 December 1919 the Dhaka Committee was founded at the ahsan manzil with Nawab khwaja habibullah as President, Syed Abdul Hafez as alternate President, and Gholam Quddus as Secretary. In response to the demands of the citizens of Dhaka, a "Sadar Khilafat Committee" was formed; Khwaja Sulaiman Kadar was its President, Maulana Abdul Jabbar Ansari, Hafez Abdur Razzak, Hafez Abdul Hakim its Vice-Presidents, and Maulvi Shamsul Huda its Secretary.

On 19 March 1920 the Second Khilafat Day was observed in Bengal. In Calcutta life almost came to a standstill and numerous Khilafat meetings were held in Dhaka, Chittagong and Mymensingh. The largest meeting was held in Tangail and was presided over by Abdul Halim ghaznavi, the liberal nationalist Muslim zamindar. At this meeting, Maniruzzaman Islambadi urged the public to adopt Satyagraha as the symbol of the Khilafat movement.

Most districts of Bengal witnessed a mushroom growth of Khilafat Committees alongside existing Congress Committees, often with common membership. This was the first significant anti-British mass movement in which Hindus and Muslims participated with equal conviction. The media, both Muslim and Hindu, played a vital role in popularising the movement. 'Mohammadi', 'Al-Eslam' and 'The Mussalman' were publications, which deserve mention. The Khilafat Movement engendered a Muslim political consciousness that reverberated throughout Bengal under the leadership of Maulana Azad, Akram Khan, Maniruzzaman Islambadi, Bipin Chandra Pal and Chitta Ranjan das. Though the Khilafat movement was orthodox in origin, it did manage to generate liberal ideas among Muslims because of the interaction and close understanding between Hindus and Muslims. Following the example of Calcutta, volunteer organisations were set up in rural Bengal to train volunteers to enforce boycott of foreign goods, courts, and government offices. They were also engaged in spinning, popularising items of necessity, and raising contributions for the Khilafat cause. In some areas in Dhaka, Muslim zamindars extracted 'Khilafat Salami' from Muslim tenants by declaring themselves the representatives of the Sultan of Turkey. Ironically, due to the ignorance of these tenants this custom continued long after the Khilafat was abolished.

Visibly shaken by the popularity of the Movement, through a Notification on 19 November 1921 the Government of Bengal declared the activities of the Khilafat and Congress volunteers illegal. Government officers raided Khilafat offices, confiscated documents and papers, banned meetings, and arrested office bearers. About a hundred and fifty personalities including Maulana Azad, CR Das, Akram Khan, and Ambika Prashad Bajpai were arrested in Calcutta on 10 December 1921.

At this critical juncture, a rift arose between Khilafat and Non-cooperation leaders on the issue of boycotting educational institutions and legislative councils. Some Muslim leaders believed that such boycott would be suicidal for Muslims. They were in favour of participating in the elections under the India Act of 1919 that assured self-governing institutions in India.

Prominent among this group of Swarajist leaders were CR Das, Bipin Chandra Pal, Motilal Nehru, Surendranath Banerjea, Ashutosh Chowdhury, Asutosh Mookerjee and Sarat Chandra Bose. Notable Muslims subscribing to the same ideas were AK Fazlul Huq, Abul Kasem, Khwaja Muhammad Azam, Khwaja

Afzal, Nawab Khwaja Habibullah, Hakim Habibur Rahman, Syed Nawab Ali Chowdhury, Sir Syed Shamsul Huda, Sir Abdullah al-Mamun Suhrawardi, Maulana Abu Bakr Siddiky (Pir of Furfura), Shah Ahsanullah, Kazem Ali and Huseyn Shaheed Suhrawardy. Indian National Congress and the Muslim nationalists were strongly opposed to the idea of joining the councils.

Eminent Hindu personalities in Bengal who supported the Khilafat movement were Bipin Chandra Pal, Shrish Chandra Chattopadhya, Kaminikumar Bandyopadhaya, Dr. Rai Kumar Chakravarty, PC Ghosh, Basanta Kumar Majumdar, Aswini Kumar Dutta, Pyarilal Roy, Gurucharan Aich, Sarat Kumar Gupta, Poet Mukunda Das, Haranath Ghosh, Nagendra Bhattacharya, Satindra Sen, Dr. Tarini Gupta, Sarol Kumar Dutta, Nishi Kanta Ganguly, Monoranjan Gupta, Sarat Kumar Ghosh, Nagendra Bijoy Bhattacharya, Nalini Das, Sailendra Nath Das, Khitish Chandra Roy Chowdhury and many others.

In addition to the front-rank leaders of the Khilafat movement, a new class of Muslim leaders emerged during this period from urban as well as from distant parts of Bengal. They gained experience in organizing and mobilizing the public. The Khilafat movement provided an opportunity to throw up a new Mofassil based leadership, which played a key role in introducing a coherent self-assertive political identity for Bengali Muslims. After the 1947 Partition, these personalities played effective roles in their respective areas of activity.

Non-Cooperation Movement was initiated by Mahatma Gandhi. To advance the Indian nationalist cause, the Indiana national congress under the leadership of of Gandhi decided in 1920 to follow a policy of passive resistance to British rule.

The Rowlatt Act, the Jalliwanwala Bagh massacre and martial law in Punjab had belied the generous war time promises of the British. The montagu-chelmsford report with its ill-considered scheme of dyarchy satisfied few. Gandhi, so far believing in the justice and fair play of the government, now felt that Non-Cooperation with the government must be started. At the same time, the harsh terms of the Treaty of Sevres between the Allies and Turkey was resented by the Muslims in India. The Muslims started the khilafat movement and Gandhi decided to identify himself with them. Gandhi's 'skilful top level political game' secured in winning over the Muslim support in the coming Non-Cooperation Movement in India.

The movement was launched formally on 1st August 1920, after the expiry of the notice that Gandhi had given to the Viceroy in his letter of 22 June, in which he had asserted the right recognised 'from time immemorial of the subject to refuse to assist a ruler who misrules'. At the Calcutta Session (September 1920) the programme of the movement was clearly stated. It involved the surrender of the titles and offices and resignation from nominated posts in the local bodies. The Non-Cooperators were not to attend Government duties, *Durbar*s and other functions and they were to withdraw their children from schools and colleges and establish national schools and colleges. They were to boycott the British courts and establish private arbitration courts; they were to use *swadeshi* cloth. Truth and non-violence were to be strictly observed by Non-Cooperators.

The Calcutta decision was endorsed at the Nagpur Session of the Congress (December 1920). There the betterment of party organisation was emphasised. Congress membership was thrown open to all adult men and women on payment of 4 annas as subscription. The adoption of the Non-Cooperation resolution by the Congress gave it a new energy and from January 1921, it began to register considerable success all over India. Gandhi along with Ali Brothers undertook a nation-wide tour during which he addressed hundreds of meetings.

In the first month, 9,000 students left schools and colleges and joined more than 800 national institutions that had sprung up all over the country. The educational boycott was particularly successful in Bengal under the leadership of Chitta Ranjan das and Subhas Chandra Bose. Punjab, too, responded to the educational boycott and Lala Lajpat Rai played the leading role. Other areas that were active were Bombay, UP, Bihar, Orissa and Assam; Madras remained lukewarm.

The boycott of law courts by lawyers was not as successful as the educational boycott. Many leading lawyers, like, CR Das, Motilal Nehru, Mr. Jayakar, S Kitchlew, V Patel. Asaf Ali Khan and others gave up lucrative practices, and their sacrifice became a source of inspiration for many. In number again, Bengal led followed by Andhra, U P, Karnataka and Punjab.

But perhaps, the most successful item of the programme was the boycott of foreign cloth. The value of imports of foreign cloth fell from Rs. 102 crore in 1920-21 to 57 crore in 1921-22.

In July 1921, a new challenge was thrown to the government. Mohammad Ali along with other leaders was arrested for holding the view that it was 'religiously unlawful for the Muslims to continue in the British army'. Gandhi as well as the Congress supported Mohammad Ali and issued a manifesto. The next dramatic event was the visit of the Prince of Wales that began on 17 November 1921. The day the Prince landed in Bombay was observed as a day of *hartal* all over India. He was greeted with empty streets and downed shutters wherever he went. Emboldened by their successful defiance of the government, Non-Cooperators became more and more aggressive. The Congress volunteer corps emerged as a powerful parallel police, and the sight of its members marching in formation and dressed in uniform was hardly one that warmed the government heart. The Congress had already granted permission to the Provincial Congress Committees to sanction mass civil disobedience including the non-payment of taxes wherever they thought that the people were ready. The Non-Cooperation Movement had other indirect effects as well. In UP it became difficult to distinguish between a Non-Cooperation meeting and a peasant meeting. In Malabar in Kerala it helped to rouse Muslim tenants against their landlords. In Assam, labourers on tea plantations went on strike. In Punjab, the Akali movement was a part of the general movement of Non-Cooperation. In Bengal, particularly, it acquired considerable strength. Not only in Kolkata, but also in rural Bengal an elemental awakening was observed. It reached a major climax following the Gurkha assault on coolies at the river port of Chandpur (20-21 May). Under the leadership of JM Sengupta the whole of Eastern Bengal was in ferment. But the best organised of the village movements was the anti-Union Board agitation in Midnapur led by Birendranath Sasmal.

As the Non-Cooperation Movement continued it became clear that the women of Bengal were willing to play an active role in the protest movement. The women nationalists here organised themselves under the *Mahila Karma Samaj* or the Ladies Organisation Board of the Bengal Pradesh Congress Committee. Women of the Samaj organised meetings and propagated the spirit of Non-Cooperation. Women volunteers were enlisted. Basanti Devi and Urmila Devi, wife and sister respectively of CR Das, Nellie Sengupta, wife of JM Sengupta, along with others like Mohini Devi, Labanya Prabha Chanda played a prominent role in this movement. Picketing of foreign wine and cloth shops and selling of *Khaddar* on the streets happened to be the main areas of their activities.

The government promulgated Sections 108 and 144 of the Code of Criminal Procedure at various centres of the agitation. Volunteers' Corps was declared illegal and by December, over 30,000 people were arrested from all over India. Among prominent leaders, only Gandhi remained out of jail. In mid-December there was an abortive attempt at negotiations, initiated by Malaviya, but the conditions offered were such that it meant sacrificing the Khilafat leaders, a course that Gandhi would hardly accept. At that time he had been also under considerable pressure from the Congress rank and file to start the phase of mass civil disobedience. Gandhi presented an ultimatum to the government but as the government did not respond he started to initiate the civil disobedience movement in Bardoli taluqa of Surat district. Unfortunately at this time the tragedy of Chauri Chaura occurred which changed the course of the movement. A mob of 3,000 killed twenty-five policemen and one inspector. This was too much for Gandhi who stood for complete non-violence. The result was that he gave order for the suspension of the movement at once. Thus on 12 February 1922, the Non-Cooperation Movement came to an end.

As regards the limitations and achievements of the Non-Cooperation Movement, it apparently failed to achieve its object of securing the Khilafat and making good of the Punjab wrongs. The Swaraj was not attained in a year as promised. Still, the retreat that was ordered on 12 February 1922 was only a temporary one. The battle was over, but the war would continue

5

The Non-Cooperation Movement

Mahatma Gandhi initiated non-Cooperation Movement. To advance the Indian nationalist cause, the Indian national congress under the leadership of Gandhi decided in 1920 to follow a policy of passive resistance to British rule.

The Rowlatt Act, the Jalliwanwala Bagh massacre and martial law in Punjab had belied the generous wartime promises of the British. The Montage Chelmsford report with its ill-considered scheme of diarchy satisfied few. Gandhi, so far believing in the justice and fair play of the government, now felt that Non-Cooperation with the government must be started. At the same time, the harsh terms of the Treaty of Sevres between the Allies and Turkey was resented by the Muslims in India. The Muslims started the Khilafat movement and Gandhi decided to identify himself with them. Gandhi's 'skilful top level political game' secured in winning over the Muslim support in the coming Non-Cooperation Movement in India.

The movement was launched formally on 1st August 1920, after the expiry of the notice that Gandhi had given to the Viceroy in his letter of 22 June, in which he had asserted the right recognized 'from time immemorial of the subject to refuse to assist a ruler who misrules'. At the Calcutta Session (September 1920) the programme of the movement was clearly stated. It involved the surrender of the titles and offices and resignation from nominated posts in the local bodies. The Non-Cooperators were not to attend Government duties, Durbars and other functions and they were to withdraw their children from schools and colleges and establish national schools and colleges. They were to boycott the British courts and establish private arbitration courts; they were to use swadeshi cloth. Truth and non-violence were to be strictly observed by Non-Cooperators.

The Calcutta decision was endorsed at the Nagpur Session of the Congress (December 1920). There the betterment of party organization was emphasized. Congress membership was thrown open to all adult men and women on payment of 4 annas as subscription. The adoption of the Non-Cooperation resolution by the Congress gave it a new energy and from January 1921, it began to register considerable success all over India. Gandhi along with Ali Brothers undertook a nation-wide tour during which he addressed hundreds of meetings.

In the first month, 9,000 students left schools and colleges and joined more than 800 national institutions that had sprung up all over the country. The educational boycott was particularly successful in Bengal under the leadership of Chitta Ranjan das and Subhas Chandra Bose. Punjab, too, responded to the educational boycott and Lala Lajpat Rai played the leading role. Other areas that were active were Bombay, UP, Bihar, Orissa and Assam; Madras remained lukewarm.

The boycott of law courts by lawyers was not as successful as the educational boycott. Many leading lawyers, like, CR Das, Motilal Nehru, Mr. Jayakar, S Kitchlew, V Patel. Asaf Ali Khan and others gave up lucrative practices, and their sacrifice became a source of inspiration for many. In number again, Bengal led followed by Andhra, U P, Karnataka and Punjab.

But perhaps, the most successful item of the programme was the boycott of foreign cloth. The value of imports of foreign cloth fell from Rs. 102 crore in 1920-21 to 57 crore in 1921-22.

In July 1921, a new challenge was thrown to the government. Mohammad Ali along with other leaders was arrested for holding the view that it was 'religiously unlawful for the Muslims to continue in the British army'. Gandhi as well as the Congress supported Mohammad Ali and issued a manifesto. The next dramatic event was the visit of the Prince of Wales that began on 17 November 1921. The day the Prince landed in Bombay was observed as a day of hartal all over India. He was greeted with empty streets and downed shutters wherever he went. Emboldened by their successful defiance of the government, Non-Cooperators became more and more aggressive. The Congress volunteer corps emerged as a powerful parallel police, and the sight of its members marching in formation and dressed in uniform was hardly one that warmed the government heart. The Congress had already granted permission to the Provincial Congress Committees to sanction mass civil disobedience including the non-payment of taxes wherever they thought that the people were ready. The Non-Cooperation Movement had other indirect effects as well. In UP it became difficult to distinguish between a Non-Cooperation meeting and a peasant meeting. In Malabar in Kerala it helped to rouse Muslim tenants against their landlords. In Assam, labourers on tea plantations went on strike. In Punjab, the Akali movement was a part of the general movement of Non-Cooperation.

As the Non-Cooperation Movement continued it became clear that the women of Bengal were willing to play an active role in the protest movement. The women nationalists here organised themselves under the Mahila Karma Samaj or the Ladies Organisation Board of the Bengal Pradesh Congress Committee. Women of the Samaj organised meetings and propagated the spirit of Non-Cooperation. Women volunteers were enlisted. Basanti Devi and Urmila Devi, wife and sister respectively of CR Das, Nellie Sengupta, and wife of JM Sengupta, along with others like Mohini Devi, Labanya Prabha Chanda played a prominent role in this movement. Picketing of foreign wine and cloth shops and selling of Khaddar on the streets happened to be the main areas of their activities.

The government promulgated Sections 108 and 144 of the Code of Criminal Procedure at various centres of the agitation. Volunteers' Corps was declared illegal and by December, over 30,000 people were arrested from all over India. Among prominent leaders, only Gandhi remained out of jail. In mid-December there was an abortive attempt at negotiations, initiated by Malaviya, but the conditions offered were such that it meant sacrificing the Khilafat leaders, a course that Gandhi would hardly accept. At that time he had been also under considerable pressure from the Congress rank and file to start the phase of mass civil disobedience.

Gandhi presented an ultimatum to the government but as the government did not respond he started to initiate the civil disobedience movement in Bardoli taluqa of Surat district. Unfortunately at this time the tragedy of Chauri Chaura occurred which changed the course of the movement. A mob of 3,000 killed twenty-five policemen and one inspector. This was too much for Gandhi who stood for complete non-violence. The result was that he gave order for the suspension of the movement at once. Thus on 12 February 1922, the Non-Cooperation Movement came to an end.

As regards the limitations and achievements of the Non-Cooperation Movement, it apparently failed to achieve its object of securing the Khilafat and making good of the Punjab wrongs. The Swaraj was not attained in a year as promised. Still, the retreat that was ordered on 12 February 1922 was only a temporary one. The battle was over, but the war would continue.

The Non-cooperation movement was a significant phase of the Indian struggle for freedom from British rule. This movement, which lasted from 1920 to 1922, was led by Mahatma Gandhi, and supported by the Indian National Congress. It aimed to resist British occupation of India through nonviolent means. Protestors would refuse to buy British goods, adopt the use of local handicrafts, picket liquor shops, and try to uphold the values of Indian honour and integrity. The Gandhian ideals of *ahimsa* or non-violence, and his ability to rally hundreds of thousands of common citizens towards the cause of Indian independence, were first seen on a large scale in this movement.

Among the significant causes of this movement were colonial oppression, exemplified by the Jallianwala Bagh massacre, economic hardships to the common man due to a large chunk of Indian wealth being exported to Britain, ruin of Indian artisans due to British factory-made goods replacing handmade goods, and popular resentment with the British over Indian soldiers dying in World War I while fighting as part of the British Army, in battles that otherwise had nothing to do with India.

The calls of early political leaders like Mohammad Ali Jinnah (Who hardened his stand in the later days of the struggle), Annie Besant, Gopal Krishna Gokhale and Bal Gangadhar Tilak for Home rule were accompanied only by petitions and major public meetings. They never resulted in disorder or obstruction of government services. Partly due to that, the British did not take them very seriously. The non-cooperation movement aimed to ensure that the colonial economic and power structure would be seriously challenged, and British authorities would be forced to take notice of the people's demands.

Champaran, Kheda, Khilafat and Amritsar

Mahatma Gandhi had shown in South Africa and in 1918 in Champaran, Bihar and Kheda, Gujarat that the only way to earn the respect and attention of British officials was to actively resist government activities through civil disobedience.

Now in Champaran and Kheda in 1918 he led impoverished farmers, mired in social evils like unhygienic conditions, domestic violence, discrimination, oppression of women and untouchability. On top of their miseries, these people were forced to grow cash crops like indigo, tobacco and cotton instead of food, and for this they were virtually not compensated. In addition, they had to pay taxes despite a famine.

The Governments of the affected regions signed agreements suspending taxation in face of the famine, allowing the farmers to grow their own crops, releasing all political prisoners and returning all property and lands seized. It was the biggest victory against the British Empire since the American Revolution.

Mahatma Gandhi was assisted by a new generation of Indian revolutionaries like Rajendra Prasad and Jawaharlal Nehru. In Kheda, the entire revolt had been led by Sardar Vallabhbhai Patel, who was to become Gandhi's lieutenant.

Millions of India's Muslims were also antagonized by the Government's support of Mustafa Kemal of Turkey, who had overthrown the Sultan of Turkey, considered the Caliph of Islam. Muslim leaders formed the Khilafat committee to protest the actions and find a way to effectively stop the British authorities from neglecting their concerns.

A public meeting of unarmed civilians at Jallianwala Bagh in Amritsar was fired upon by troops under the command of Reginald Dyer. Hundreds of people died and perhaps thousands were injured. Women, children and the elderly were not spared. The outcry in Punjab led to thousands of arrests, beatings and more deaths at the hands of police and some violent protesters. The Amritsar Massacre became the most infamous event of British rule in India. To Gandhi and many others, it became clear that a reckoning with the British was not far off.

Satyagraha

Gandhi's call was for a nationwide protest against the Rowlatt Acts. All offices and factories would be closed. Indians would be encouraged to withdraw from Raj-sponsored schools, police services, the military and the civil services, and lawyers were asked to leave the Raj's courts. Public transportation and English-manufactured goods, especially clothing, would be boycotted.

Veterans like Bal Gangadhar Tilak, Bipin Chandra Pal, Mohammad Ali Jinnah, Annie Besant opposed the idea outright. The All India Muslim League also criticized the idea.

But the younger generation of Indian nationalists were thrilled, and backed Gandhi. The Congress Party adopted his plans, and he received extensive support from Muslim leaders like Maulana Azad, Mukhtar Ahmed Ansari, Hakim Ajmal Khan, Abbas Tyabji, Maulana Mohammad Ali and Maulana Shaukat Ali. Gandhi was elected President of the Indian National Congress in 1919 and 1920, as well as the All India Home Rule League — the latter once dominated by Gandhi's critics like Jinnah, Besant and Tilak.

Success and Suspension

The success of the revolt was a total shock to British authorities and a massive encouragement to millions of Indians. Then on February 4, 1922, in the Chauri Chaura, after violent clashes between the local police and the protestors in which three protestors were killed by police firing, the police *chowki* (pron.-chau key) (station) was set on fire by the mob, killing 22 of the police occupants.

Gandhi felt that the revolt was veering off-course.Gandhi was disappointed that the revolt lost its Non-Violent nature. He did not want the movement to degenerate into a contest of violence, with police and angry mobs attacking each other back and forth, victimizing civilians in between. Gandhi appealed to the Indian public for all resistance to end, went on a fast lasting 3 weeks, and called off the mass civil disobedience movement.

Aftermath

The Non-Co-operation Movement was withdrawn because of the Chauri-Chaura incident. Although he had stopped the national revolt single-handedly, on March 10, 1922, Gandhi was arrested. On March 18, 1922, he was imprisoned for two years for publishing seditious materials.

Although most Congress leaders remained firmly behind Gandhi, the disillusioned broke away. The Ali brothers would soon become fierce critics. Motilal Nehru and Chittaranjan Das formed the Swaraj Party, rejecting Gandhi's leadership. Many nationalists had felt that the Non-Cooperation Movement should not have been stopped due to isolated incidents of violence, and most nationalists, while retaining confidence in Gandhi, were discouraged.

Contemporary historians and critics suggest that the movement was successful enough to break the back of British rule, and possibly even result in the independence most Indians strove for until 1947.

But many historians and Indian leaders of the time also defend Gandhi's judgment. If he had not stopped the revolts, India could have descended into a chaotic rebellion which would have alienated common Indians and impress only violent revolutionaries.

Chauri Chaura

Chauri Chaura is a town near Gorakhpur, Uttar Pradesh, India. The town is famous for an event that took place on 22 February 1922 during British rule when a police *chowki* (pron.-chau key) (station) was set on fire by a nationalist mob, killing 22 of the police occupants.

Background

In the years 1920 and 1921, Indians launched a nationwide revolt now recognized as the Non-Cooperation Movement, which protested authoritarian laws like the Rowlatt Acts of 1919, and lack of human freedom and self-government for Indians in their own country.

Mahatma Gandhi was the leader of the nationwide revolts organised by the Indian National Congress based upon civil disobedience, or *Satyagraha* by peaceful means alone.

The Incident

On February 4, 1922, around 2,000 protesters gathered for picketing of the liquor shop at the local market in Chauri Chaura. Sensing the trouble, armed policemen were sent to the city police station to control the situation. The crowd marched towards the market and started shouting anti-government slogans. The policemen fired into the air as a warning signal. However, it had the reverse effect on the crowd who were in no mood to retreat and started pelting stones at the armed policemen. Seeing the situation was getting out of control, the sub inspector ordered the policemen to commence firing on the advancing crowd. Three protesters were killed on the spot and several others were injured. Seeing this, the crowd became violent and attacked the police from all the sides. The armed policemen lost their courage to fire, seeing thousands of protesters marching towards them. They retreated to the shelter of the police station. The crowd decided to take revenge for their dead comrades and set fire to the building from all the sides. Twenty-three policemen were burnt alive, including the station sub inspector.

Consequences

Mahatma Gandhi asked all Indians to end the Non-cooperation movement, and went on a five-day fast to absolve himself of what he perceived as his role in inciting the attacks. Gandhi felt that he had acted too hastily in encouraging a revolt against the British Raj, while not emphasizing the importance of ahinsa (non-violence) and not training the resisters enough. Due to his fast and the exhortation of Congress leaders, Indians gave up civil resistance.

Other consequences is a Birth of INA, Opposing the step towards endof Non-cooperation movement, Subash Chandra Bose formed INA and belived army struggle is the only way to get freedom from British rule faster.

Limelight of Lengendary freedom fighters Bhagath Singh and Chandershekhar Azad, Opposing the decision of endof Non-cooperation movement they both joined HRA (Hindustan republic association) formed in the year 1923 to fight against British rule. Incidents like Chauri Chaura (1922) contributed in getting faster independence for India. Its one of the greatest and historical incident which always to be discussed.

The Trial and the Judgement

The British government was furious after this incident and imposed martial law in the city of Chauri Chaura and surrounding areas. All the areas were raided and hundreds of people were arrested. 172 people were charged and put on the trial. On April 20, 1923 Allahabad high court awarded death sentence to 19, various jail terms including life imprisonment to 2 years jail to 113 accused, and acquitted 38 due to lack of evidence, whereas 3 accused died during the course of the trial.

Modern Assessment

Many modern historians view the Chauri Chaura incident as a minor episode of violence, which while regrettable, did not merit the cancellation of a nation's demand for political freedom.

Supporters of Gandhi's point of view agree with his decision, as it was feared by Gandhi that Chauri Chaura was not an isolated incident, but a shocking episode in a rising trend of violence between protesters and police, which could have degenerated into an orgy of mob violence, which would justify martial law and police suppression of even more civil liberties.

Thus (in Gandhi's view) the spiral of violence would have wrecked the wider agenda and organization, while maligning India's patriots as bloodthirsty murderers in the eyes of the world.

The nationalist version of historiography in India has linked it with the larger conscious call of Gandhi in Non-cooperation movement. However, the recent subaltern scholarship has tried to dug more substantive meanings of the incidence. The metaphor of Gandhi in the consciousness of masses, the way he moved in masses and his symbolic gestures had a myriad 'meanings' to the masses. Shahid Amin in his book *Event, Metaphor, Memory* has portrayed the chain of events that were occurring in Gorakhpur in that time. He had tried to argue that the nationalist meta-narrative of Indian National Congress has failed to bring out the history from below. The reason of the masses to act in a manner they did in Gorakhpur was as diverse as caste tensions, belief as Gandhi as liberator that enabled them to defy authority of local zamindars or the British.

Therefore, there can be alternative versions of history. The over-arching explanation of event like Chauri Chaura in the Nationalist historiography can be concealing if not read with other accounts.

Chauri Chaura : Famous Historical Town

Chauri Chaura is a small town in Gorakhpur district in the state of Uttar Pradesh, India. History students remember this place for its famous Chauri Chaura Incident which took place on 4th of February 1922. It is also known for its Dal and Gud (Pulses and Jaggery) Mandi. There is a big leather market too, known as Chamadahiya Bazaar (Leather Market) to supply hide (Khal or raw leather) to markets as far away as Kanpur and Calcutta. Chauri Chaura witnessed the historical incident during 1922 after which Mahatma Gandhi was shocked and withdrew his year old Asahayoga Andolan (Non Cooperation movement). Several freedom fighters were hanged by the British Government of that period and several others were sentenced to the cellular jail on the Andaman Islands, known as Kala Pani (Black waters). Shahid Amin, a professor of history at University of Delhi, who hails from Deoria (15 miles from Chauri Chaura), has written a famous book on Chauri Chaura titled "Event, Metaphor, Memory: Chauri Chaura 1922-1992" published by University of California Press. This book has complete details regarding the Chauri Chaura incident.

Chauri Chaura is a small town in Gorakhpur district in the state of Uttar Pradesh, India. History students remember this place for its famous Chauri Chaura Incident which took place on 4th of February 1922. It is also known for its Dal and Gud (Pulses and Jaggery) Mandi. There is a big leather market too, known as Chamadahiya Bazaar (Leather Market) to supply hide (Khal or raw leather) to markets as far away as Kanpur and Calcutta. Chauri Chaura witnessed the historical incident during 1922 after which Mahatma Gandhi was shocked and withdrew his year old Asahayoga Andolan (Non Cooperation movement). Several freedom fighters were hanged by the British Government of that period and several others were sentenced to the cellular jail on the

Andaman Islands, known as Kala Pani (Black waters). Shahid Amin, a professor of history at University of Delhi, who hails from Deoria (15 miles from Chauri Chaura), has written a famous book on Chauri Chaura titled "Event, Metaphor, Memory: Chauri Chaura 1922-1992" published by University of California Press. This book has complete details regarding the Chauri Chaura incident. Chauri Chaura is a Tehsil comprising of Sardar Nagar and Brahmpur blocks.

Chauri Chaura has a population of 3,84,335 comprising 194833 males and 189502 females. Chauri Chaura tehsil's urban population is only 11,228. Most of the urban population is in Mundera Bazar (also shown in old maps as Murera). Chauri Chaura, being tehsil headquarters, caters for most of the needs of people residing in neighbouring villages as far as 10-15 kilometres. It also serves as a ready market for agriculture and craft product of the area. Nearby attractions in Chauri Chaura include the famous Tarkulaha Devi Temple. There is a month long mela (funfair) every year starting from Chaitra Ramnavami at the Tarkulaha Devi Temple. People from far flung locations visit 'Tarkulaha Mela' to shop for their annual requirements of Garam Masala (Indian Spices) and to enjoy the traditional 'Nautanki' (drama), Nag Kanya shows and small circuses. Also, Tarkulaha Devi Temple was Shaheed Bandhu Singh's favourite place.

People here are peace loving and courteous. Majority of urban population is from the business community with a mix of Marwaris (migrated from Rajasthan) and Deswalis (local Vaishya community), with a very small number of Punjabi community. Several other people like teachers, doctors and government employees have made Chauri Chaura their residence due to its being the only urban hub for more than 200 villages; with facilities like Schools, Colleges, Railway Station, Tehsil Headquarters, Banks and Postoffice etc. One can find people from all religions like Hinduism, Islam, Sikhism, Jainism and Christianity living peacefully in Chauri Chaura.

Chauri Chaura was able to get the road connecting Gorakhpur to Deoria widened and re-made due to its close proximity to the famous Buddha circuit (Buddha Paripath) comprising of Naugarh (Kapilvastu), Sarnath, Bodh Gaya and Kushi Nagar.

Chauri Chaura : History

Chauri Chaura is situated in Lat. 26 Degree 38' N. and Long. 83 Degree 35' E. on the State highway between Gorakhpur and Deoria, 26 km. from Gorakhpur. It has a railway station which is25 km. south-east of the Gorakhpur railway junction. Prior to abolition of zamindari the village was held by Sikh zamindars of Dumri (Gagaha), who established a bazar near the railway station and made the place a local commercial centre of hide trade. Adjoining Chauri Chaura on the north is Mundera Bazar, another flourishing market. Chauri Chaura came into prominence in 1922..

Chauri Chaura is situated in Lat. 26 Degree 38' N. and Long. 83 Degree 35' E. on the State highway between Gorakhpur and Deoria, 26 km. from Gorakhpur. It has a railway station which is 25 km. south-east of the Gorakhpur railway junction. Prior to abolition of zamindari the village was held by Sikh zamindars of Dumri (Gagaha), who established a bazar near the railway station and made the place a local commercial centre of hide trade. Adjoining Chauri Chaura on the north is Mundera Bazar, another flourishing market.

Chauri Chaura came into prominence in 1922 when its inhabitants wholeheartedly participated in the Non-co-operation movement started by Gandhiji.

In February 1922 on hearing that the sub inspector of Chauri Chaura police-station had assaulted some of the Congress volunteers at Mundera Bazar, an infuriated mob assembled before the police-station Chauri Chaura in February 4,1922 demanding explanation from the guilty official. It ultimately resulted in police firing killing 3 persons from crowd and several injured. After the police had exhausted their ammunition and went inside the police-station, the enraged crowd challenged the policemen to come out of their den and on their paying no heed, it set fire to the thana in which 23 policemen including the station officer were burnt alive. Consequently, Gandhiji suspended the Non-co-operation movement. The people of the district did not forget their freedom fighters. In 1971, they formed Chauri Chaura Shaheed Smarak Samiti. In 1973, this Samiti constructed near the lake at Chauri Chaura a 12.2 metres high triangular minaret on each side of which a martyr is depicted hanging with a noose round his neck.

The minaret was built at a cost of Rs 13,500 generously contributed by the people. Later another Shaheed Smarak (now it is the main Shaheed Smarak) was built by Government of India to honour those hanged for Great Freedom Struggle. This tall memorial has names of those hanged engraved. Railways also introduced 2 trains to honour martyrs. These trains are Shaheed Express and Chauri Chaura Express.

Non-cooperation

In Punjab, the Jallianwala Bagh massacre of civilians by British troops caused deep trauma to the nation, and increased public anger and acts of violence. Gandhi criticized both the actions of the British, and the retaliatory violence of Indians. He authored the resolution offering condolences to British civilian victims and condemning the riots, which after initial opposition in the party, was accepted after Gandhi made an emotional speech pushing forth his principle that all violence was evil and could not be justified. R. Gandhi, *Patel: A Life*, pp. 82 But it was after the massacre and violence that Gandhi's mind focused upon obtaining complete self-government and control of all Indian government institutions, maturing soon into *Swaraj* or complete individual, spiritual, political independence.

Gandhi was invested with executive authority on behalf of the Indian National Congress in December 1921. Under Gandhi's leadership, the Congress was reorganized with a new constitution, with the goal of *Swaraj*. Membership in the party was opened to anyone prepared to pay a token fee. A hierarchy of committees was set up to improve discipline, transforming the party from an elite organization to one of mass national appeal.

Gandhi expanded his non-violence platform to include the *swadeshi* policy – the boycott of foreign-made goods, especially British goods. Linked to this was his advocacy that *khadi* (homespun cloth) be worn by all Indians instead of British-made textiles. Gandhi exhorted Indian men and women, rich or poor, to spend time each day spinning *khadi* in support of the independence movement. This was a strategy to inculcate discipline and dedication to weed out the unwilling and ambitious, and include women in the movement at a time when many thought that such activities were not "respectable" for women. In addition to boycotting British products, Gandhi urged the people to boycott British educational institutions and law courts, to resign from government employment, and to forsake British titles and honours.

"Non-cooperation" enjoyed widespread appeal and success, increasing excitement and participation from all strata of Indian society, yet just as the movement reached its apex, it ended abruptly as a result of a violent clash in the town of Chauri Chaura, Uttar Pradesh, in February 1922. Fearing that the movement was about to take a turn towards violence, and convinced that this would be the undoing of all his work, Gandhi called off the campaign of mass civil disobedience. Gandhi was arrested on March 10, 1922, tried for sedition, and sentenced to six years. Beginning on March 18, 1922, he only served about two years of the sentence, being released in February 1924 after an operation for appendicitis. Without Gandhi's uniting personality, the Indian National Congress began to splinter during his years in prison, splitting into two factions, one led by Chitta Ranjan Das and Motilal Nehru favouring party participation in the legislatures, and the other led by Chakravarti Rajagopalachari and Sardar Vallabhbhai Patel, opposing this move. Furthermore, cooperation among Hindus and Muslims, which had been strong at the height of the nonviolence campaign, was breaking down. Gandhi attempted to bridge these differences through many means, including a three-week fast in the autumn of 1924, but with limited success.

Swaraj Party

The Swaraj Party was a political party in India that sought greater self-government and political freedoms for the Indian people from the British Raj. It was inspired by the concept of Swaraj. In Hindi and many other languages of India, *swaraj* means "independence" or "self-rule".

Chauri Chaura

The Swaraj Party was formed by Indian politicians and members of the Indian National Congress who had opposed Mahatma Gandhi's suspension of all civil resistance in 1922 in response to the Chauri Chaura tragedy, where policemen were killed by a mob of protestors. Gandhi felt responsible for the killings, reproached himself for not emphasizing non-violence more firmly, and feared that the entire Non-Cooperation Movement would degenerate into an orgy of violence between the British-controlled army and police and mobs of freedom-fighters, alienating and hurting millions of common Indians. He went on a fast-unto-death to convince all Indians to stop civil resistance. The Congress and other nationalist groups disavowed all activities of disobedience.

But many Indians felt that the Non-Cooperation Movement should not have been suspended over an isolated incident of violence, and that its astonishing success was actually close to breaking the back of British rule in India. These people became disillusioned with Gandhi's political judgments and instincts.

Council Entry

Gandhi and most of the Congress Party rejected the provincial and central legislative councils created by the British to offer some participation for Indians. They argued that the councils were rigged with un-elected allies of the British, and too un-democratic and simply *rubber stamps* of the Viceroy.

In December 1922, Chittaranjan Das, N.C. Kelkar and Motilal Nehru formed the Congress-Khilafat Swarajaya Party with Das as the president and Nehru as one of the secretaries. Other prominent leaders included Huseyn Shaheed Suhrawardy and Subhas Chandra Bose of Bengal, Vithalbhai Patel and other Congress leaders who were becoming dissatisfied with the Congress. The other group was the 'No-Changers', who had accepted Gandhis' decision to withdraw the movement.

Now both the Swarajists and the No-Changers were engaged in fierce political struggle. But both were determined to avoid the disastrous experience of the 1907 split at Surat. On the advice of Gandhi, the two groups decided to remain in the Congress but to work in their separate ways. There was no basic difference between the two.

Swarajist members were elected to the councils. Vithalbhai Patel became the President of the Central Legislative Assembly. However, the legislatures had very limited powers, and apart from some heated parliamentary debates, procedural stand-offs with British authorities, the core mission of obstructing British rule failed. With the death of Chittaranjan Das in 1925, and with Motilal Nehru's return to the Congress the following year, the Swaraj party was greatly weakened.

Changers and No-Changers, and the Simon Commission

After his release from prison in 1924, Gandhi sought to bring back the Swarajists to the Congress and re-unite the party. Gandhi's supporters were in a vast majority in the Congress, and the Congress still remained India's largest political party, but Gandhi felt it necessary to heal the divide with the Swarajists, so as to heal the nation's wounds over the 1922 suspension.

The Swarajists sought more representation in the Congress offices, and an end to the mandatory requirement for Congressmen to spin khadi cloth and do social service as a prerequisite for office.

These was opposed by Gandhi's supporters, men like Vallabhbhai Patel, Jawaharlal Nehru and Rajendra Prasad, who became known as the *No Changers* as opposed to the Swarajist *Changers*. Gandhi relaxed the rules on spinning and named some Swarajists to important positions in the Congress Party. He also encouraged the Congress to support those Swarajists elected to the councils, so as not to embarrass them and leave them rudderless before the British authorities.

When the Simon Commission arrived in India in 1928, millions of Indians were infuriated with the idea of an all-British committee writing proposals for Indian constitutional reforms without any Indian member or consultations with the Indian people.

The Congress created a committee to write Indian proposals for constitutional reforms, headed by now Congress President Motilal Nehru. The death of Lala Lajpat Rai, beaten by police in Punjab further infuriated India. People rallied around the Nehru Report and old political divisions and wounds were forgotten, and Vithalbhai Patel and all Swarajist councillors resigned in protest.

Between 1929 and 1937, the Indian National Congress would declare the independence of India and launch the Salt Satyagraha. In this tumultuous period, the Swaraj Party was defunct as its members quietly dissolved into the Congress fold.

Madras Province Swarajya Party

The Madras Province Swarajya Party was established in 1923. S. Sathyamurthy and S. Srinivasa Iyengar led the party. Though the character of the organisation was heterogeneous compared to the communal Justice Party, it was largely dominated by Brahmins. The party contested in all provincial elections between 1923 and 1934 with the exception of the 1930 election which it did not participate officially due to the Civil Disobedience Movement though some of the members of the party contested as independents. The party emerged as the single largest party in the 1926 and 1934 Assembly elections but refused to form the provincial government under the existing dyarchy system. In 1934, the Madras Province Swarajya Party merged with the All India Swarajya Party which subsequently merged with the Indian National Congress when it contested the 1935 elections to the Imperial Legislative Council held as per the Government of India Act 1935.

Chittaranjan Das

Chittaranjan Das (popularly called Deshbandhu "Friend of the country") (November 5, 1870-June 16, 1925) was an eminent Bengali lawyer and a major figure in the Indian independence movement.

Personal Life

He belonged to the famous Das family of Telirbagh, in Bikrampur, Dhaka (now in Bangladesh). He was the son of Bhuban Mohan Das, and nephew of the Brahmo social reformer Durga Mohan Das. Some of his cousins were Satish Ranjan Das, Sudhi Ranjan Das, Sarala Roy and Lady Abala Bose. His eldest grandson is Siddhartha Shankar Ray and granddaughter is Justice Manjula Bose.

Career

Educated in England, where he became a Barrister, his public career began in 1909 when he successfully defended Aurobindo Ghosh on charges of involvement in the previous year's Alipore bomb case.

He was a leading figure in Bengal during the Non-Cooperation Movement of 1919-1922, and initiated the ban on British clothes, setting an example by burning his own European clothes and wearing Khadi clothes.

He brought out a newspaper called *Forward* and later changed its name to *Liberty* to fight the British Raj. When the Calcutta Corporation was formed, he became its first Mayor. He resigned his presidency of the Indian National Congress at the Gaya session after losing a motion on "No Council Entry" to Gandhi's faction. He then founded the Swaraj Party, with Motilal Nehru, to express his immoderate opinions.

He was a believer of non-violence and constitutional methods for the realisation of national independence, and advocated communal harmony and championed the cause of national education. His legacy was carried forward by his disciples, and notably by Subhash Chandra Bose.

He is generally referred to by the honorific Desh Bandhu meaning "friend of the nation."

In 1925, Das's health began to fail and in May he withdrew to a mountain home in Darjeeling, where Mahatma Gandhi visited him. On 16 June 1925, with a severe fever, he died.

The funeral procession in Calcutta was led by Gandhi, who said:

Deshbandhu was one of the greatest of men... He dreamed... and talked of freedom of India and of nothing else... His heart knew no difference between Hindus and Mussalmans and I should like to tell Englishmen, too, that he bore no ill-will to them. Das, Chitta Ranjan (1870-1925) better known as CR Das and popularly known as *Deshabandhu*, was one of the most dynamic political leaders of twentieth century Bengal. Born in Calcutta on 5 November 1870, he belonged to an upper middle class family of vikramapura in the district of Munshiganj. His father Bhuban Mohan Das was a solicitor of the Calcutta High Court. He received his early education at the London Missionary Society's Institution at Bhawanipur (Calcutta). He passed the Entrance Examination in 1885 and obtained his graduation degree in 1890 from the Presidency College, Calcutta. He went to England, joined the Inner Temple and was called to the Bar in 1894. In the same year he returned to India and enrolled himself as a Barrister at the

Calcutta High Court. The trial of Aurobindo Ghosh in 1908 brought CR Das to the forefront of his profession. He defended the case so brilliantly that Aurovinda was finally acquitted. He was the defence counsel in the Dhaka Conspiracy Case, which was initiated in 1910-11. He was an expert in both civil and criminal law.

Responding to the call of MK Gandhi during the non-cooperation movement he left his lucrative practice at the Bar and took a leading part in the boycott of the visit of the Prince of Wales to Calcutta in 1921. The government imprisoned him on many occasions. CR Das, however, strongly criticised the announcement of the suspension of the Non-cooperation Movement by Gandhi and condemned it as a serious mistake. In his opinion, this action of Gandhi demoralised the political workers to a great extent.

At this critical hour, he came forward with his formula of the Council Entry Programme, or non-cooperation from within the Councils. He was vehemently opposed to the Congress principle of boycotting the Legislatures. He held that entry must be gained into the Legislatures with a view to offering uniform, continuous and consistent obstruction to the government. His proposal of Council-Entry was, however, rejected by the annual session of the Indian national congress, held at Gaya in December 1922. Thereafter he resigned the presidentship of the Congress and laid the foundation of the Swarajya Party within the Congress in collaboration with Pandit Motilal Nehru, Hakim Azmal Khan, the Ali brothers and others. In the election to the Bengal Legislative Council, held in 1923, the Swarajya Party achieved a remarkable victory.

Deshabandhu was of the opinion that the obstructionist policy of the *Swarajists* would not succeed without the wholehearted cooperation of the Muslim members who formed a substantial group in the Bengal Legislative Council. Indeed he was a political realist with deep-rooted convictions and never diverted himself even in the face of the most vigorous opposition. Himself an ardent advocate of Hindu-Muslim unity, he succeeded in resolving the communal problem of Bengal in a memorable way. He won over the Muslims of Bengal to his side through an agreement commonly known as the bengal pact. The terms of the agreement were accepted at a meeting of the Swarajya Council Party held on

16 December 1923. Unfortunately the Pact was opposed by many of the Congress leaders of Bengal. The Bengali middle class Hindus, led by SN Banerjee, BC Pal and others, offered stubborn resistance to it. They feared that the Pact would weaken the political influence of the Hindu community. They accused CR Das of surrendering the rights of the Hindus. Even many moderate Hindu leaders held that CR Das had gone too far in trying to win the confidence of the Muslims.

The Muslims of the province welcomed the Pact wholeheartedly. But they were disillusioned when the Pact was rejected by the Cocanada Session of the Indian National Congress, held in December 1923. In their opinion the blunder that the Cocanada Congress had committed was the worst in the history of the Congress movement and dealt a serious blow to the cause of Hindu-Muslim unity and the cause for which the Congress stood.

CR Das stood solid as a rock in the face of all oppositions. He criticised the stand of the Indian National Congress and declared: "You may delete the Bengal Pact from the resolutions but you cannot delete Bengal from the Indian National Congress Bengal will not be deleted in this unceremonious fashion. I cannot understand the arguments of those who cry 'delete the Bengal Pact'... Is Bengal untouchable? Will you deny Bengal the right of suggestion on such a vital question? If you do, Bengal can take care of itself. You can not refuse Bengal the right to make a suggestion". Though rejected by the Indian Congress, he, however, succeeded in getting the terms of the Pact ratified by the Bengal Provincial Congress Conference, held at Sirajganj in June 1924.

CR Das was elected the first Mayor of the Calcutta corporation following the victory of the *Swarajists* in the election of that organisation in 1924 and was reelected for the next term also. He presided over the All India Trade Union Congress held at Lahore and Calcutta in 1923 and 1924 respectively. He presided over the Bengal Provincial Conference held at Faridpur in 1925. He founded the weekly *Forward*, the organ of the Swarajya Party in 1923. He also founded the *Municipal Gazette*, the official organ of the Calcutta Corporation in 1924. He was against caste distinctions and untouchability. He favoured women's emancipation and encouraged female education as well as widow remarriage. His advocacy of inter-caste marriage is proved by the marriage of his own daughters with Brahmin and Kayastha families.

Deshabandhu died in June 1925 when he was only fifty-five. His premature death came as a blow to the cause of communal harmony of Bengal and India as well. 'If he had not died a premature death', observed Abul Kalam Azad, 'he would have created a new atmosphere in the country'. He added, 'It is a matter of regret that after he died, some of his followers assailed his position and his declaration was repudiated. The result was that the Muslims of Bengal moved away from the Congress and the first seed of partition was sown'

Motilal Nehru

Motilal Nehru (6 May 1861 – 6 February 1931) was an early Indian independence activist and leader of the Indian National Congress. He was the founder patriarch of India's most powerful political family, the Nehru-Gandhi family.

Early Life

Motilal Nehru was born in Garden Grove, to Ganga Dhar in a Kashmiri Pandit family. He became one of the first generation of young Indians to receive a 'Western-style' college education. He attended Muir Central College at Allahabad, but failed to appear for the final year B.A examinations. Later he qualified "Bar at law" from Cambridge and then enlisted as a lawyer in the English courts.

Career

Nehru became a barrister and settled in the city of Allahabad, Uttar Pradesh. Many of Motilal's suits involved civil cases and soon he made a mark for himself in the legal profession of Allahabad. With the success of his practice, ne bought a large family home in the Civil Lines of the city and aptly christened the house Anand Bhavan (lit. Abode of happiness). In 1909 he reached the pinnacle of his legal career by gaining the approval to appear in the Privy Council of Great Britain. His frequent visits to Europe, angered the Kashmiri Brahmin community as he refused to perform the traditional "prayashchit" or reformation ceremony after crossing the ocean (according to Orthodox Hinduism, one lost his caste after crossing the ocean, and was required to perform certain rites to regain caste).

Nehru was a man of many elitist habits and had a westernized lifestyle. He was one of the moderate, wealthy leaders of the Indian National Congress. Under the influence of Mahatma Gandhi in 1918, Nehru became one of the first to transform his life to exclude western clothes and material goods, adopting a more native Indian lifestyle. To meet the expenses of his large family and large family homes (he built Swaraj Bhavan later), Nehru had to occasionally return to his practice of law.

Political Career

Motilal Nehru twice served as President of the Congress Party. He was arrested during the Non-Cooperation Movement. Although initially close to Gandhi, he openly criticized Gandhi's suspension of civil resistance in 1922 due to the murder of policemen by a riotous mob in Chauri Chaura in Uttar Pradesh. Motilal joined the Swaraj Party, which sought to enter the British-sponsored councils.

In 1923, Nehru was elected to the new Central Legislative Assembly of British India in New Delhi and became leader of the Opposition. In that role, he was able to secure the defeat, or at least the delay, of Finance bills and other legislation. He agreed to join a Committee with the object of promoting the recruitment of Indian officers into the Indian Army, but this decision contributed to others going further and joining the Government itself.

In March 1926, Nehru demanded a representative conference to draft a constitution conferring full Dominion status on India, to be and enacted by the parliament. This demand was rejected by the Assembly, and as a result Nehru and his colleagues left the Assembly and returned to the Congress.

The entry of Motilal's glamorous, highly-educated son Jawaharlal Nehru into politics in 1916, started the most powerful and influential Indian political dynasty. When in 1929, Motilal Nehru handed over the Congress presidency to Jawaharlal (Jawaharlal was elected, with Gandhi's backing), it greatly pleased Motilal and Nehru family admirers to see the son take over from his father. Jawaharlal had opposed his father's preference for dominion status, and had not left the Congress Party when Motilal helped found the Swaraj Party.

Motilal Nehru chaired the famous Nehru Commission in 1928, that was a counter to the all-British Simon Commission. Nehru's Report, the first constitution written by Indians only, conceived a dominion status for India within the Empire, akin to Australia, New Zealand and Canada. It was endorsed by the Congress Party, but rejected by more radical Indians who sought complete independence, and by many Muslims who didn't feel their interests, concerns and rights were properly represented.

N. C. Kelkar

Sahityasamrat Narsimha Chintaman or Tatyasaheb Kelkar (24 August 1872-14 October 1947) was close associate of Tilak. He was editor and trustee of Kesari. He was assoicated with Shikshana Prasarak Mandali Pune, e education society in Pune established in 1904.

After the death of Tilak in 1920, he became one of the foremost leaders of the Tilakites in the Congrss. He was member of the Viceroy's Council during 1924-1929. He was president of Akhil Bharat Hindu Mahasabha twice at Jabalpur in 1928 and Delhi at 1932.

Madan Mohan Malaviya

Madan Mohan Malaviya (1861–1946) was an Indian politician, educationist, and freedom fighter notable for his role in the Indian independence movement and his espousal of Hindu nationalism. Later in life, we was also addressed as 'Mahamana'.

He was the President of the Indian National Congress on three occasions and today is most remembered as the founder of the largest residential university in Asia, with over 12,000 students living on its campus, Banaras Hindu University (BHU) at Varanasi in 1916, of which he also remained the Vice Chancellor, 1919–1938 He was one of the founders of Scouting in India.

Early Life and Education

Malaviya was born at Allahabad, Uttar Pradesh on 25 December 1861, to an orthodox Hindu Brahman family of Brijnath and Moona

Devi. The fifth child in a family of five brothers and two sisters. His ancestors, known for their Sanskrit scholarship, originally hailed from Malwa, hence came to be known as 'Malaviyas'. His father Pandit Brijnath was also a learned man in Sanskrit scriptures, and used to recite the *Bhagvat Katha* to earn a living.

Madan Mohan's education began at the age of five in Sanskrit, when he was sent to Pandit Hardeva's Dharma Gyanopadesh Pathshala, where he completed his primary education and later another school run by Vidha Vardini Sabha. Mohan soon joined a Hindi medium, Allahabad Zila School (Allahabad District School), now a diligent boy, started writing poems under the pen name *Makarand* which were published in journals and magazines, eventually he matriculated in 1879 from and joined the Muir Central College, now known as Allahabad University. With his family facing tough financial condition, Harrison college's Principal started giving a monthly scholarship, and finally he passed his B.A. from the Calcutta University in 1884, as Allahabad University was formed only in 1887.

Career

Though he wanted to pursue an M.A. in Sanskrit his family conditions didn't allowed it and his father wanted him to take his family profession of Bhagavad recital, thus in July 1884 Madan Mohan Malaviya started his career as teacher in Allahabad District School. In December 1886, he attended the IInd Congress session in Calcutta under chairmanship of Dadabhai Naoroji, where he spoke on the issue of representation in Councils. His address not only impress Dadabhai but also Raja Rampal Singh, ruler of Kalakankar estate near Allahabad, who has started a Hindi weekly *Hindustan* but was looking for a suitable editor to turn it into a daily. Thus in July 1887, he left his school job and joined as the editor of the nationalist weekly, he remained her for two and a half years, and left for Allahabad to joined L.L.B., it was here that it was offered co-editorship of *The Indian Union*, an English daily. After finishing his law degree, he started practicing law at Allahabad District Court in 1891, and moved to Allahabad High Court by December 1893

Malaviya became the president of the Indian National Congress in 1909 and in 1918. Like many of the contemporary leaders of

Indian National Congress he was a Moderate. Though, Scouting in India was officially founded in British India in 1909, at the Bishop Cotton's Boys School in Bangalore, Scouting for native Indians was started by Justice Vivian Bose, Pandit Madan Mohan Malaviya, Pandit Hridayanath Kunzru, Girija Shankar Bajpai, Annie Besant and George Arundale, in 1913, he also started a Scouting inspired organisation called *Seva Samithi*.

In April 1911, Annie Besant met him and they decided to unite their forces and work for a common Hindu University at Varanasi. Annie and fellow trustees of the Central Hindu College, which she has founded in 1898 also agreed to Government of India's precondition that the college should become a part of the new University. Thus Banaras Hindu University (BHU) was established in 1916, through under the Parliamentary legislation, 'B.H.U. Act 1915', today it remains a prominent institution of learning in India.

He remained a member of the Imperial Legislative Council from 1912 and when in 1919 it was converted to the Central Legislative Assembly it remained its member as well, till 1926.

In early 1920s, he became one of the important figures in the Non-cooperation movement of Mahatma Gandhi, and was subsequently arrested on 25 April 1932, along with 450 other Congress volunteers in Delhi, only a few days after he was appointed the President of Congress after the arrest of Sarojini Naidu.

Then in 1928 he joined Lala Lajpat Rai, Jawaharlal Nehru and many others in protesting against the Simon Commission, which had been set up by the British to consider India's future. Just as the "Buy British" campaign was sweeping England, he issued, on 30 May 1932, a manifesto urging concentration on the "Buy Indian" movement in India.

He also represented India at the First Round Table Conference in 1931. In 1939, he left the Vice chancellorship of BHU and was succeeded by none other than S. Radhakrishnan, who went on to become the President of India.

Malaviya popularised the slogan *Satyameva Jayate* (Truth alone will triumph).

Lala Lajpat Rai

Lala Lajpat Rai was an Indian author and politician who is chiefly remembered as a leader in the Indian fight for freedom from the British Raj. He was popularly known as *Punjab Kesari* (The Lion of Punjab). He was also the founder of Punjab National Bank and Lakshmi Insurance Company.

Early Life

(Born in Jagraon, on 28 January, India in 1865 in a Hindu Vysya Family, Lajpat Rai created a career of *reforming Indian policy through politics and writing.* (When studying law in Lahore, he continued to practice Hinduism. He became a large believer in the idea that Hinduism, above nationality, was the pivotal point upon which an Indian lifestyle must be based.) Hinduism, he believed, led to practices of peace to humanity, and the idea that when nationalist ideas were added to this peaceful belief system, a non-secular nation could be formed. His involvement with Hindu Mahasabhaite leaders gathered criticism from the Bharat Sabha as the Mahasabhas were anti-secularism, which did not conform with the system laid out by the Indian National Congress. This focus on Hindu practices in the subcontinent would ultimately lead him to the continuation of peaceful movements to create successful demonstrations for Indian independence.

Political Life

As the need for partition and independence took an important turn for the possible, Lajpat Rai's involvement became imperative to the Indian Independence Movement. His actions in anti-imperialist movements led to numerous arrests. He became an important member of the Arya Samaj. This political group was full of British-educated Indians who believed that Hinduism had a specific and direct impact on what it meant to be Indian. The group also took the ideas of a merged western and eastern world and promoted the view that the subcontinent had benefited from its coagulation. The involvement of the Arya Samaj in constitutional reform supported the freedom movement which took hold of the Indian population. Lajpat Rai led political rallies which taught how the history of the subcontinent had always been heading to the philosophical idea that it would become an independent nation.

(Lajpat Rai presided over the first session of the All India Trade Union Congress in 1920. In 1923, he became a member of the Imperial Legislative Assembly. He also went to Geneva to attend the eighth International Labour Conference in 1926 as a representative of Indian labour. He had an opportunity to watch the labour movement in the USA and England where he was required to prolong his stay for political reasons.)

In addition to espousing his philosophical principles, Lajpat Rai engaged heavily in direct action and protest against British rule. (He led the Punjab protests against the Amritsar Massacre (1919), the Non-Cooperation Movement (1919-1922), and the "Simon go back" demonstrations against the Simon Commission (1928)). He was repeatedly arrested.He disagreed, however, with Mohandas Gandhi's suspension of the movement due to the Chauri Chaura incident.(He formed the *Congress Independence Party*, which was particularly pro-Hindu in voice and policy)SS.

He was not only a good orator but also a prolific and versatile writer. His journal *Arya Gazette* concentrated mainly on subjects related to the Arya Samaj. *Bande Mataram* and *People*, contained his inspiring speeches to end oppression by the foreign rulers. He founded the Servants of the People Society, which worked for the freedom movement as well as for social reform in the country. He also wrote an autobiography in English titled *The Story of My Life*.

Simon Commission Protests

In 1928, Lajpat Rai led a procession with Pandit Madan Mohan Malaviya to demonstrate against the Simon Commission. During this procession, Rai became the target of a lathi charge (a form of crowd control in which the police use heavy staves or 'lathis' in Hindi) led by British police.

He was severely injured in the charge. Nevertheless, at a meeting held the same evening, he spoke with great vigour. His words at this meeting, *"Every blow aimed at me is a nail in the coffin of British imperialism"*, have become historic. Though he recovered from the fever and pain within three days, his health had received a permanent setback and on November 17, 1928, he died of his injuries. His death led to great disturbances in the country and it inspired national struggle for freedom.

Huseyn Shaheed Suhrawardy

Huseyn Shaheed Suhrawardy was a politician from Bengal in undivided India, and later in East Bengal, who served as the fifth Prime Minister of Pakistan from 1956 until 1957. He is also known for his controversial role in the Direct Action Day of August 16, 1946, following riots in Bengal on that day.

He was considered a favourite of Muhammad Ali Jinnah. He is also considered to be the first populist leader in Pakistan's history. He joined Awami League that Maulana Bashani formed and finally took ovrt the leadership from the Maulana. Awami League was the first opposition party in Pakistan those days against the Muslim League.

Early Life and Family

Suhrawardy was born on 8 September 1892 to a Muslim family in the town of Midnapore, now in West Bengal. He was the younger son of Justice Sir Zahid Suhrawardy, a prominent judge of the Calcutta High Court and of Khujastha Akhtar Banu (c. 1874–1919) a noted name in Urdu literature and scholar of Persian. Kujastha was the daughter of Maulana Ubaidullah Al Ubaidi Suhrawardy and sister of, amongst others, Lt. Col. Dr. Hassan Suhrawardy, OBE and Sir Abdullah Al-Mamun Suhrawardy.

Suhrawardy had an elder brother Shahid Suhrawardy.

Education and Marriage

Suhrawardy completed his undergraduate studies at St. Xavier's College, and completed a masters degree at the University of Calcutta. Afterwards, he moved to the United Kingdom to attend St. Catherine's College, Oxford University from where he obtained a BCL degree. On leaving Oxford, he was called to the bar at Gray's Inn. He then started his practice at Calcutta High Court.

In 1920, Suhrawardy married Begum Niaz Fatima, daughter of Sir Abdur Rahim, the then home minister of the Bengal Province of British India and later President of India's Central Legislative Assembly. Suhrawardy had two children from this marriage; Ahmed Shahab Suhrawardy and Begum Akhtar Sulaiman. Ahmed Suhrawardy died from pneumonia whilst he was a student in

London in 1940. Begum Akhtar Sulaiman was married to Shah Ahmed Sulaiman (son of Justice Sir Shah Sulaiman) and had one child, Shahida Jamil (who later became the first female Pakistani Federal Minister for Law). Shahida Jamil has two sons, Zahid Jamil (a lawyer in Pakistan) and Shahid Jamil (a solicitor in London).

Begum Niaz Fatima died in 1922. In 1940 Suhrawardy married Vera Alexandrovna Tiscenko Calder Begum Noor Jahan, a Russian actress from the Moscow Art Theatre and protege of Olga Knipper. The couple divorced in 1951 and had one child, Rashid Suhrawardy (aka Robert Ashby), who is an actor living in London. Vera later settled in America.

Return to India

Suhrawardy returned to the subcontinent in 1921 as a practising barrister of the Calcutta High Court. He became involved in politics in Bengal. Initially, he joined the Swaraj Party, a group within the Indian National Congress, and became an ardent follower of Chittaranjan Das. He played a major role in signing the Bengal Pact in 1923.

Suhrawardy became the Deputy Mayor of the Calcutta Corporation at the age of 31 in 1924, and the Deputy Leader of the Swaraj Party in the Provincial Assembly. However, following the death of Chittaranjan Das in 1925, he began to disassociate himself with the Swaraj Party and eventually joined Muslim League. He served as Minister of Labour, and Minister of Civil Supplies under Khawaja Nazimuddin among other positions. In the Bengal Muslim League, Suhrawardy and Abul Hashim led a progressive line against the conservative stream led by Nazimuddin and Akram Khan.

In 1946, Suhrawardy established and headed a Muslim League government in Bengal. It was the only Muslim League government in India at that time.

Direct Action Day

Sir Frederick Burrows declared August 16, 1946 to be a public holiday following the Direct Action Day called by Jinnah to protest against the Cabinet Mission plan for the independence of India. Suhrawardy, acting on the advice of R.L. Walker, the then chief secretary of Bengal, requested Governor Burrows to declare a public holiday on that day. Walker made this proposal with the hope that the risk of conflicts, especially those related to picketing, would be minimized if government offices, commercial houses and shops remained closed throughout Calcutta on the 16th.

The intensity of Direct Action Day was at its worst in the capital Calcutta. Suhrawardy was controversially blamed by Congress leaders for both orchestrating and not taking steps to prevent the carnage and for trying to suppress the news of the same from the media.

However, commentators view the riots of Direct Action Day as being caused as a result of a combination of factors including a power vacuum created by the impending withdrawal of the British from Government that lead to the lack of immediate and adequate army and police involvement in trying to control the riots.

Political brinkmanship by both the Congress and Muslim League leadership played a major factor in stirring the passions of the supporters of both the Hindu and Muslim communities.

On the day, Suhrawardy put forth a great deal of effort to bring reluctant British officials around to calling the army in from Sealdah Rest Camp. Unfortunately, British officials did not send the army out until 1.45am on the 17th. Accordingly, commentators conclude that a substantial number of lives could have been saved if the army had been deployed earlier.

Independence

In 1947, the balance of power in Bengal shifted from the Muslim League to the Indian National Congress, and Suhrawardy stepped down from the Chief Ministership. Unlike other Muslim League stalwarts of India, he did not leave his hometown immediately for the newly established Pakistan. Anticipating revenge of Hindus against Muslims in Calcutta after the transfer of power, Suhrawardy sought help from Gandhi. Gandhi was persuaded to stay and pacify tempers in Calcutta, but he agreed to do so on the condition that Suhrawardy share the same roof with him so that they could appeal to Muslims and Hindus alike to live in peace. "Adversity makes strange bed-fellows," Gandhi remarked in his prayer meeting.

Political Life in East Bengal

Upon the formation of Pakistan, Suhrawardy maintained his work in politics, continuing to focus on East Bengal as it became after partition of by the British colonialist. In 1949 he formed the Awami Muslim League, which would develop into the Awami League.

In the 1950s, Suhrawardy worked to consolidate political parties in East Pakistan to balance the politics of West Pakistan. He, along with other leading Bengali leaders A.K. Fazlul Huq and Maulana Abdul Hamid Khan Bhashani, formed a political alliance in the name of *Jukta Front* which won a landslide victory in 1954 general election of East Pakistan. Under Muhammad Ali Bogra, Huseyn Shaheed Suhrawardy would serve as Law Minister and later become the head of opposition parties.

Prime Minister of Pakistan

In 1956, he was made Prime Minister by President of Pakistan Iskander Mirza after the resignation of Chaudhry Muhammad Ali. Suhrawardy inherited a political schism that was forming in Pakistan between the Muslim League and newer parties, such as the Republican party. The schism was fed by the attempt to consolidate the four provinces of West Pakistan into one province, so as to balance the fact that East Pakistan existed as only one province. The plan was opposed in West Pakistan, and the cause was taken up by the Muslim League and religious parties. Suhrawardy supported the plan, but the vast opposition to it stalled its progress.

In order to divert attention from the controversy over the "One Unit" plan as it was called, Suhrawardy tried to ease economic differences between East and West Pakistan. However, despite his intentions, these initiatives only led to more political frictions, and was worsened when Suhrawardy tried to give more financial allocations to East Pakistan than West Pakistan from aids and grants. Such moves led to a threat of dismissal looming over Suhrawardy's head, and he resigned in 1957.

His contribution in formulating 1956 constitution of Pakistan was substantial as he played a vital role in incorporating provisions for civil liberties and universal adult franchise in line with his adherence to parliamentary form of liberal democracy. In the foreign policy arena, he is considered to be one of the pioneers of Pakistan's pro-United States stand. He was also the first Pakistani Prime Minister to visit China and establish an official diplomatic friendship between Pakistan and China (a friendship that Henry Kissinger would later use to make his now-famous secret trip to China in July 1971).

Atomic Policy and Civilian Nuclear Program

During 1950s, Pakistan was suffering from severe energy crises. It was Huseyn Shaheed Suhrawardy's Prime Ministerial term when Pakistan Atomic Energy Commission (PAEC) was established by a Parliamentary Act of 1956. He also appointed Dr. Nazir Ahmad, a noted physicist and scientist, to be its first Chairman. Under Dr. Nazir Ahmad's direction, Pakistan started its civilian nuclear program. Prime Minister Suhrawardy also allotted PAEC to sat up its new pilot-nuclear labs. He played an important role in establishing of Nuclear research institutes in West Pakistan. He also allowed PAEC to established the first nuclear power plant in Karachi. However, after his removal from office, the Nuclear Power Plant Project was undermined by a political turmoil in the country. The Pakistani Civilian Nuclear Program was also frozen by Ayub Khan's military regime for more than a decade.

Post-political Life and Death

Disqualified from politics under the military regime of Ayub Khan, Huseyn Shaheed Suhrawardy died in Lebanon in 1963. His death was officially due to complications from heart problems, though some have alleged he was poisoned. After a befitting funeral attended by a huge crowd, he was buried at Suhrawardy Udyan in Dhaka

Vithalbhai Patel

Vithalbhai Patel (1873-22 October 1933) was an Indian legislator and political leader, and co-founder of the Swaraj Party.

Early Life

Born in Nadiad, in the Indian state of Gujarat, Vithalbhai Jhaverbhai Patel was the third of five Patel brothers, four years elder to Vallabhbhai Patel, raised in the village of Karamsad.

Vithalbhai educated himself in Nadiad and in Bombay, and worked as a pleader (a junior lawyer) in the courts of Godhra and Borsad. At a very young age, he was married to a girl from another village, Diwaliba.

His younger brother, Vallabhbhai Patel, had similarly studied by himself and worked as a pleader. Studying in England was a dream for both men. Vallabhbhai had saved enough money and ordered his passport and travel tickets, when the postman delivered them to Vithalbhai, it having been addressed to a *Mr. V.J. Patel, Pleader*. Vithalbhai insisted on travelling on those documents actually meant for Vallabhbhai, pointing out that it would be socially criticized that an older brother followed the lead of the younger. Respecting his brother despite the obvious cruelty of fate on his own hard work, Vallabhbhai allowed him to proceed to England, and even paid for his stay.

Vithalbhai entered the Middle Temple Inn in London, and completed the 36-month course in 30, emerging at the top of his class. Returning to Gujarat in 1913, Vithalbhai became an important barrister in the courts of Bombay and Ahmedabad. However, his wife died in 1915, and he remained a widower.

Political Career

Patel entered politics before his more renowned brother, winning a seat on the Bombay Legislative Council, a body with no real functions. Although failing to achieve anything concrete in terms of the fight for national independence, self-government or public welfare, Patel grew popular and respected by his oratorical and witty mastery and belittling of the Raj's officials, winning many a battle of wit, which bore little overall significance. In 1923 he was elected to the Central Legislative Assembly, a chamber of elected and appointed Indian and British representatives with limited legislative powers, and in 1925 became the Assembly's president, or speaker.

Although never truly accepting the philosophy and leadership of Mohandas Gandhi, Patel joined the Congress and the struggle for freedom. He had no regional base of support, yet he was an influential leader who expanded the struggle through fiery speeches and articles published. When Gandhi aborted the struggle in 1922 following the Chauri Chaura Incident, Patel left the Congress to form the Swaraj Party with Chittaranjan Das and Motilal Nehru, which would seek to foil the Raj by sabotaging the government after gaining entry in the councils. The party only succeeded in dividing the Congress and finally itself, but Patel and others were important voices who rebelled against the leadership of Gandhi when the nation anguished over the abortion of the Non-Cooperation Movement

Last Years

In 1929, supporters of the government of India tried to have Patel removed as president of the Imperial Legislative Assembly, but were thwarted by the Viceroy, Lord Irwin, who at the time was trying to win over radical nationalists. He failed to do so, which led to Gandhi's launching of the civil disobedience movement in 1930, and Patel resigned from the Legislative Assembly in sympathy with this movement. He rejoined the Congress upon the declaration of *Purna Swaraj* (*Complete Independence*), and was subsequently imprisoned, but with his health deteriorating, he was released from prison in 1931 and went to Europe for medical treatment.

Patel gave up the Congress after the end of the Salt Satyagraha, became a fierce critic of Gandhi and a strong ally of Subhas Chandra Bose. Bose had been released in 1933 from the Bhowali Sanitorium in UP for treatment in Europe-Vienna and Vithalbhai had also gone to Vienna for treatment. As both the invalids had similar political views, they came nearer to each other. They in fact in a joint statement stated, inter alia, "...as a political leader Mahatma Gandhi has failed.... ad a change of leadership is necessary..."

Bose and Patel travelled across Europe, gathering funds and political support-among others, they met Éamon de Valera, President of Ireland. While Bose's health improved, Patel's illness worsened. However, impressed by the work of Subhas and aware that he had no private means nor would he receive any "penny" from the Congress for his political work, he willed the residual part of his property amounting to Rs.1,20,000/-to Subhas for his political work on Oct 2, 1933 and died Geneva, Switzerland, on 22 October 1933 and was cremated in Bombay on 10 November.

Gandhi and Sardar Patel wanted Subhas to spend the money as per the whims and fancies of the Congress, and when he refused, there was a litigation in Bombay High Court. The English masters of the High Court felt that the term "Political Upliftment of India" was too vague a term and deprived Bose of the proceeds. The strangest thing in the whole affair was that Sardr Patel had kept a neutral attitude during the whole affair, but in his official biography published by Navajivan Press, Ahmedabad the very authenticity of the will was questioned...

Patel, Vithalbhai (1873-1933)

Some persons are born great, some achieve greatness and greatness is thrust on others. Vithalbhai Patel, who was born at Nadiad in 1873 and rose to Himalayan heights on the Indian National scene, belonged to the second category.

His early education began at a village school at Karamsad when he was only five. While at school, when he was only nine, he had to get married only to please his parents. After passing the School Final examination in 1891, he passed the District Pleader's examination four years later. He along with his younger brother, the late Sardar Vallabhabhai, then moved to Borsad and started legal practice.

During the seven years of legal practice at Borsad, Vithalbhai conducted several civil and criminal cases. One of the important cases in which he appeared was what was known as the Shukla Case. Mr. Shukla, the then Sub-Judge of Borsad, was alleged to be corrupt and several complaints were made against him. Vithalbhai moved the High Court to hold a public enquiry into the doings of this notorious officer who was later found guilty and was forced to retire.

After a successful career at the Bar for nearly eight years, Vithalbhai decided to go to England to become a Barrister. During his three years' stay in that country, he came into contact with Dadabhai Naoroji and learned from him the complex Indian problems and the need for an all-round agitation-through the Press, the Platform and the Legislative-to awaken British conscience for the grant of freedom for his motherland. So, he decided to enter the Bombay Legislative Council through the constituency of District Local Board of Gujarat. He got himself elected to the Kaira District Local Board, defeating a powerful rival by a liberal margin.

The Morley-Minto reforms gave Vithlabhai an opportunity of entering the Legislative Council in 1912. In a House of 48 members including officials and ex-offcio members, 21 were elected and 14 non-officio had been nominated. This was an opportunity for him to bring together all the non-official members, both elected and nominated, together on one platform.

With the active help of Dr. R. P. Paranjpye and Mr. B. S. Kamat, both nominated non-officials, he founded an Association of Non-Official Members of the Bombay Legislative Council. Sir Dinshaw Petit joined along with Vithalbhai. By thus bringing together all non-official forces, Vithalbhai succeeded to a great extent in influencing the decisions of the Government in several matters affecting public interests.

In March 1915 he moved a resolution in the Council for the fixation of the salary of the Official Assignee who by way of commission earned an income of Rs. 10,000 a month. He urged that the officer should be paid a fixed salary. Lord Willingdon, the Governor of Bombay who was in the Chair, fully appreciated the viewpoint of Vithalbhai and promised to consider the desirability of putting that dignitary on a payscale commensurate with his duties and responsibilities.

Vithalbhai's great achievement was the passage of the Primary Education Bill which was an enabling measure permitting Municipalities to introduce free and compulsory primary education in their respective areas. It was based more or less on Gokhale's Bill which had been introduced in the Imperial Legislative Council. As a member of the Bandra Minicipality, Vithalbhia was responsible for introducing compulsory primary education in that suburb. Lord Willingdon, in his capacity as president, paid Vithalbhai a glowing tribute for his painstaking efforts in piloting such a useful measure.

The members of the Bombay Legislative Council showed their appreciation of the valuable services rendered by Vithalbhai by electing him unanimously to the Imperial Legislative Council in the vacancy caused by resignation of Ibrahim Rahimtoola.

In the Imperial Council, Vithalbhai introduced a Bill to make valid by law marriages between Hindus of different castes. This was on the lines of Basu's Bill which had lapsed. There was an uproar from the orthodox members of the Council led by Pandit Madan Mohan Malaviya, while Sapru, Shastri and Khanparde warmly supported this measure. The Home Member, William Vincent, on behalf of the Government said that they were prepared to accept the motion for leave to introduce the Bill and circulate it for eliciting public opinion. Owing to the dissolution of the Council, the Bill lapsed.

Early in 1919, two Bills, viz., the Criminal Law (Emergency Powers) and the Indian Criminal Law (Amendment) Bill, popularly known as "Black Bills", based on the recommendations of the Indian Sedition Committee presided over by Lord Rowlatt, were introduced by the Government in the Imperial Council. Earlier, the Bombay Special Congress, of which Vithalbhai was the moving spirit and Chairman of the Reception Committee, had condemned the recommendations of this Committee (Rowlatt Committee) as they interfered with the "Fundamental Rights" of the Indian people and "came in the way of the healthy growth of public opinion".

In order to fight this few Legislative, Gandhiji threatened to start a Satyagraha if it was proceeded with. Vithalbhai decided to fight the same from inside the Legislative Chamber with all his might. First, he would move for the postponement of the very introduction of the Bills for six months. He told the House that revolutionary crime was the outcome of political and administrative stagnation. In his opinion, the remedy did not lie in repressive measures, which in turn brought revolutionary crime into existence.

When the Government persisted in proceeding with the Bills, he moved over 250 amendments to several clauses of the Bill, with the result that it took several days to get the legislative passed by the official majority. Even night sittings had to be resorted to in order to expedite the passing of this unwanted measure.

But unfortunately for the Government, the sustained agitation put up by Gandhiji and other progressive political organisations had its effect and the Act remained a dead letter.

In August 1917, the new Secretary of State for India, Mr. Edwin Montagu, made an important announcement in Parliament in which he declared that the goal of British policy in India was the progressive realisation of responsible government. To that end, he hoped to visit India and make the necessary recommendations to the British Government. The report when published was strongly critised by all Parties except the Moderates. The Special Congress (1918), at which Vithalbhai played a prominent role, expressed its opinion that the recommendations made in the Montagu-Chelmsford Report were unsatisfactory and disappointing.

Early in 1919, Montagu introduced in the House of Commons his India Bill and after its second reading, a Select Committee with Lord Selbourne as Chairman was appointed to examine the provisions and to hear evidence. Several Indian political parties sent members to England to do propaganda work in connection with this Bill. The Congress Party was represented by Vithalbhai and Madhav Rao and later they were joined by Tilak, Khaparde, Hasan Imam and Bepin Chandra Pal. Vithalbhai acted as Secretary.

An effort was made to reconcile the difference between the moderates and nationalist opinion on the Bill but it failed. The British Committee of the Congress also did not co-operate with the Congress delegation and Vithalbhai had to plough a lonely furrow along with his colleagues.

In order to create a favourable opinion among the British public on India, Vithalbhai in a reasoned memorandum to the Committee urges the necessity for the repeal of all repressive laws including the Rowlatt Act and inclusion in the proposed Bill of a Declaration of Rights in order that the reforms may be acceptable to the people of India as a sincere attempt to place the country on the road to responsible government.

He and Madhav Rao were closely examined by the Selbounce Committee and they were very much impressed by Vithlabhai" knowledge of constitutional questions. Whenever Vithalbhai was free, he addressed along with his colleagues, Tilak and Pal, several meetings both in London and in the suburbs. The British Committee of the Congress, although it did not co-operate with the Congress delegation, recorded its appreciation of the valuable services rendered by the Delegation and especially by Vithalbhai Patel, "to whose industry, tact and good judgement much of the success is due."

In 1921 Vithalbhai resigned from the Indian Assembly to join the Satyagraha movement started by Gandhiji and Vallabhbhai at

Bardoli. Though he had not much faith in this no-tax movement, he plunged into it for the sake of his leader, Gandhiji. He believed that undermining and overthrowing British Imperialism was a material problem and no amount of nonviolent non-cooperation would serve this purpose.

In 1922 he desired to enter the Bombay Municipal Corporation but there was a hitch. He was not a voter because he had not been paying any taxes. He got a friend's car transferred to his name and became a tax-payer. He was elected from the Mandvi Ward. Soon after, he founded the National Party and was elected Chairman of that Party. Thereafter, he was elected Chairman of the Schools Committee and persuaded that Committee to introduce free and compulsory education in 'F' and 'G' Wards.

He also introduced the teaching of Hindi and gave special encouragement to the education of the scheduled castes. Swadeshi was introduced in all departments of the Corporation. At his instance the Corporation passed a resolution banning the use of articles manufactured in any other part of the British Empire by any Department of the Corporation except when they were not available in any other part of the world.

A year later, he was elected President of the Corporation. He took great interest in the founding of the G. S. Medical College and the K. E.M. Hospital. One of the most important acts of his presidential regime was the civic address to Gandhiji, the resolution for which was carried against the strongest opposition led by Homi Mody. His refusal to receive Lord Reading, the new Viceroy, and attend the functions in his honour greatly upset his Progressive Party colleagues. When he resigned his membership of the Corporation a year later, the then Municipal Commissioner, H. B. Clayton, said that no Councillor had ever the least occasion to doubt the impartiality of his decisions. This was a great tribute paid to any President by a prominent member of the Indian Civil Service.

Vithalbhai entered the Indian Legislative Assembly in January 1924 on the Swarajya Party ticket and was elected Deputy Leader of the Party. During the first year, two important Bills to further amend the Indian Penal Code and Code of Criminal Procedure were introduced by him. By the first one, he wanted that the punishment for sedition should not be transportation or rigorous imprisonment but simple imprisonment; while by the other, he wanted to do away with some of the racial discrimination provided in the original Act. He, however, did not succeed in getting them passed by the Assembly.

In August 1925 when the Assembly was called upon to have an elected President in pursuance of the provisions of the Government of India Act, 1919, Vithalbhai was elected President. The first thing he did was to do away with racial discrimination in the matter of toilet facilities. There were separate toilet rooms for Europeans and Indians in the Assembly Chamber and he ruled that these distinctions should go. Secondly, he wanted every member including those on the Treasury Benches to bow to the Chair whenever he entered or left the Chamber. This rule was very much resented by the European Members of the Assembly.

This Assembly was dissolved in the following year and Vithalbhai got himself re-elected to that august body. This time he was unanimously re-elcted as President. Later in the year, he paid a visit to England on a study tour or Parliamentary affairs. He paid a courtesy call on Lord Birkenhead who was them the Secretary of State for India, but that dignitary was absent and did not care to reply although Vithalbhai left his card before leaving the India incident Council. Vithalbhai complained about this incident to the King on whom he called a few days after.

The introduction of the Reserve Bank Bill met with many reverses. The Government wanted to bar members of the Legislative from being appointed on the Board of the Reserve Bank, but this proposal was lost by a large majority. According to Vithalbhai, the methods adopted by the Government in dealing with this Bill vitiated the proprieties of the House and constituted an abuse of its forms and procedure. Further, it provided a Shareholder's Bank as against the decision of the Assembly in favour of a State Bank. The Government felt that Vithalbhai had made their position weak and withdrew the Bill.

A little later, the Government introduced a Public Safety Bill which was a measure to sabotage the growth of Indian Nationalism in the country and for the suppression of the legitimate activities for the political and economic advancement of the masses. It received the strongest opposition and even nominated Indian members opposed the measure. After a heated debate, the report of the Select Committee on the Bill was put to the vote but there was a tie, and Vithalbhai in following the strict parliamentary tradition, gave his casting vote for the status quo. This action naturally enraged the Treasury Benches.

Three months later, the Government introduced a second Public Safety Bill with the object of putting down certain types of political propaganda which the Government considered objectionable. The speech with which the Home Member, Crerar, had initiated it, contained almost verbatim the charge-sheet against the Communists in the Conspiracy Case that was being heard before a Special Tribunal presided over by Mr. Justice Yorke at Meerut. Vithalbhai pointed out to the Government that in view of the Conspiracy Case in which thirty-one persons had been brought to trial the Government's arguments in support of the proposed Bill would prejudice the trial. He, therefore, suggested that the Bill should be postponed till the trial was over. But the Government was adamant.

Vithalbhai desired members to express their views whether it was possible to have a real and reasonable debate on the motion before the House in view of the pending prosecutions at Meerut. Further, the President asked the members to express their opinion on the powers of the Chair to intervene at that stage. These two points were argued at great length while the Government benches disputed the interpretation of the rules and standing orders by the Chair. They did not accept the advice offered by him. Vithalbhai felt that no real or reasonable debate on the Bill was possible. The only course left to him was to give his ruling which was his inherent right to do. In this surcharged atmosphere, two bombs were dropped from the visitor's gallery causing injury to some members. After the confusion subsided, Vithlabhai read out his ruling. He said that the Chair had inherent powers to rule out any motion on the ground that it involved an abuse of the forms and procedure of the House and, as such, he had no option but to rule it our of order. The Treasury benches were stunned at this ruling.

The Government lost no time in advising the Viceroy to take immediate steps to restrict the powers and authority of the

President. The Viceroy came to the Assembly Chamber and declared that he would avail himself of the authority conferred upon him under section 72 of the Government of India Act by issuing an Ordinance giving his Government the necessary powers to re-introduce the Public Safety Bill.

Vithlabhai greatly resented this move to publicly censure him in the very precincts of the House over which he was presiding with grace and dignity. As the Assembly was to be shortly prorogued and he was proceeding to England on a political mission, the only course left for him was to protest against the Viceregal pronouncement. No further move was, however, made to re-introduce this obnoxious Bill.

Vithlabhai's personal relations with Lord Irwin, however, remained as cordial as before. Both of them met often and exchanged views on a variety of topics of general interest.

During the latter part of 1927, the British Government appointed an all-white Commission under the Chairmanship of Sir John Simon. The whole country decided to boycott the Commission which arrived in India in 1928. The day of their arrival in Bombay was observed as a "Black Day" and demonstrations were held all over the country. Vithalbhai did not take any notice of the Commission although several attempts were made by the officials and others to persuade him to invite Simon to the Assembly Chamber. Vithalbhai would not oblige unless Simon paid a courtesy call on him at his house before an invitation could be extended. This Simon did later.

The Lahore Session of the Congress under the Presidency of Jawaharlal Nehru defined the political goal of India to be "complete Independence". Vithalbhai desired to be with the people rather than with the Legislature, of which he was the resignation which was accepted by Lord Irwin with very great regret.

He then plunged himself into the National Movement and courted attest but was released earlier on a serious illness. He left for Europe where he died in 1933.Thus ended the magnificent political career of a man of iron will. Vithalbhai had a mind sharp as a razor's edge and a keen intellect capable of solving difficult and intricate legal problems and disentangling the most complicated facts.

He had a subtle humour and readiness of wit which made his repartees often delightful and produced phrases and fancies of characteristic daintiness. He touched nothing that he did not adorn. His geniality was infectious.

Above all, Vithalbhai was a humanist and believed in the spirit of humanism transcending all barriers of caste, creed or colour.

Chittaranjan Das

Born-5 November 1870

Died-16 June 1925

Achievements-CR Das was an important personality in Bengal during the time of the non-cooperation movement from 1919 to 1922. It was he who started the boycott of British or western dresses. He was appointed the mayor of Calcutta Corporation after it was formed and also supervised the Gaya round of the Indian National Congress.

Though a lawyer by profession, Chittaranjan Das or C.R. Das went on to play a very important role in Indian struggle for independence from the British. He was born on 5 November 1870 and acquired his education from England. His career in law kicked off in the year 1909 when he successfully defended Aurobindo Ghosh when the latter was involved in the Alipore bomb blast case. Fondly, he was called Deshbandu by near and dear ones.

Read this biography to know more about the life history of Chittaranjan Das or CR Das, who was an important personality in Bengal during the time of the non-cooperation movement from 1919 to 1922. It was he who started the boycott of British or western dresses. He set an example for others to follow by burning his own western clothes and in its stead, adopting the hand made desi khadi garments. He later set up the Swaraj Party to propagate his non-moderate views with Motilal Nehru.

CR Das also launched a newspaper named Forward to spread his message to the public and fight the British raj, but later rechristened it as Liberty. He was appointed the mayor of Calcutta Corporation after it was formed and also supervised the Gaya round of the Indian National Congress. Deshbandu was continuously ill throughout his political life. But despite this, he showed spunk and unwavering determination in opposing the foreign rule.

Chittaranjan Das was a staunch non-believer of non-violence and advocated the adherence of constitutional ways in order to attain independence for India. He preached communal concord and supported the cause of national education. After him, his teachings and legacy was taken forward by his followers like Subhas Chandra Bose and others. Chittaranjan Das will always remembered for his struggle in the Indian war of independence.

Motilal Nehru

A boyhood of poverty. In later life wealth, luxury and pomp as those princes could not match. An honoured guest of the Emperor. And then, in later life, a great leader of India's fight for freedom. Motilal went to prison, too. His son was Jawaharlal Nehru. His grand daughter is Srimathi Indira Gandhi.

There are few in this country who have not heard of Jawaharlal Nehru. Motilal was his father and Swaroop Rani his mother. Vijayalakshmi Pandit who was India's High Commissioner in England andambassador in America and Mrs. Krishna Huthisingh the famous writer were the two daughters of Motilal. And Jawaharlal's daughter is Mrs. Indira Gandhi, the Prime Minister of India.

Thus every one in the Nehru family attained fames.

Pandit Motilal Nehru (1861-1931).

President-Amritsar, 1919; Calcutta, 1928.

Pandit Motilal Nehru, an eminent lawyer and politician, was born on May 6, 1861. The Nehrus hailed from Kashmir, but had settled in Delhi since the beginning of the eighteenth century. Motilal's grandfather, Lakshmi Narayan, became the first Vakil of the East India Company at the Mughal Court of Delhi. Motilal's father, Gangadhar, was a police officer in Delhi in 1857, when it was engulfed by the Mutiny. When the British troops shelled their way into the town, Gangadhar fled with his wife Jeorani and four children to Agra where he died four years later. Three months after his death Jeorani gave birth to a boy who was named Motilal.

Motilal spent his childhood at Khetri in Rajasthan, where his elder brother Nandial became the Diwan. In 1870 Nandlal quit Khetri, qualified as a lawyer and began to practice law at Agra. When the High Court was transferred to Allahabad, be moved with it.

Meanwhile Motilal passed the matriculation examination from Kanpur and joined the Muir Central College at Allahabad. Athletic, fond of outdoor sports, specially wrestling, brimming over with an insatiable curiosity and zest for life, he soon attracted the attention of Principal Harrison and his British colleagues, in the Muir Central College, who took a strong liking to this intelligent, lively and restless Kashmiri youth.

Motilal decided to become a lawyer, topped the list of successful candidates in the Vakil's examination in 1883, set up as a lawyer at Kanpur, but three years later shifted to Allahabad where his brother Nandlal had a lucrative practice at the High Court. Unfortunately, Nandlal died in April 1887 at the age of forty-two, leaving behind five sons and two daughters. Young Motilal found himself, at the age of twenty-five, as the head of a large family, its sole bread-winner.

In 1889 Motilal's wife Swarup Rani gave birth to a son, who was named Jawaharlal. Two daughters, Sarup (later Vijayalakshmi Pandit) and Krishna (later Krishna Hutheesing) were born in 1900 and 1907 respectively. In 1900 Motilal purchased a house at Allahabad, rebuilt it, and named it Anand Bhawan (the abode of happiness). His legal practice was meanwhile growing. A rise in his standard of living was paralleled by a progressive westernization, a process which was accelerated by his visits to Europe in 1899 and 1900. Thorough-going changes, from knives and forks at the dining table to European governesses and tutors for the children, ensued.

In May 1905 Motilal again sailed for Europe, this time with his whole family. He returned in November of the same year after putting Jawaharlal to school at Harrow. From Harrow, Jawaharlal went to Cambridge where he took a Tripos in Natural Science before being called to the Bar in 1912.

Motilal's early incursions into politics were reluctant, brief and sporadic. The list of 1,400 delegates of the Allahabad Congress (1888) includes: "Pandit Motilal, Hindu, Brahmin, Vakil, High

Court, N.W.P. (North-Western Provinces)." He attended some of the subsequent sessions of the Congress, but unlike his Allahabad contemporary Madan Mohan Malaviya, he was no more than a passive spectator. It was the tug-of-war between the Moderates and the Extremists in the aftermath of the Partition of Bengal which drew Motilal into the arena and, strangely enough, on the side of the Moderates. In 1907 he presided over a Provincial Conference of the Moderate politicians at Allahabad.

In 1909 he was elected a member of the U.P. Council. He attended the Delhi Durbar in 1911 in honour of the visit of King George V and Queen Mary, became a member of the Allahabad Municipal Board and of the All India Congress Committee. He was elected President of the U.P. Congress. Nevertheless, it was not politics but domestic and professional pre-occupations which were the dominant interest of his life during this period. But from 1912 onwards when Jawaharlal returned from England, there were forces at work, both at home and in the country, which were to lead Motilal into the maelstrom of national politics.

The First World War generated deep discontent in several sectors of Indian Society which found a focus in the Home Rule Movement. Motilal had been reluctant to join the Home Rule League, but the internment of Mrs. Besant in June 1917 brought him into the fray. He became the President of the Allahabad branch of the Home Rule League. Now began a perceptible shift in Motilal's politics. In August 1918 he parted company with his Moderate friends on the constitutional issue, and attended the Bombay Congress which demanded radical changes in the Montagu-Chelmsford Reforms. On February 5, 1919 he launched a new daily paper, the Independent, as a counterblast to the well-established local daily paper, the Leader, which was much too moderate for Motilal's taste in 1919.

The emergence of Mahatma Gandhi on the Indian political stage changed the course of Indian history; it also profoundly influenced the life of Motilal Nehru and his family. The Rowlatt Bills and the publication of the Satyagraha pledge in February 1919 deeply stirred Jawaharlal; he felt an irresistible call to follow the Mahatma. Motilal was not the man to be easily swept off his feet; his legal background predisposed him against any extraconstitutional agitation. It was clear to both father and son that they were at the crossroads. Neither was prepared to give in, but at Motilal's instance Gandhiji intervened and counselled young Nehru to be patient.

Shortly afterwards events marched to a tragic climax in the Punjab; the holocaust of Jallianwala Bagh was followed by Martial Law. Motilal did what he could to bring succour and solace to that unhappy province. He gave his time freely, at the cost of his own legal practice, to the defence of scores of helpless victims of Martial Law, who had been condemned to the gallows or sentenced to long terms of imprisonment.

Elected to preside over the Amritsar Congress (December 1919), Motilal was in the centre of the gathering storm which pulled down many familiar landmarks during the following year. He was the only front rank leader to lend his support to non-cooperation at the special Congress at Calcutta in September 1920. Motilal's fateful decision to cast in his lot with Gandhiji was no doubt influenced by the tragic chain of events in 1919. Apart from the compulsion of events, there was another vital factor without which he may not have made, in his sixtieth year, a clean break with his past and plunged into the unknown. This was the unshakeable resolve of his son to go the way of Satyagraha.

Immediately after the Calcutta Congress Motilal resigned from the U.P. Council, abandoned his practice at the Bar, curtailed the vast retinue of servants in Anand Bbawan, changed his style of living, consigned cartloads of foreign finery to public bonfires and put on khadi.

In December 1921 both father and son were arrested and sentenced to six months' imprisonment. In February 1922 came the anti-climax, when Gandhiji first announced and then suddenly cancelled mass civil disobedience. In March the Mahatma himself was arrested, tried for sedition and sentenced to six years' imprisonment.

When Motilal came out of gaol in the summer of 1922, he found that the movement had declined, the Congress organisation was distracted by internal squabbles, and the constructive programme could not evoke the enthusiasm of the intelligentsia. Motilal felt that the time had come to revise the programme of non-cooperation so as to permit entry into Legislative Councils. This revision was resisted by those who regarded themselves as the faithful followers of the Mahatma. A long and bitter controversy, which nearly split the Congress, ensued. However, Motilal and C. R. Das founded the Swarajya Party in January 1923, had their way, and contested the elections at the end of 1923. The Swarajya Party was the largest Party in the Central Legislative Assembly as well as in some of the Provincial Legislatures. From 1925 onwards it was recognised by the Congress as its political wing.

The spotlight shifts for the next six years to the Legislative Assembly where Motilal was the leader of the Opposition. With his commanding personality, incisive intellect, great knowledge of law, brilliant advocacy, ready wit and combative spirit, he seemed to be cut out for a Parliamentary role. The Legislative Assembly, however, was no Parliament. It was a hybrid legislature elected on a narrow and communal franchise; it had a solid bloc of official, nominated, European and some Indian members who took their cue from the irremovable executive. At first Motilal was able to secure sufficient support from the Moderate and the Muslim legislators to outvote the Government. He ruled his own party with an iron hand, but found his task increasingly difficult from 1926 onwards when communal and personal squabbles divided and weakened the Swarajya Party.

Towards the end of 1927, with the appointment of the Simon Commission, there came a political revival. The exclusion of Indians from the Commission united Indian parties in opposition to the Government. An All-Parties Conference was convened by Dr. Ansari, the Congress President, and a Committee, including Tej Bahadur Sapru and headed by Motital, was appointed to determine the principles of a constitution for free India. The report of the Committee-the Nehru Report as it came to be called-attempted a solution of the communal problem which unfortunately failed to receive the support of a vocal section of Muslim opinion led by the Aga Khan and Jinnah.

The Nehru Report, representing as it did the highest common denominator among a number of heterogeneous Parties was based on the assumption that the new Indian Constitution would be based on Dominion Status. This was regarded as a climb-down by a radical wing in the Congress led by Subhash Bose and Motilal's own son who founded the "Independence for India League". The Calcutta Congress (December 1928) over which Motilal presided was the scene of a head-on clash between those who were prepared to accept Dominion Status and those who would have nothing short of complete independence. A split was averted by a via media proposed by Gandhiji, according to which if Britain did not concede Dominion Status within a year, the Congress was to demand complete independence and to fight for it, if necessary, by launching civil disobedience.

The way was thus opened for Gandhiji's return to active politics and for the revival of Satyagraha. Motilal was at first more amused than impressed by Gandhiji's plans for the breach of the salt laws, but as the movement caught on. It found him against the advice of his doctors in the centre of the political arena. He was arrested and imprisoned; but his health gave way and he was released. But there could be no peace for him when most of his family was in gaol and the whole of India was passing through a baptism of fire. In the last week of January 1931 Gandhiji and the Congress Working Committee were released by the Government as a gesture in that chain of events which was to lead to the Gandhi-Irwin Pact. Motilal had the satisfaction of having his son and Gandhiji beside him in his last days. On February 6, 1931 he passed away.

Motilal had a rational, robust, secular and fearless outlook on life. A brilliant lawyer, an eloquent speaker, a great parliamentarian, and a greater organizer, Motilal was one of the most notable and attractive figures of Indian nationalism in the Gandhian era

Father of Moti Lal Nehru; The Story of Gangadhar

This is the true story of Ganga Dhar (not Ganga Dhar Nehru), father of Moti Lal Nehru. The adjunct 'Nehru' derived from the Persian word 'Nahr' meaning a canal or nullah, was adopted by Moti Lal, who, like all members of his family, had a fascination for alien Mohammedan names mostly in Arabic or Persian. The adjunct 'Nehru' added a Persian flavor to his otherwise Hindu name. That was very desirable for the family, as will be explained later. Otherwise, under normal circumstances, his name would have been Moti Lal Dhar.

The adjoining picture of Ganga Dhar was obtained from Robert Hardy Andrews' book titled A LAMP FOR INDIA-The Story of Madame Pandit (meaning Jawahar's first sister Vijay Lakshmi, alias Nan.) That book was first published by Prentice-Hall in 1967, a long time after the division of the country. But the fact on the scion of the dynasty, namely Ganga Dhar, had been kept a secret from the Indian public, primarily, the Hindus.

It is now quite clear, as you will soon see, that Ganga Dhar was an assumed name. The man we now know as the paternal grandfather of Jawahar Lal (son of Moti Lal) was in reality a sunni Mohammedan; in fact he was a Mogul nobleman. The important question is why did he then adopt a Hindu kafir's name? In this case a Kashmiri Brahmin's name?

The accompanying picture featured was the same one that Jawahar Lal had referred to when he wrote in his autobigraphy that he had seen a picture of his grandfather Ganga Dhar which protrayed him as a Mogul nobleman. Krishna Hutheesing (Jawahar's second sister) had also mentioned in her memoirs, that their grandfather Ganga Dhar was the city Kotwal of Delhi (an important post) prior to 1857's uprising. Bahadur Shah Zafar was still the sultan of Delhi. It was extremely unlikely that he would hire a Hindu for that very important post.

Apparently, some investigations had been made on this count but no one could discover Ganga Dhar's name as the Kotwal of Delhi. Well, how could they? Ganga Dhar's real name then was Ghiyasuddin Ghazi (or something like that) which had been quietly changed to his new Hindu name, just before the English forces entered the city. The sultan had replaced the earlier Kotwal as well as the City Governor Mirza Maniruddin. The latter had been dismissed by Bahadur Shah Zafar on charges of spying for the English. The Naib Kotwal, a subordinate officer, was a Hindu; his name was Bhao Singh. And another Hindu, one Sri Kashinath was the thanedar of the Lahori Gate area of Delhi. Their names were found in the records but Ganga Dhar was missing. Be that as it may, the fact remains that Ganga Dhar indeed was the grandfather of Jawahar and Krishna Hutheesingh.

And how did he look like? Ganga Dhar had a thick beard which would put even Pakistani president Tarar's beard to shame!

Ganga Dhar's thick moustache extended beyond his ears. He used to wear a Mogul cap and had in his both hands a long sword. Does that look like a Kashmiri Brahmin? No, not at all!

The Muslim Grandfather of Jawaharlal Nehru

Ghiyasuddin Ghazi (the word means 'kafir-killer') looked exactly like a sunni Mogul. Don't they say: 'If it looks like a duck, walks like a duck and quacks like a duck, well, then it IS a duck.' The same was the case with Ganga Dhar, the Kashmiri Brahmin alias Ghiyasuddin Ghazi the sunni Mogul. Only this vital information had been kept a secret from the Hindus of India, like so many other secrets of the family!

Our readers! If you can, please read up all references made in the memoirs of Jawahar Lal and Krishna Hutheesingh on Ganga Dhar. True to the last whisker, the picture portrayed on our web-site, does represent a Mogul nobleman, so proudly mentioned by both the brother and the sister. The element of secrecy crept in when it became clear that the Nehrus' Mogul ancestry, if made known to India's Hindu public, might spell trouble for the forthcoming 'reign'. The 'Hindu by accident' got wise to the fact and acted as if he was indeed, son of a Kshmiri Brahmin, Moti Lal Nehru by name.

Now, why was it at all necessary for Ghiyasuddin Ghazi to change his name to Ganga Dhar? Dhar is a well-known Kashmiri Hindu surname. Many of these 'Dhars' were forced converted into Islam; their names were then changed to 'Dar' just to distance themselves from the Hindu 'Dhar'. The smart Moti Lal added the Persian epithet 'Nehru' thus making the name sound even more 'un-Hindu'.

The English army, quite unlike the Hindu army, was made of a different material. While Hindus let the defeated enemy go free (like Prithviraj Chauhan had done and then regretted), the English were after each and every Mogul. They were shooting down all Mohammedans for fear of facing another claimant to the Delhi throne. Panic and fear ran like wildfire among the Moguls. There was nowhere to flee. The city had been surrounded by the 'firangi' forces and their allies, the Sikhs and the Gurkhas. It was then that the wily Mohammedans came up with the brilliant idea of name-changing. Ghiyasuddin became Ganga Dhar, almost like Yusuf Khan who had become Dilip Kumar, many years later.

Delhi was rånsacked. All residents (both Hindus and Mohammedans) had to leave and take shelter under tents set up by the 'firangis' outside city ramparts. For full two months they remained there in the tents (like the Kashmiri Hindu refugees do today). During this time, the English searched thoroughly each vacated home and discovered immense wealth, which was, by the rules of the game, confiscated by the new rulers. A month later, the Hindus were asked to return to their homes. The Mohammedans were allowed to return even later.

In the aftermath, many Mohammedans fled to nearby cities not yet fully under the control of the English. Agra was such a city. It still had considerable Mogul influence. And Jawahar's Mogul grandfather Ganga Dhar, with his entire family, left for Agra. How do we know that? Jawahar states in his own autobiography that on their way to Agra, the English troops detained Ganga Dhar's family. Ganga Dhar told them that they were not Mohammedans but Kashmiri Hindus. Jawahar explains in his autobigraphy that the primary reason for the detention was their Mogul features. The Kashmiri Hindus looked very much like Mohammedans from Iran, Turkey, Afghanistan and so on. And behold the English let Ganga Dhar and his family go to Agra. The rest is history.

Afterword: The unbecoming fascination of the Nehrus for alien Mohammedan connections persisted even beyond the Mogul roots. Reference is made there to Indira's (falsely described as the wife of Parsi Firoz Gandhi when he was no such thing; he was a pure and simple sunni Mohammedan whose father Nawab Khan was a liquor supplier of Allahabad) letters in the publication Two Alone, Two Together (letters between Indira Gandhi and Jawahar Lal Nehru) edited by Sonia Gandhi. The publishers of this book were London's Hoddard and Stoughton. In that book is featured a letter by Indira to her father, Jawahar and it says:

"Some months ago when I was at Metheran, Masi (aunt) wrote saying that she had heard from some Parsis that it was written in their ancient book that a Hindu of high family would marry into a Parsi family (here, a 'Hindu of high family' is Indira and 'Parsi' is Firoz, son of sunni Nawab Khan) and their son would do great things-religious reform and so on. Masi asked me to inquire into the matter but it quite slipped my mind. Last evening my mother in law (meaning Nawab Khan's so called Parsi wife, converted to islam at the time of her nikaah) came in a state of great excitement. She had also heard something of the sort, a slightly different version. According to her, the son was the reincarnation of the Shah Behram of Persia.

"Baby's (meaning Rajiv Gandhi's) patri (horoscope) has arrived. I am enclosing it. It is written in Gujarati but I suppose you will be able to get it read. I am enclosing an English translation of the jyotishi's remarks. I am sending all this registered-please do the same when you return it. The good thing about it is supposed to be that there are five planets in one house," and so on.

Quite clearly, the Nehrus could oscillate from the Mogul to the Persian at will as long as the roots appeared to be Mohammedan, alien or home made, and farther removed from indigenous roots the better. May we ask what great things did Rajiv do, other than stealing the Bofors money and jeopardizing the lives of our jawans by supplying them with inferior canon? And what reform was she talking about other than legalizing polygamy among the Mohammedans of India and granting them special privileges to talaaq their womenfolk, sans alimony? No doubt Indira would not move against the fornication-prone Pakistani ruffians when they were shooting down unarmed Bengali Hindu civilians. Some three millions were thus decimated but she had not even lifted a finger until the uproar inside the country became literally uncontrollable. Then again, she let go the 93,000 Pakistani soldiers scot free without exacting a quid pro quo from the enemy. Neither did she ask for the trial of Tikka Khan. And during that time, our jawans captured by the Paki army on the western front, were summarily shot in prisons, against the Geneva regulations. Is it surprising that in Europe today one can purchase picture post cards of Hari Mandir Temple with a comment on the back that Indira had secretly become Mohammedan and that is why she had chosen the Gurpurnima day (when the temple was choc a bloc with women and children) to shoot the pilgrims down, in thousands. And when the 93,000 Pakis left for their home, they had put on weight, were well-dressed and so on. She was some musalmanani of great piety although out of fear for divulging her Islamic roots, she had refused to visit the Kaaba as desired by the Saudi Royal family. Since when the Saudis have taken to inviting non-Mohammedans to visit Mecca?

Let us not be impressed by the 'five planets' and all such 'bakwaas'. What really happened is in front of our eyes, is this. In a country where they would not even hurt a chicken, there were not one, not two but three assassinations in quick succession. And all three were Gandhis. One was shot by a Hindu, the second was turned into pulp by two Sikhs and the third was pulverized by a Catholic lady of Tamil extraction. In the mean time, the bastard son of Mohammad Yunus (still the custodian of the Netaji Papers), Sanjay aka Sanjiv, killed himself in that plane accident. And the 'sarkari chacha' had died of syphilis, which apparently he had contracted in a local dhaba from a glass of drinking water! Well! Who will believe that? What really happened can only be described as divine dispensation to preserve and protect our 'dharma rajya' of Bharat, that the Congress and the secularists along with the Mohammedan traitors were bent upon destroying for good!

Government of India Act 1919

The Government of India Act 1919 (9 & 10 Geo. V c. 101) was an Act of the Parliament of the United Kingdom. It was passed to expand participation of the natives in the government of India. The Act embodied the reforms recommended in the report of the Secretary of State for India, Sir Edwin Montagu, and the Viceroy, Lord Chelmsford. The Act covered ten years, from 1919 to 1929. This retraction of British imperialism was a result of India's enthusiastic participation in World War I.

The Act provided a dual form of government (a "dyarchy") for the major provinces. In each such province, control of some areas of government, the "transferred list", were given to a Government of ministers answerable to the Provincial Council. The 'transferred list' included Agriculture, Health and Education. The Provincial Councils were enlarged.

At the same time, all other areas of government (the 'reserved list') remained under the control of the Viceroy. The 'reserved list' included Defence (the military), Foreign Affairs, and Communications.

The Imperial Legislative Council was enlarged and reformed. It became a bicameral legislature for all India. The lower house was the Legislative Assembly of 144 members, of which 104 were elected and 40 were nominated and tenure of Three years. The upper house was the Council of States consisting of 34 elected and 26 nominated members and tenure of five years. This structure allowed Britain to use the Princely States (who were directly represented in the Council of States) to offset the growing power of the native political parties.

The Act also provided for a High Commissioner who resided in London, representing India in Great Britain.

The Indian National Congress was unhappy at these reforms and termed them as 'disappointing.' A special session was held in Mumbai under Hasan Imam and the reforms were condemned. However, leaders such as Surendranath Banerjea were inclined to accept the reforms, so they left the Congress and formed the Indian Liberal Federation, which played a minor role in subsequent affairs.

Simon Commission

The Indian Statutory Commission was a group of seven British Members of Parliament that had been dispatched to India in 1927 to study constitutional reform in that colony. It was commonly referred to as the Simon Commission after its chairman, Sir John Simon. One of its members was Clement Attlee, who subsequently became the British Prime Minister who would oversee the granting of independence to India and Pakistan in 1947.

Background

The Government of India Act 1919 had introduced the system of dyarchy to govern the provinces of British India. However, the Indian public clamoured for revision of the difficult dyarchy form of government, and the Government of India Act 1919 itself stated that a commission would be appointed after 10 years to investigate the progress of the governance scheme and suggest new steps for reform. In the late 1920s, the Conservative government then in power in Britain feared imminent electoral defeat at the hands of the Labour Party, and also feared the effects of the consequent transference of control of India to such an "inexperienced" body.

Hence, it appointed seven MPs (including Chairman Simon) to constitute the commission that had been promised in 1919 that would look into the state of Indian constitutional affairs. The people of the Indian subcontinent were outraged and insulted, as the Simon Commission, which was to determine the future of India, did not include a single Indian member in it. The Indian National Congress, at its December 1927 meeting in Chennai, resolved to boycott the Commission and challenge Lord Birkenhead, the Secretary of State for India, to draft a constitution that would be acceptable to the Indian populace. A faction of the Muslim League, led by Muhammad Ali Jinnah, also decided to boycott the Commission.

An All-India Committee for Cooperation with the Simon Commission was established by the Council of India and by selection by the Viceroy The Lord Irwin. The members of the committee were: Sir C. Sankaran Nair (Chairman), Sir Arthur Froom, Rajah Nawab Ali Khan, Sardar Shivdev Singh Uberoi, Nawab Sir Zulfiqar Ali Khan, Sir Hari Singh Gour, Sir Abdullah Al-Mamun Suhrawardy, Kikabhai Premchand and Rao Bahadur M. C. Rajah.

In Burma (Myanmar), which was included in the terms of reference of the Simon Commission, there was strong suspicion either that Burma's unpopular union with India would continue, or that the constitution recommended for Burma by the Simon Commission would be less generous than that chosen for India; these suspicions resulted in tension and violence in Burma leading to the rebellion of Saya San.

Protest and Death of Lala Lajpat Rai

Almost immediately with its arrival in Bombay on February 3, 1928, the Simon Commission was confronted by throngs of protestors. The entire country observed a *hartal* (strike), and many people turned out to greet the Commission with black flags. Similar protests occurred in every major Indian city that the seven British MPs visited. However, one protest against the Simon Commission would gain infamy above all the others.

On October 30, 1928, the Simon Commission arrived in Lahore where, as with the rest of the country, its arrival was met with massive amounts of protestors. The Lahore protest was led by Indian nationalist Lala Lajpat Rai, who had moved a resolution against the Commission in the Legislative Assembly of Punjab in February 1928. In order to make way for the Commission, the local police force began beating protestors with their *lathis* (sticks). The police were particularly brutal towards Lala Lajpat Rai, who later that day declared, "The blows which fell on me today are the last nails in the coffin of British imperialism." On November 17, Lajpat Rai died of his injuries on his head.

Aftermath

The Commission published its 17-volume report in 1930. It proposed the abolition of dyarchy and the establishment of representative government in the provinces. It also recommended that separate communal electorates be retained, but only until tensions between Hindus and Muslims had died down. Noting that educated Indians opposed the Commission and also that communal tensions had increased instead of decreased, the British government opted for another method of dealing with the constitutional issues of India. Before the publication of the report, the British government stated that Indian opinion would henceforth be taken into account, and that the natural outcome of the constitutional process would be dominion status for India. The outcome of the Simon Commission was the Government of India Act 1935, which established representative government at the provincial level in India and is the basis of many parts of the Indian Constitution. In 1937 the first elections were held in the Provinces, resulting in Congress Governments being returned in almost all Provinces. In September 1928, Mr. Motilal Nehru presented his Nehru Report to counter British charges that Indians could not find a constitutional consensus among themselves, it advocated that India be given dominion status of complete internal self-government

Simon Commission Boycott

In 1927, however, the Conservative Government of Britain, faced with the prospect of electoral defeat at the hands of the Labour Party, suddenly decided that it could not leave an issue which concerned the future of the British Empire in the irresponsible hands of an inexperienced Labour Government; and it was thus that the Indian Statutory Commission, popularly known as the Simon Commission after its Chairman, was appointed.

The response in India was immediate arid unanimous. That no Indian should be thought fit to serve on a body that claimed the right to decide the political future of India was an insult that no Indian of even the most moderate political opinion was willing to swallow.

The call for a boycott of the Commission was endorsed by the Liberal Federation led by Tej Bahadur Sapru, by the Indian Industrial and Commercial Congress, and by the Hindu Mahasabha; the Muslim League even split on the issue, Mohammed Ali Jinnah carrying the majority with him in favour of boycott.

It was the Indian National Congress, however, that turned the boycott into a popular movement. The Congress had resolved on the boycott at its annual session in December 1927 at Madras, and in the prevailing excitable atmosphere, Jawaharlal Nehru had even succeeded in getting passed a snap resolution declaring complete independence as the goal of the Congress. The action began as soon as Simon and his friends landed at Bombay on 3 February 1928. That day, all the major cities and towns observed a complete hartal, and people were out on the streets participating in mass rallies, processions and black-flag demonstration. Everywhere that Simon went-Calcutta, Lahore, Lucknow, Vijayawada, Poona-he was greeted by a sea of black-flags carried by thousands of people. And ever new ways of defiance were being constantly invented.

But the worst incident happened in Lahore where Lala Lajpat Rai, the hero of the extremist days and the most revered leader of Punjab, was hit on the chest by lathis on 30 October and succumbed to the injuries on 17 November 1928. It was his death that Bhagat Singh and his comrades avenged by killing Saunders, in December 1928. The Simon boycott movement provided the first taste of political action to a new generation of youth. Subhash Bose and Jawaharlal Nehru merged as the leaders of this new wave of youth and students, and they travelled from one province to another addressing and presiding over innumerable youth conferences.

Simon Commission

Macaulay's Speech on the 1833 Renewal of the Charter of the British East India Company.

The two most important official statements of British policy concerning India were Queen Victoria's Royal Proclamation, of 1858, when the crown took control of the East India Company's Indian territories, and the statement of Secretary of State for India, Edwin Montagu (July 17, 1917-March 19, 1922) to the House of Commons on 20 August 1917.

Queen Victoria's Proclamation included the promise that "... so far as may be, Our Subjects, of whatever Race or Creed, be freely and impartially admitted to Offices in Our Service, the Duties of which they may be qualified, by their education, ability, and integrity, duly to discharge." The British Government of India studiously subverted this promise denying Indians commissions in the Indian Army and almost completely excluding them from the Indian Civil Service and the higher ranks of the Indian Police.

Edwin Montagu's statement included the following –

"The policy of His Majesty's government, with which the Government of India are in complete accord, is that of the increasing association of Indians in every branch of the administration, and the gradual development of self-governing institutions, with a view to the progressive realization of responsible government in India as an integral Part of the British Empire.... I would add that progress in this policy can only be achieved by successive stages. The British Government, and the Government of India, on whom the responsibility lies for the welfare and advancement of the Indian people, must be the judges of the time and measure of each advance, and they must be guided by the cooperation received from those upon whom new opportunities of service will thus be conferred and by the extent to which it is found that confidence can be reposed in their sense of responsibility."

Montagu had no political base and was a junior minister. Golant wrote –

"Conscious from the start of the rift between the waves of reasonable expectations in India and the tide of conservative opinion within the wartime coalition, the Montagu-Chelmsford

Report gravitated towards a policy where 'a substantial step is to be taken at once'. The sheltered existence which Britain had given India, labelled not uncritically 'constitutional autocracy', was to be altered according to the logical application of past promises. 'Indians must be enabled in so far as they attain responsibility to determine for themselves what they want done. The process will begin in local affairs, which we have long since intended and promised to make over to them; the time has come for advance in some subjects of provincial concern; and it will proceed to the complete control of provincial matters, and thence, in the course of time and subject to the proper discharge of Imperial responsibilities, to the matters concerning all India.'

"This statement contained many of the ambivalent aspects of constitution-making: reform with qualifications, clear intentions muffled by vague reference to Imperial interests, the present made a hostage to the future. The phrase 'in so far as they attain responsibility' still made Indians free to determine policy *only after* they had shown themselves able and had been given the right to do so by the British Government. 'Attain' suggested trying to reach but not yet accomplished, which left the British authorities arbiters of what was attained. 'In so far' implied a continuing limitation. In another part of the paper a parlia-mentary commission was to report on the, working of the new constitution. The reference to '*some* subjects' meant that others, and these were significant, were kept from provincial control. This was subsequently known as dyarchy, a form of dual control and responsibility dividing government power between an elected and an official authority with transferred and reserved subjects respectively. 'In the course of time' held out the future promise of self-government for the whole of India, in a vague and uncharted way. 'Subject to the proper discharge of Imperial responsibilities' could be construed to mean that British and Imperial needs were still superior to any popular measure. The word 'subject' applied a condition which could alter or under-mine any decision.

"Though subtle in his wording there can be little doubt that the Secretary of State intended a definite relaxation of British authority and power."

The promise of "responsible government" together with the subsequent Indian representation on international bodies clearly implied a commitment to move India to dominion status as was explicitly confirmed by the viceroy, Lord Irwin (1926–1931) on 31 October 1929.

The goal of British policy was stated in the declaration of August 1917 to be that of providing for the gradual development of self-governing institutions, with a view to the progressive realization of responsible government in India as an integral part of the British Empire.... I am authorized on behalf of His Majesty's Government to state clearly that in their judgement it is implicit in the declaration of 1917 that the natural issue of India's constitutional progress, as there contemplated, is the attainment of Dominion Status.

Indian Lack of Confidence in British Good Faith and its Basis

The commitment to dominion status seems as clear as that of Queen Victoria to opening all positions to Indians and there was every reason to believe that most supporters of the dominant Conservative Party would have liked to make it as ineffectual.

Views and Statements of Senior British Officials and Politicians;

- "(British prime minister) Mr. Lloyd George's "Steel Frame" speech in the House of Commons on August 2, 1922, was another contribution to the radical cause. In the course of his remarks ... he made several references to the Indian Reforms as an experiment. He also spoke of the British Civil Service as the steel frame of the Indian administration and said that he could see no time when India could dispense with its guidance and assistance. This language was regarded in India as a repudiation of the Reforms.... The government of India tried to put a conciliatory interpretation upon the Premier's language, but the Legislative Assembly ... passed a resolution expressing the grave apprehension of the people of India. The question was kept alive by the appointment of the Lee Commission on the Public Services. The fear that India would have to pay larger salaries and pensions to European officials and that the improved conditions would encourage European recruitment was too strong to be offset by the prospect that the commission would also recommend a more speedy rate of Indianization. It is doubtful whether the feeling would have been so bitter if the British civilians as a class had not been so obviously Reforms. hostile to the Reforms."

- Ambiguities in Irwin's Dominion Status announcement "This declaration, hailed as a solemn oath 'to Indian advance', was no more forthright than previous declarations. In a country inured to sincere words with substantial qualifications, Irwin's 'we cannot at present foresee on what lines this development may be shaped' left undefined (1) what was being offered in the present, (2) the meaning of 'dominion status', (3) what part Indians had in the 'attainment', a word which had more future than present connotation."
- The reaction to Irwin's Dominion Status announcement.

"He (Irwin) had already, in January 1929, emphasized that the 1917 Declaration still stood as a solemn pledge to assist India to obtain full national political stature; but this was stale and too vague. An 'indefeasible assurance' of Dominion Status, a declaration of India's right to it, would do much to remove the surface misunderstandings and distrust. For whereas to the English Dominion Status connoted an achieved constitutional position, to Indians it was mainly a promise of full rights to come. Motilal Nehru himself informed Geoffrey Dawson, then on tour in India, that what was really wanted was an assurance that Dominion Status was on the way.... Simon at first resented the suggestion of a conference, but later, following Reading's lead, focused his criticism on the reference to Dominion Status. This soon became the general attitude in both (Conservative and Liberal) parties. While they accepted the suggestion that Indian opinion be formally consulted after the report was published they disliked a categoric recognition of Dominion Status as India's goal.... The contention of the Viceroy and The Times that Dominion Status was implicit in the 1917 Declaration and the Instrument of Instructions to the Governor-General did not find unanimous acceptance in England. Even in May 1928 Birkenhead had informed Irwin that the British Government were averse to using the phrase to describe even the ultimate and remote goal of Indian political development because this meant 'the right to decide their own destinies', and this right the Government were not prepared to accord to India just then or in any way to prejudge the,question whether it should ever be accorded. So, in other words, references to 'full partnership', 'selfgovernment within the Empire', and India's 'acquiring her due place among the Dominions really meant little."

- "The pronouncement of August 1917 spoke of 'the gradual development of self-governing institutions with a view to the progressive realization of responsible government in India'. That is also the term used in the Preamble to the Act; that is the term used in the Royal Warrant of Instructions which adds that 'thus will India be fitted to take her place among the other Dominions'. The term has its significance; we know that it was deliberately chosen. The Congress and the League had asked the Imperial Government to proclaim its intention to confer self-government on India at an early date and the Cabinet chose the present term. The expression used in the Act is a term of precision, conveying that the Executive in India would be responsible to the Indian Legislature instead of to the British Parliament. If you analyse the term 'full Dominion Self-Government', you will see that it is of somewhat wider extent,conveying that not only will the Executive be responsible to the Legislature, but the Legislature will in itself have the full powers which are typical of the modern Dominion. I say there is some difference of substance, because responsible government is not necessarily incompatible with a Legislature with limited or restricted powers. It may be that full Dominion self-government is the logical outcome of responsible government, nay, it may be the inevitable and historical development of responsible government, but it is a further and a final step." (Sir Malcolm Hailey, Home Member to the Government of India on the grant of full self-governing Dominion Status to India, 8 February 1924 – Gwyer and Appadorai).

Appointment of Lord Birkenhead as Secretary of State for India

Birkenhead, who was Secretary of State for India from

November 1924 to October 1928. "He believed that if Britain lost India it would be 'a tragedy of inconceivable magnitude'."

"He was very bad at receiving deputations of visiting Indians, tended to treat them with scant courtesy if not actual rudeness, and often refused to see them on the constitutional ground that Indians should not think they could appeal over the Viceroy's head to London....

(He wrote) 'To me it is frankly inconceivable that India will ever be fit for Dominion self-government. My view is that .... it is not likely, unless matters change in the interval, that such a re-examination (i.e. the Statutory Commission) will slightest extension (of self-government)....'

"In January 1925, commenting on a speech of Reading's, he went further and revealed the deeply cynical basis of his certainty that India would never be fit for self-government.

'In a later passage of your speech, you lamented the recent renewal of outbreaks between Hindu and Mohammedan. Both you and I must of course speak of these outbreaks in the terms you used... But surely the breakdown of a Hindu-Mohammedan anti-reform unity, looked at very broadly, spells a death blow to Das [leader of the swaraj party since 1923] and the whole of his campaign... His task is absolutely hopeless when the fundamental strength of our position is advertised to all India by the resolute determination of the powerful and virile Mohammedan community that they cannot and will not have any form of Home Rule on terms which are acceptable to Das and Nehru.

'I have always placed my highest and most permanent hopes ... upon the eternity of the communal situation. The greater the political progress made by the Hindus the greater ... will be the Moslem distrust and antagonism....'

"Of course, he was not so frank in public. In public he was committed, as the representative of the British government, to preserve with the 1919 reforms and bound to pay lip-service to the 1917 promise that self-government, however distant, was the ultimate goal. But he was easily able to shelter behind the disunity and obstructiveness, the unrealism and irresponsibility of the Indian politicians, whom he regarded as a small westernized caste utterly unrepresentative of the numberless peasant masses, clamouring for further advance before they had shown that they could work the present system, as a persuasive reason for moving cautiously"

Derisory British Support for Education and the Indianization of the Army

Two key reasons, given by the British, as to why India was not ready for self-government at the Centre were lack of education (e.g. Montagu's 5 June 1919 speech to the House of Commons on the Government of India Bill) and an inability to run the Indian army without British officers who must remain under the control of parliament.

- British economic priorities during the economically stressed decades between the wars were to give: (a) top priority to meeting Stirling liability (debt payment, pensions of ex-ICS and army officers, payments to the British Government for services, repatriation of capital and profits, imports of all sorts of goods and services etc.); (b) second priority for the needs of the Indian Army, the central Government of India, provincial governors and civil servants, provincial services related to law and order and revenue collection. N.b. at this time the Government of India was funding the construction of its magnificent new capital New Delhi designed by Edwin Lutyens; and, (c) the miniscule residual resources were divided among the many needy services including education which received meager financing. As noted by Brown,"Government expenditure on education actually dropped in the early 1930s, then levelled off in 1936-7 at a lower figure than at the start of the decade." All this while the population was increasing.
- British sabotage of the Indianization of the army officer corps is described by Mason.

"In 1918 it had been announced that in future the King's Commission would be open to Indians and that ten places a year would be reserved for Indians at Sandhurst. They were to be in every way on a footing with British officers and were posted in the same way.... The fear that British officers 'of the right kind' would not come forward was strong in the 'twenties and it was to meet this that the 'eight unit scheme' was devised. The scheme was announced on February 17th, 1923; the essence of it was that two cavalry regiments and six infantry battalions should be 'Indianized' as a first step; Indians with the King's Commission in other units should be encouraged to transfer to them and no new British officers would be posted there. This, it was said officially, would give Indians 'a fair chance' to show that such units as efficient as those with British officers. But there can be no doubt that it was primarily a solution of the difficulty of 'serving under natives.'... the India Office proposed that a beginning should be made with four units only. Now nobody thought the British officer's fear of serving under an Indian was quite the sort of reason for segregated units that ought to be given in public. The official reason was that only by this means could we be sure that a unit officered by Indians was thoroughly efficient. Considering the whole operation as a scientific experiment, this could not be proved until there were Indian lieutenant-colonels in command of regiments; this would occur in twenty-six years' time. If the experiment took so long and was confined to four units it was hard to see when the process would be complete. It cannot really be regarded as an honest attempt to implement the policy; it meant that the War Office refused to take seriously the proclamation of 1918 and put up a token proposal as a way of shelving the question.... it did not take much knowledge to see that the real reason for segregated units was dislike for serving under a 'native'-and the reason publicly given was not much less wounding, while it seemed to postpone completion of the process indefinitely. No one could disguise the fact that most Englishmen believed that hardly any Indians were really good enough to lead Indian troops."

British Objectives in Designing a New Indian Constitution

The Key Objective Shared by British Political Leaders

The most important aim of a new constitution, from a British point of view, was to retain control of the Indian Army, Indian Foreign relations, finance and ultimately of the machinery of internal law and order while attracting to their support the Liberals, moderate Congress members and moderate Muslim Indian nationalists and retaining the support of most Muslims and the rulers of the princely states. This was summarized by Irwin as;

"I don't believe that...it is impossible to present the problem in such a form as would make the shop window look respectable from an Indian point of view, which is really what they care about, while keeping your hand pretty firmly on the things that matter."

Irwin to Stonehaven, 12 November 1928

Most British political leaders considered that one of Britain's greatest gifts to India was unity. The whole of the subcontinent was under British control saving it from internecine fighting and allowing integrated economic development. British leaders wanted this unity to persist into the future.

As a matter of practical politics, virtually all British political leaders recognized that, as a minimum, responsible government, would have to be conceded at the provincial level. However, safeguards could be built in to ensure the meeting of overriding British responsibilities and interests. It should be remembered, that the period 1922-1939 was one of Conservative party domination in the UK.

Beyond this, British political leaders, and the leadership of the Government of India, in the 1920s could be divided into three categories regarding Indian self-government:

Objectives of Supporters of Indian Progressive Achievement of Dominion Status Within a Westminster Type, Democratic Framework

This was the Labour Party position see Ahmed espoused most notably by Sir [Stafford Cripps] see Moore 1979. Labour's inclination was to transfer power as soon as Indian's were capable of taking on the job. However, the Labour Party was never securely in power between the wars and, really, its priorities and experience lay in domestic issues. As Gopal states

"But when the usual mid-term leave enabled Irwin to discuss his plan in England, the elections were over and Ramsay Macdonald had formed the Labour Government, and Irwin could again bring forward his plan in full. The new Prime Minister, while greatly interested in India, had no policy of his own; and he gladly agreed with the Viceroy if only because he had earlier, when still out of office, looked forward to India becoming a Dominion within a period of months."

Objectives of Supporters of Indian Progressive Achievement of Dominion Status Within a Constitutional Framework Excluding Congress from Power

This group included Stanley Baldwin, Sam Hoare and much of the official leadership of the Conservative Party. This position was supported by the last two viceroys prior to World War II; the Marquess of Willingdon and Lord Linlithgow. This group represents the purest continuation of the traditional British policy in India.

"The rationale for British Empire in India varied with time and personality, but a persistent theme runs through the period of colonial rule. Maintenance of order and with it survival of the bureaucracy rested on the government's ability to operate within a complex and expanding political system. The British stood at the apex of the system.... High on the list of imperial priorities was retention of decision-making and policy functions. This control in turn necessitated satisfactory handling of pressures and expectations from numerous sources.... The foreign-dominated bureaucracy learned to compromise and to manipulate patronage so as to maintain support groups and isolate opponents."

The Conservative view was well described by Lord Linlithgow, in a letter to the Secretary of State in 1939 when he wrote.

"After all we framed the constitution as it stands ... because we thought that way the best way given the political position in both countries-of maintaining British influence in India. It is no part of our policy, I take it, to expedite in India constitutional changes for their own sake, or gratuitously to hurry the handing over of the controls to Indian hands at any rate faster than that which we regard as best calculated, on the long view, to hold India to the Empire."

The [Government of India Act 1935] largely reflects the views of this group pushed somewhat further to the right by the "diehards." Their gameplan was to gradually develop a conservative, strongly pro-British unified India within the Empire by strengthening the position of the Muslims and the Princes to the point that Congress could never capture leadership regardless of its degree of popular support. The Conservatives' hope was that by granting responsible government at the provincial level, including much opportunity for patronage, while delaying or denying it in the Centre, they would gain several advantages from a British point of view:

- It might undermine the unity of the Indian National Congress by encouraging the development of provincial parties, inside or outside congress, which would have major incentives to play ball with the British;
- Muslims would be sure to control two major provinces – Punjab and Bengal whereas they would be a permanent minority in a democratic Centre and thus might be expected to support continued British control of the Government of India; and,
- The best hope for the Princes to retain their states, status and wealth was by maintaining British control of the Centre.

Objectives of the "Diehards"

This group, representing the views of Birkenhead and Winston Churchill, was out of favour with the Conservative party leadership but enjoyed wide support within the Conservative and Liberal parties. Their views could be summarized as:

- If it were possible, they would have liked to go back to the pre-1917 situation where:
  - o There was no publicly proclaimed long-term goal for British rule in India. In particular, they considered that authoritarian bureaucratic government was, and would always remain, the most suitable form of government in Indian conditions;
  - o Indians were consulted but held no power at the central or provincial government levels;
  - o The Indian Civil Service and the senior ranks of the police would be overwhelmingly British and the officers of the British Indian Army would be exclusively so; and,

  - o If it were desired to associate Indians more closely with the bureaucracy running India, the Indians so favoured would be rich and conservative with a special emphasis on colourful princes.

- Although the Royal Warrant for the Commission spoke of reporting "... as to whether and to what extent it is desirable to establish the principle of responsible government, or to extend, modify. or restrict the degree of responsible government then existing therein. However, as politicians living in the real world, they recognized that the clock could not be put back and that they would have to accept responsible government at the provincial level. Their reluctance to do so is shown in Churchill's April 22, 1931 speech in Parliament where he said "I thought the Simon Report went much too far, but the Simon Report has long been left behind." The motives of the diehards, including the protection of British commercial interests and the desire to permenantly maintain British rule were exposed in the following-

"On February 11, at the close of the second reading of the Bill, Churchill made the final opposition speech, warning that to give India self-government at the centre would give Indians the power to whittle away all trading safeguards, and to hold Lancashire 'as hostages', and would enable a small group of politically motivated men to trample on the rights of millions of inarticulate and ill-represented minorities. Those who would speak against the Bill at each of its stages, he said, hoped 'to kill the idea that the British in India are aliens moving out of the country as soon as they have been able to set up any kind of governing organism to take their place'. Instead, they wished to establish the idea 'that we are there for ever', as 'honoured partners with our Indian fellow-subjects whom we invite in all faithfulness to join with us in the highest functions of Government and administration for their lasting benefit and for our own'".

In this connection, Aiyer wrote-

What is the next step to be taken? Three courses may be suggested; to go back, to stand still, or to go forward. The first course is hardly likely to be suggested by any Indian politicians.

But it has been recommended as an escape from the present position in some schemes of a reactionary and fantastic character put forward by retired bureaucrats. It is hardly necessary to deal with these proposals at length, for though the provisions of the Act empower the Statutory Commission to report whether it is desirable to restrict the degree of responsible government now existing, it is difficult to imagine that Parliament will stultify itself by going back upon the policy of the declaration of 1917 and the Act of 1919. The common feature of these schemes is the assumption that British India will never be fit for responsible government and that the interests of India require that she should be under the perpetual tutelage of Britain or, at any rate, for as long a period as their imagination can con template. The advocates of these schemes belong to the school which holds that the policy of giving western education to an oriental people, which was embarked upon in pursuance of Lord Macaulay's minute, was a grievous blunder, inasmuch as it tended to fill the heads of the educated classes with dangerous aspirations to political freedom and constitutional government wholly unsuited to Indian conditions.... They consider that the declaration of 1917 by the Parliament was a solemn mistake of thoughtless generosity and that parliament should now retrace its steps. According to them, India was never more than a mere geographical expression. It was never a united country and can never hope to be one. Its only destiny in the scheme of a benevolent Providence is to be a perpetual dependency of the British Empire.

The diehards probably realised that provincial autonomy, full Indianization of the Provincial Services and substantial Indianization of the Higher Services meant that British rule in India would have to be put on a completely new basis if it were to endure.

- Britain's responsibilities and interests were mainly at the Government of India level. The Diehards wanted to exclude Indian politicians from power, and to minimize their influence, at this level. Although they did not spell it out, their ideal outcome would have probably been modelled with the Crown's relationship with the Princely States. it would have probably taken the form of a very loose confederation of Princely States and Indian provinces with Britain controlling foreign affairs, the army and finances with a right to intervene in the case of the breakdown of law and order. This could be seen as a continuation of earlier British political thinking. Thus J.L. Jenkins (in "Note by the Hon'ble J.L. Jenkins," June 24,1911" in "Transfer of the Seat of Government of India from Calcutta to Delhi and the Creation of a New Lieut.-Governorship at Patna." quoted in Johnson-

"The maintenance of British rule depends on the ultimate supremacy of the Governor-General in Council...Yet it is certain that in the course of time the just demands of Indians for a greater share in the government of the country will have to be satisfied,and the question is how they can be satisfied without impairing the supreme authority of the Governor-General in Council,which is the basis of British rule. It appears to me that the only possible answer is-by gradually giving the provinces a greater measure of self-government,until, at last, India will consist of a number of provinces, autonomous in all provincial affairs, with the Government of India above all of them, possessing power to intervene in case of misgovernment, but whose functions will ordinarily be restricted to matters of imperial concern."

- Distrust, conflicts of interest, indeed hostility between the Hindu political class, on the one hand, and the Muslim leadership, the Princes and the mass of land owners and peasants and the "martial races" would likely prevent the emergence of a self-governing India. Some of these reactionaries would have really liked to achieve the Indian unity that they fundamentally believed to be impossible. Others, such as Birkenhead and Churchill, would do everything possible to carry on ruling India by the age-old stratagem of "divide and rule." Even in 1939, according to Moore

"Churchill advocated a firm stand against Congress.... he did not share the anxiety to encourage and promote unity between the Hindu and Muslim communities. (His view was that) Such unity was, in fact, almost out of the realm of practical politics, while, if it were to be brought about, the immediate result would be that the united communities would join in showing us the door. He regarded the Hindu-Muslim feud as the bulwark of British rule in India."

British Responsibilities as Viewed by Most British Political Leaders in the 1920s

- defence of India;
- preserving law and order;
- protection of minorities, mainly Muslims in Hindu majority areas;
- maintaining the unity of Indian which had been increasingly expressed by India, encompassing both British India and the Princely States, having separate intra-empire and international (e.g. at the League of Notions) representation;
- maintaining the treaty provisions between the crown and the Princely States; and,
- ensuring that British members of the higher Services (Indian Civil Service, Police and Army) would be treated fairly.

British Interests

British leaders' view of long-term British Interests in India was probably similar to that outlined, for an earlier period by Tomlinson (1979);

"In the years before 1914 India's imperial commitment meant three things in practice: that India should be retained as a market for British exports which meant that the Government of India should not impose insurmountable barriers, especially tariffs, to the flow of British merchandise to India; that the Indian army be kept available for the imperial cause; and that the Indian administration should ensure that repayment of interest on guaranteed debt bonds was made smoothly and that adequate revenue and remittance was available for the Home Charges. Isolating the imperial factor in India policy allows us to pin-point the fundamental dichotomy of British rule in India. Each prong of its triple commitment cost the Government of India money.... As an India Office memorandum pointed out in June 1931: If a Federal Government were established in India, the aggregate charges under these three heads (Defence, Service of the Debt, and Salaries and Pensions) would, at a very conservative estimate, absorb three-quarters of the total revenues of the Federation, and a very large proportion of these payments would have to be made in sterling. This fact illustrates vividly the direct interest which the British Government must continue to retain in the financial administration of India, and explains why it is necessary to impose such measures of Parliamentary control as may be sufficient to ensure that these obligations are met... There is no escape from the conclusion that so long as the British Government retains obligations which absorb so large a proportion of the total revenues of India, it must retain a direct interest in the financial administration of the country. This by no means implies that financial administration must remain under close or detailed control, but merely that provision must be made to ensure that the financial stability and credit of the country will be maintained, as unless this can be ensured the obligations falling on the British Government could not be met. This, from the purely British point of view, is the primary object of the [financial] safeguards."

In practice British latitude was constrained.

- India as a market for British exports – The Fiscal Autonomy Convention of 1922, a bid to win the support of industrial and political India, allowed the Government of India to set protective tariffs even if they hurt UK exports. As described by Tomlinson (1979).

"The real crisis over the cotton tariff came in September 1931. The Government of India, in financial difficulties again and under pressure from London to balance its budget to boost confidence in the rupee, proposed a further 5 per cent increase in all tariff levels. ... Sir Samuel Hoare (Secretary of State for India August 25, 1931 – June 7, 1935), thought that as 'an extreme measure in a time of national emergency' the Convention could be set aside.... But although Hoare thought that the Government of India's new tariff proposals were 'disastrous upon [sic] Lancashire', there was little that he was able to do about them.... But the new Viceroy, Lord Willingdon.... Argued that any dictation by London of Indian tariff policy would cause a storm in India, and revealed that three of the Indian and two of the British members of his Executive Council were prepared to resign if the Cabinet's proposals went through. In the face of this opposition there was little that the

British Government could do but give in.... By the end of 1931 the National Government had accepted that it could not interfere directly in the general tariff policy of the Government of India and that this method of maintaining a British commercial advantage was closed to it. The stick of imperial command now had to be replaced by the carrot of bilateral' consultation."

- Sterling Charges on the Government of India – The British Government ensured that the Rupee was maintained at the high rate of R.1=1s 6d in the face of strong India opposition. This required an extremely tight monetary policy at a time of depression. It is clear now, and was clear then, that the interests of the Indian economy were being subordinated to those of the British tax payer who would have had to pick up the tab if the government of India could not meet its Sterling obligations.
- Indian Army-The financial stress on the Government of India put severe limits on the Indian Army. In the period after 1918 military expenditures continued to be the largest item of government expenditure. "35.7% of India's national expenditure was devoted to the military... compared to that of Britain itself (16.8%) and Canada (0.6%)" (Cell). In this context, there was a strong reaction when Imperial planners attempted to use Indian troops to cheaply garrison Britain's new empire in the Middle East. This led to a struggle between, on the one side, the India Office, the Government of India and Indian political opinion vs., on the other side the Imperial General Staff.

The Indian position was (Tomlinson 1979);

"The principle should be generally accepted that, except in the gravest emergency, the Indian Army should be employed outside the Indian Empire only after consultation with the Governor-General in Council.... The view of the Government of India that the Indian army should not be required permanently to provide large overseas garrisons is supported. Units required for such purposes should be maintained in addition to the establishment laid down for the Indian Army, and the whole cost, direct or indirect, of recruiting and maintaining such units should be borne by His Majesty's Government, or by the dependency or colony requiring their services. This position held for the rest of the decade; the Indian army could still play a limited imperial role, but at London's expense."

The Statutory Commission

Under section 84 of the Government of India Act, 1919, a Statutory Commission was to be appointed "at the expiration of ten years after the passing of the Act...for the purpose of inquiring into the working of the system of Government, and the development of representative institutions in India, with a view to extend, modify or restrict the degree of responsible government then existing in India."

In 1927, the national movement was at one of its periodic low points. Hindu-Muslim riots, financial stringency and the frustration of living under an almost unworkable constitution had taken their toll. A unifying and galvanizing issue was required and Britain supplied it.

Public Agenda-the Objectives, Makeup and Method of Operation of the Commission as Presented to the India Public by Lord Irwin on 8 November 1927;

"The question of what should be the composition of the Commission is one to which the answer must inevitably be greatly influenced by the nature of the task which Parliament has to perform in the light of its advice. In order that the decision at which His Majesty's Government have arrived may be fully understood, it is necessary to state in a few words what they conceive that task to be. If it were simply the drawing up of a Constitution which Parliament, which must in any circumstances be the final arbiter, would impose on India from without, the problem would be comparatively simple. But that is not how His Majesty's Government conceive it. The preamble to the Act of 1919 recognized, in effect, that with the development of Indian political thought during the last generation, legitimate aspirations towards responsible government had been formed of which account must be taken. His Majesty's present Government desire no less to take account of those aspirations, and their hope is to lay before Parliament-after the investigation into facts prescribed by the Act-conclusions which shall, so far as is practicable, have been reached by agreement with all parties concerned. It is with this object steadily in view that His Majesty's Government have considered both the, composition of the Commission and the procedure to be followed in dealing with its Report.

"It would be generally agreed that what is required is a Commission which would be unbiased and competent to present an accurate picture of the facts to Parliament, but it must also be a body on whose recommendations Parliament should be found willing to take action which a study of these facts may indicate to be appropriate.

"To fulfil the first requirement it would follow that the Commission should be such as may approach its task with sympathy and a real desire to assist India to the utmost of its power, but with a mind free from preconceived conclusions on either side. It is, however, open to doubt whether a Commission constituted so as to include a substantial proportion of Indian members and, as it rightly would, British official members also, would be thought to satisfy the first condition of reaching conclusions unaffected by any process of a priori reasoning. On the one hand, it might be felt that the desire, natural and legitimate, of the Indian members to see India a self-governing nation, could hardly fail to colour their judgement of her present capacity to sustain the role; on the other hand, there are those who might hold that British official members would be less than human if their judgement were not in some degree affected by long and close contact with the questions to which they would now be invited to apply impartial minds.

"But even after such a Commission had written its report Parliament would inevitably approach consideration of it with some element of mental reservation due to an instinctive feeling that the advice in more than one case represented views to which the holder was previously committed. It would move uncertainly among conclusions the exact value of which, owing to unfamiliarity with the minds of their framers, it would feel unable to appreciate.

"We should, however, make a great mistake if we supposed that these matters were purely constitutional or could be treated merely as the subject of judicial investigation. Indian opinion has a clear title to ask that in the elaboration of a new instrument of government their solution of the problem or their judgement on other solutions which may be proposed should be made an integral factor in the examination of the question and be given due weight in the ultimate decision. It is, therefore, essential to find means by which Indians may be made parties to deliberations so nearly affecting the future of their country."

Covert Agenda-the Timing, Objectives and Makeup of the Commission;

Indian nationalists had been demanding an early launching of the Commission since, under the 1919 Act, this was an necessary precursor to the further devolution of power from British to Indian hands. Thus when Birkenhead announced of the appointment of the Statutory Commission on November 8, 1927, two years ahead of the scheduled date, he could present it as a concession to Indian political opinion. However, the reality, as Birkenhead himself wrote was rather different-

When I made my speech in the House of Lords suggesting that it might be possible to accelerate the Commission of 1928, if some measure of cooperation were forthcoming in India, I always had it plainly in mind that we could not afford to run the slightest risk that the nomination of the 1928 Commission should be in the hands of our successors. You can readily imagine what kind of Commission in its personnel would have been appointed by (Colonel Wedgwood and his friends. [Wedgwood was a strongly pro-Indian ex-Radical tipped as a possible Secretary of State in a future Labour Government.] I have, therefore, throughout been of the clear opinion that it would be necessary for us, as a matter of elementary prudence, to appoint the Commission not later than the summer of 1927.

If, therefore, we take the view that we are not prepared to run the slightest political risks in a problem so grave and so decisive of the future of India, it becomes evident that we ought to aim for the best possible terms from our opponents in compensation for a concession which, rightly considered, is no concession at all, because our own interests imperatively require that we should make it.

The Act of 1919 did not clearly state that the Statutory Commission should be mainly, or wholly made up of members of parliament. In fact, major enquiries going back into the 19th century always included both British and Indian members. The newly appointed viceroy, Lord Irwin, making the worst misjudgment of his Indian career, wrote to Birkenhead that he would recommend a small parliamentary commission – "five men of the type of the late (Lord Cromer), – which would come to a well-considered judgement; while Birkenhead preferred a mixed commission, as "divergent Hindu and Muslim reports might... be of great assistance... to us if the Commission took the view that a very considerable advance was not to be recommended". However, Birkenhead was also worried that the Indians might sink their differences and team up with the labour representatives to recommend a major shift of power to Indians.

Probably, on the basis of this concern he accepted Irwin's recommendation. (However,) "The official rationale for limiting to Englishmen membership of the Simon Commission... was that if Indians or bureaucrats became members, they would bring to the evaluation preconceived notions and thereby affect the commission's findings and the readiness with which Parliament would accept its report." (Barrier)

To head the Commission he selected Sir John Simon. The other commission members were little known. However, one of the two labour members was Clement Attlee who, as British prime minister, was to grant India independence in 1947.

Simon was on the right wing of the declining Liberal party and would later become the leader of the National Liberals. Like Birkenhead he was a brilliant lawyer. The following is quoted from Bridge –

Simon was Bikenhead's choice. Although a front-rank Liberal, he had all the attributes Birkenhead required. He was persona' grata with the: Conservatives after his anti-Labour stance in the General Strike of May 1926.

Moreover, he had been a close friend of Birkenhead's since they had played in the Wadham XV together at Oxford and gone on to the Bar and politics. Both were politicians'-politicians as is witnessed by the probably apocryphal story that the two had tossed a coin to decide which would be a Liberal and which a Tory. Like Birkenhead, Simon had a brilliant legal career; unlike him, he had what Birkenhead called "great subtlety" and "tact", though others less friendly, like Neville Chamberlain, detected a "slyness which is rather disconcerting in a man of the first rank".

Another Tory ... reported later that "every-thing this brilliant man does seems shifty or even, worse; he has a lamentable reputation as a twister"; "adroit" and "suave".... Birkenhead reported that "his views upon the fundamentals of the matter; are very largely in agreement with my own" ; and they played golf together "'nearly every day" in the summer recess that their views might be in even better accord.... Out of office since 1916 Simon welcomed the opportunity "to play my part in this tremendous' business".... Geoffrey Dawson thought the Conservatives were taking quite a risk. Though Simon had great intelligence, the Commission was "a terribly weak team" and "it is really trusting him very highly to turn him loose with such a feeble band of colleagues."

Golant wrote- "Attlee-along with Vernon Hartshorn, the Labour Party representative-wrote of Simon: 'He was at,his best when a decision had not to be taken.

' The other four commissioners were staunchly conservative: Lord Burnham, editor of the Daily Telegraph was an unashamed imperialist, Edward Cadogan believed 'in the great imperial idea', George Lane-Fox was related to both Baldwin and Lord Irwin, and Lord Strathcona was decidedly anti-black.

Strathcona believed they were 'sent on the Commission to give it a certain elegant demeanour and make things socially easier for Lord Irwin; the main purpose of the Commission was for it to be a show of strength, Indians liking the aristocracy and being great snobs'.... (They were called) the 'simple seven'."

Before these men, brilliant Indians (the 2 Nehrus, Sapru, Jinnah etc.) were to appear merely as witnesses. They would have done well to consider what Montagu had written about Jinnah a decade earlier (Read)- "Chelmsford tried to argue with him, and was tied up into knots. Jinnah is a very clever man, and it is, of course, an outrage that such a man should have no chance of running the affairs of his own country".

Racial and Cultural Assumptions

As put by (Johnson);

"Though offering far more advanced constitutional reforms than ever before, the Government of India Act of 1919 expressed the underlying racial, cultural and social dichotomies of its authors. The continued authority of the British at the centre, the reliance on race as an important element of politics, the pedagogical nature of the reforms, and the decision to appoint commissions to review and assess Indian compatibility with democratic institutions clearly reflected Britain's negative opinion of Indian political and intellectual thought.

Hence, as Britain made political gestures toward greater Indian independence, it continued to undermine this political stance with its deeply embedded bias toward the west.

The Simon Commission and constitutional reform in India must be seen within tills tension between Britain's political move to provide greater independence in India, through constitutional reform, and its inability to escape the racial, cultural, and social dichotomies that had long justified imperial rule assumptions shared by the Simon Commission.

"The Simon Commission was given two directives by Parliament: first, to assess India's progress toward responsible government since the Government of India Act of 1919, and second, to draft a report that made recommendations for further constitutional reform.... British officials and Indian leaders alike were well aware that its unspoken mission was to create the groundwork upon which a new constitution, which gave Indians more responsibility while securing British imperial rule.... The Round Table Conference was a direct response to the Simon Commission.

By dismissing the Simon Report outright, Indian leaders were stating their rejection of British imperial paternalism of which the Simon Commission was the latest example.... Lord Irwin chose the path of conciliation because the administration of British-India had become impossible in the midst of the non-cooperation movement.... [F]or Govemment of India officials who understood the weakened position of British rule in India, the only viable option was to give India independence within an imperial framework. The offer of dominionhood would do precisely this. In contrast, the Simon Commission represented a form of British imperial discourse that no longer had any legitimacy in India.

Its embedded paternal and racial constructions clearly expressed in the writings of Cadogan, Simon and the report itself, were hotly contested by Indian nationalist leaders.... Simon made the relationship clear in front of the House of Commons before leaving for India for the first visit: 'The British have a tremendous responsibility to the peoples of India... which cannot be denied or evaded, for it is rooted in history and in the facts of the world today.

If therefore the future of India is to be one of peaceful progress...it can only come about by the action of the British Parliament combined with the cooperation of India itself...The Commission does not go to India with any idea of imposing Western ideas or constitutional forms from without; we go to listen, to learn, and faithfully to report our conclusions as to actual conditions and varying proposals from within.'

"Yet the very structure of the Commission-an all-white membership-made it impossible for the Commission to speak for the Indian public "within," and Indians were no longer convinced by the "rooted[ness]"of the historical fact that Britain was the only guide for India or that it even needed a mentor. The Commission's report as well as the way it was produced could only be seen by many Indians as another British imposition."

Indian Reaction to the Make-up of the Commission

The most important aim of a new constitution, from a British point of view, was to attract to their support the Liberals, moderate Congress members while retaining the support of most Muslims and the rulers of the princely states.

However, when news reached India that the Commission would be "all-white", the Congress and the Muslim followers of Jinnah announced that they would boycott all its proceedings. Much to the surprise of the British leadership the Liberals, led by Tej Bahadur Sapru and Jaykar also announced that they would boycott the Commission. Reed wrote-

"Lord Lloyd rang me up in my Chiltern abode and said: "I have seen the personnel of the Commission; you will not like it, nor do I." Who could? Just consider the implications of this step. The Commission was to frame for the decision of Parliament the form of government under which Indians were to live for probably a generation.

From it Indians were excluded. The chairman was a very distinguished lawyer; Lord Burnham was personally known to some Indian journalists for his kindly and generous hospitality as head of the Empire Press Union; Mr. Attlee had not emerged into the limelight, "As for the other members, well, a kindly veil had better be drawn over their qualifications. Ministers who walk to their seats with steps solemn, ponderous and slow, with Parliamentary Private Secretaries proudly bearing the red boxes behind them; back-benchers who hold their heads higher when the police stop traffic for their march to Palace Yard, quite naturally think no small beer of themselves. They would be shocked at the repute in which they are held abroad....

"Indian politicians who had grown grey in the public life of their country were summoned to headquarters and told that they might be heard as witnesses; but they were to have no major part in fashioning the instrument of government.... No wonder they saw red and the greater the sense of esponsibility the hotter the indignation voiced by men like Sir Tej Bahadur Sapru, ... the consequences of this act of folly were apparent to all who knew their India....

"The Commission staggered round India boycotted by all reputable people. It was soon apparent that no recommendations would have the slightest value unless Indian opinion was associated with them.... Within the fabric of the terms of reference the Commission did seek to enlist Indian support, and step by step the Joint Committee to work with it was established, but it was fatally handicapped by nomination; its members could not agree amongst themselves....

"The Simon Report, with all the labour it represented, was a dead letter.... (However, The first volume is the most masterly survey of the conditions of the problem in official literature; if the recommendations in the second volume run away from all this analysis that is no fault of the writer or writers, who did their own work well".

Mehrota hit the nail on the head-

"All political parties in India in the 'twenties recognized the legislative supremacy of the Imperial Parliament. Even the Congress, which took its stand on the principle of self-determination, bowed to the sovereign and ultimate authority of Parliament. What it challenged was the assertion contained in the Preamble to the Act of 1919 that 'the time and manner of each advance can be determined only by Parliament'. 'Now, that is a proposition', said Motilal Nehru, 'which we cannot accept...., Liberals, Independents and Muslim Leaguers-all alike claimed that Indians should have an equal voice in framing the future constitution for their country, however much they might have differed from Congressmen in the manner of asserting that claim. Dominion precedents were frequently quoted by Indian nationalists in support of their demand to frame their own constitution and submit the same to Parliament for ratification. The recent example of Ireland and the remarks made by Imperial statesmen justifying the procedure followed in her case only strengthened the claim of Indian nationalists.

The latter noted and remembered what Lloyd George had remarked during the debate on the Anglo-Irish Treaty on December 14, 1921: 'Here we are going to follow the example which has been set in the framing of every constitution throughout the Empire. The constitution is drafted and decided by the Dominion, the Imperial Parliament taking such steps as may be necessary to legalize these decisions.'... Sir John Simon .... (in a) speech he ... delivered in Parliament on November 27, 1922 ... (said) 'I believe it would be true to say that Constitutions which promote prosperity and loyalty, and which have been found to be lasting Constitutions for subordinate States in our Empire, have, almost without exception, either actually or virtually, been formed by those who were to live under them themselves.'

"... What India needed in 1927 was not a judicial inquest into the 1919 reforms, such as was entrusted to the Simon Commission. The working of dyarchy had proved nothing and settled nothing. It had been a foggy episode in which all parties had been groping.

Its results had been so diverse and confused as to make it impossible to base any confident conclusions upon it and extract from its records any sure guidance for the future.

Howsoever intelligent the 'jury' they could not find a solution to the Indian puzzle.... The great need of the hour in India was to restore confidence in the good intentions of the Imperial Government. This could only be done by a sympathetic understanding of the Indian problem and by determining the political advance of the country in cooperation with its leaders. The most perfect and impartial findings of an excellent Commission could be of little use if they were not acceptable to the main body of Indian nationalists. The difficulties in the way of composing a mixed Commission were obvious and many, but certainly there were other ways of approaching the problem, and the considerations which prompted the Government of India and the Secretary of State not to search for these alternative methods do not reflect much credit on either."

Lala Lajpat Rai

The Simon Commission

The non-cooperation movement failed. Therefore there was a lull in political activities. In 1927 the British Government wanted a report on political reforms in India and on amending the Government of India Act. So it appointed a commission. The commission consisted of Sir John Simon and six other members. All of them were members of the British Parliament. There was not a single Indian as member. It was composed solely of White people. The commission was an insult to Indians. These White men were to shape the future of India. The people of India rose as one man against this step. Under Lalaji's leadership, it was resolved to boycott the Simon Commission.

Lajpat Rai moved a resolution in the Central Legislative Assembly in February 1928. "The present constitution of the Commission and its terms of reference are unworthy of acceptance by this House; therefore, this House advises the Government that it should have nothing to do with the Commission." He made an impassioned speech on that occasion. There were several English men and government officers in the Legislative

Assembly: It was known that they would vote against the resolution. Lalaji appealed to the Indian members thus: "Let the members understand that they are slaves in the eyes of the British Government and of the world. When they vote on the resolution let them remember that in 1919, because of a s...gle epidemic, six crores of people died in our country. Let them remember that in this country ten crores of people do not have even one meal a day."

What right did the British Parliament have to frame a constitution for India? That was Lalaji's fearless question. Only Indians had the right to decide about their future. They were determined about it. The report of Motilal Nehru and his colleagues was ready. It had protested against the British attitude. Lalaji toured the whole of India to give publicity to the Nehru report.

Bibliography

Adikaram, E. W.: *Early History of Buddhism in Ceylon,* D. S. Puswella, Migoda, 1946.

Agrawala, V. S.: *Shiva Mahadeva: The Great God,* Veda Academy, Varanasi, 1966.

Ahmad, Imtiaz: *State and Foreign Policy: India's Role in South Asia,* Vikas, New Delhi, 1993.

Ahmad, Jamil-ud-din: *Some Recent Speeches and Writings of Mr. Jinnah,* Lahore, Ashraf, 1952.

Aiyar, R. Krishnaswami: *Outlines of Vedaanta,* Chetana, Bombay, 1978.

Archer, W. G.: *The Kama Sutra,* Unwin Hyman, London, 1990.

Ashton, S.R. : *British Policy Towards the Indian States, 1905-1939,* London, Curzon, 1982.

Aurobindo, Sri: *Vyasa and Valmiki,* Acharya Press, Pondicherry, 1956.

Avalon, Arthur and Ellen: *Hymns to the Goddess,* Ganesh and Co., Madras, 1964.

Aziz, Ashraf: *Light of the Universe: Essays on Hindustani Film Music,* Three Essays Collective, New Delhi, 2003.

Bagchi, P. C.: *Studies in Dharmashastra,* University of Calcutta Press, Calcutta, 1939.

Bahadur, K.P.: *The Wisdom of Vedaanta,* Sterling Publishers Private Limited, New Delhi, 1996.

Banerjea, J. N.: *Pauranic and Vedanta Religion,* University of Calcutta, Calcutta, 1996.

Bankimchandra, C.: *Essentials of Dharma,* Sanskrit Book Depot, Calcutta 1979.

Basu, Manoranjan: *Dharmashastra: A General Study,* Shrimati Mira Basu, Calcutta, 1976.

Beaumont, Roger : *Sword of the Raj: The British Army in India, 1747-1947*, Indianapolis, Bobbs-Merrill, 1977.

Benjamin, Joseph : *Scheduled Castes in Indian Politics and Society*, New Delhi, Ess Ess Publications, 1989.

Bhattacharyya, B.: *Nispannayogavali of Mahapandita Abhyakara Gupta*, Oriental Institute, Baroda, 1949.

Borchert, Bruno: *Mysticism: Its History and Challenge*, Samuel Wiser, York Beach, 1994.

Bose, D. N.: *Dharmashastra: Their Philosophy and Occult Secrets*, Kali Press, Calcutta, 1965.

Bowle, John: *The Imperial Achievement: The Rise and Transformation of the British Empire*, Little, Brown, 1974.

Brockington, J. L.: *Righteous Rama: The Evolution of an Epic*, Oxford, London, 1984.

Bromley, D.: *Krishna Consciousness in the West*, Bucknell University Press, Lewisburg, 1989.

Brooks, E.: *The Original Analects: Sayings of Confucius and His Successors*. Columbia University Press, New York, 1988.

Bruhn, Klaus: *The Jina-Images of Deogarh*, MacMillan, Leiden, 1969.

Burke, Mary Louise: *Swami Vivekananda in America: New Discoveries*, Advaita Ashrama, Calcutta, 1966.

Chaudhary, M.: *Partition and the Curse of Rehabilitation*, Calcutta, Bengal Rehabilitation Organization, 1964.

Chaudhuri, Nirad: *Thy Hand, Great Anarch! India: 1921-1952*, London, Chatto & Windus, 1987.

Coomeraswamy, Ananda K.: *Buddha and the Gospel of Buddhism*, MacMillan, London, 1928.

Crawford, Cromwell S.: *Ram Mohan Roy: His Era and Ethics*, Acharya Press, New Delhi, 1984.

Dalton, Dennis : *Gandhi's Power : Nonviolence in Action*, New Delhi, OUP, 2001.

Danielou, Alain: *The Complete Kama Sutra*, Park Street Press, Rochester, 2000.

Dasgupta, Shahana: *Rani Lakshmibai: The Indian Heroine*, Rupa & Company, Calcutta, 2002.

Datta, V.N.: *Sati: Widow Burning in India*, Manohar, New Delhi, 1990.

David, M. D.: *John Wilson and his Institutions*, Mumbai, 1957.

De Bary: *Self and Society in Ming Thought*, Columbia University Press, New York, 1970.

De, Sushil Kumar: *Ancient Indian Erotics and Erotic Literature*, Firma K. L. Mukhopadhyay, Calcutta, 1959.

Deak, Istvan: *The Lawful Revolution: Louis Kossuth and the Hungarians 1848-1849*, Columbia University Press, 1979.

Dhar, Niranjan: *Vedanta and Bengal Renaissance*, Minerva Associates, Calcutta, 1977.

Dikshit, D.P. *Political History of the Chalukyas of Badami*. New Delhi: Abhinav, 1980.

Donat, K.: *Meditate the Tantric Yoga Way*, George Allen and Unwin, London, 1973.

Doniger, W.: *The Rig Veda: An Anthology*, Penguin, New York, 1981.

Duboi, Abbe: *Hindu Manners, Customs and Ceremonies*, Fifth Indian Impression, CUP, 1985.

Dwivedi, M.: *The Principal Upanishads*, Adyar Library, Madras, 1931.

Eaton, Richard M.: *Sufis of Bijapur, 1300-1700: Social Roles of Sufis in Medieval India*, Princeton University Press, Princeton, 1978.

Edwardes, Michael: *Battles of the Indian Mutiny*, London; B. T. Batsford Ltd., 1963.

Erickson, Erik H.: *Gandhi's Truth: On the Origins of Militant Nonviolence*, Norton, New York, 1970.

Farquhar, J.N.: *Modern Religious Movements in India*, Munshiram, New Delhi, 1967.

Fay, Peter Ward: *The Opium War, 1840-42*, University of North Carolina Press, 1975.

Fisher, Michael H.: *The Politics of British Annexation of India - 1757-1857*, Oxford, 1996.

Frauwallner, E..: *History of Indian Philosophy*, Motilal, Delhi, 1973.

Gambhirananda, S.: *Brahma Sutra Shamkar Bhasya*, Adavita Ashrama, Calcutta, 1977.

Gambhirananda, Swami: *Brahma Sutra Shamkar Bhasya*, Adavita Ashrama, Calcutta, 1977.

Gandhi, M. K.: *The Story of My Experiment With Trust*, Washington, Public Affairs Press, 1948.

Garbe, R.: *The Philosophy of Ancient India*, Chicago University Press, Chicago, 1899.

Goradia, Nayana: *Lord Curzon: The Last of the British Moghuls*, New Delhi, Oxford University Press, 1993.

Goudriaan, T.: *Ritual and Speculation in Early Tantrism*, State University of New York Press, New York, 1992.

Gough, A.E.: *The Philosophy of the Upanisads and Ancient Indian Metaphysics*, MacMillan, London, 1882.

Grant, G. P.: *Philosophy in the Mass Age*, Copp Clark, Toronto, 1959.

Grisenold, H.D.: *Insights into Modern Hinduism*, Oxford, New York, 1934.

Growse, F. S.: *The Ramayana of Tulasidasa*, Motilal Banarsidass, Delhi, 1995.

Gurumurthy, S. : *Hindu Heritage, Assimilative, Not Divisive*, Vigil, Madras 1993.

Haich, E.: *Sexual Energy and Yoga*, Aurora Press, New York, 1982.

Hasan, Murhirul: *Legacy of a Divided Nation: India's Muslims Since Independence*, New Delhi, Oxford, 1997.

Hasan, Mushirul: *India's Partition: Process, Strategy and Mobilization*, New Delhi, Oxford UP, 1993.

Heifetz, Hank: *The Origin of the Young God: Kalidasa's Kumara-sambhava*, University of California Press, Berkeley, 1985.

Heimann, Betty: *Facets of Indian Thought*, Geroge Allen & Unwin, London, 1964.

Heinsath, Charles: *Indian Nationalism and Hindu Social Reform*, Princeton University Press, Princeton, 1964.

Heschel, J.: *God in Search of Man: A Philosophy of Judaism*, Noonday Press, New York, 1997.

Hirschman, Edwin: *White Mutiny: The Ilbert Bill Crisis in India and the Genesis of the Indian National Congress*, New Delhi, Heritage, 1980.

Hixon, L.: *Mother of the Universe: Visions of the Goddess, Tantric Hymns of Enlightenment*, Quest Books, Wheaton, 1994.

Hopkins, J.: *Kalachakra Tantra Rite of Initiation*, Wisdom Publications, Boston, 1982.

Hopkirk, Peter: *The Great Game: The Struggle for Empire in Central Asia*, Kodansha, 1992.

Hume, R.E.: *The Thirteen Principle Upanishads*, Oxford University Press, London, 1971.

Hutchins, Francis: *Spontaneous Revolution: The Quit India Movement*, New Delhi, Manohar, 1971.

Irene, S.: *Vedic Heritage Teaching Program*. Arsha Vidya Gurukulam, Coimbatore, 1994.

Iyar, K.: *Vedanta: The Science of Reality*, Ganesh and Co., Mardas, 1930.

Iyengar, B.K.S.: *Light on the Yoga Sutras of Patanjali*, Aquarian Press, London 1993.

Jacob, K.: *Religion and Ethics in Advaita*, C.M.S. Press, Kottayam, 1982.

Jafar, Malik Muhammad: *Jinnah as a Parliamentarian*, Lahore, Afzar Publications, 1977.

Jain, Kailash Chand, *Lord Mahavira and His Times*, Saraswati Press, Delhi, 1974.

James, Lawrence: *The Rise and Fall of the British Empire*, St. Martin's, 1997.

James, Robert Rhodes: *The British Revolution, 1880-1939*, New York, Knopf, 1976.

Jean, M.: *Tantrik Yoga*, The Aquarian Press, Wellingborough, 1970.

John, B.: *Mantras: Sacred Words of Power*, George Allen and Unwin, London, 1977.

John, Elsner: *Pilgrimage: Past and Present in the World Religions*, Harvard University Press, Cambridge, 1995.

John, K.: *The Origin and Development of the State Cult of Confucius*, Paragon Book, New York, 1966.

Karmarkar, D.: *Sankara's Advaita*, Karnatak University, Dharwar, 1976.

Kaushik, Asha : *Globalization, Democracy and Culture : Situating Gandhian Alternatives*, Jaipur, Pointer, 2002.

Kaviraj, G.: *Aspects of Indian Thought*, University of Burdwan, Calcutta, 1966.

Kavlekar, K.K. : *Non-Brahmin Movement in Southern India, 1873-1949*, Kolhapur, Shivaji University, 19790

Keith, A.B. : *Rigveda Brahmanas*, Harvard University Press, Cambridge, 1920.

Keith, Arthur Berriedale: *The Religion and Philosophy of the Veda and Upanishads*, MacMillan, Delhi, 1925.

Kishwar, Madhu : *Religion at the Service of Nationalism, and Other Essays*, OUP, Delhi, 1998.

Klaus, K.: *A Survey of Hinduism*, State University of New York Press, Albany, 1989.

Knipe, M.: *Hinduism: Experiments in the Sacred*, Harper, San Francisco, 1991.

Knott, K.: *Hinduism, A Very Short Introduction*, Oxford University Press, New York, 1998.

Kosambi, D. D. : *The Culture and Civilisation of Ancient India in Historical Outline*, London, Routledge and Kegan Paul, 1956.

Kottackal, Jacob: *Religion and Ethics in Advaita*, C.M.S. Press, Kottayam, 1982.

Kuiper, F.B.J. : *Aryans in the Rigveda*, Rodopi, Amsterdam, 1991.

Kuppuswamy, Sastri S.: *Compromises in the History of Advaitic Thought*, Kalyani Press, Madras, 1940.

Louis, Fischer: *Essential Gandhi: An Anthology of His Writings*, Vintage, New York, 1983.

Low, D. A. and Brasted, Howard: *Freedom, Trauma, Continuities: Northern India and Independence*, New Delhi, Sage Publications, 1998.

Maheshwari, Shriram: *Rural Development in India: A Public Policy Approach*, New Delhi, Sage, 1995.

Makhan, L.: *The Ramayana of Valmiki*, Munshiram Manoharlal, New Delhi, 1978.

Mathew, Arnold: *Culture and Anarchy*, The University Press, Cambridge, 1935.

Mayer, A. : *Caste in an Indian Village: Change and Continuity 1954-1992*, Delhi, OUP, 1996.

Mazumder, Sukhendu : *Politico-Economic Ideas of Mahatma Gandhi: Their Relevance in the Present Day*, New Delhi, Concept Pub., 2004.

Mearns, David J.: *Shiva's Other Children: Religion and Social Identity amongst Overseas Indians*, Sage, Walnut Creek, 1995.

Mearns, J.: *Shiva's Other Children: Religion and Social Identity amongst Overseas Indians*, Sage, Walnut Creek, 1995.

Mehra, Parshotam: *A Dictionary of Modern Indian History, 1707-1947*, New Delhi, Oxford University Press, 1985.

Metcalf, Thomas R.: *The Aftermath of the Revolt: India, 1857-1870*, Princeton, Princeton University, 1964.

Mohan, K.: *The Mahabharata*, Munshiram Manoharlal, Delhi 1997.

Mookerjee, Ajit: *Kali The Feminine Force*, Thames and Hudson, London, 1988.

Mookerji, Satkari: *Modern Polity and Vedanta*, Sanskrit College, Calcutta, 1972.

Moon, Penderel: *The British Conquest and Dominion of India*, London, Duckworth, 1989.

Morris-Jones, W.H.: *The Government and Politics of India*, London, Hutchinson, 1971.

Nanda, B. R. : *Gandhi and His Critics*, Oxford University Press, Delhi, 1993.

Neale, Walter C.: *Economic Change in Rural India: Land Tenure and Reform in the United Provinces, 1800-1955*, New Haven, 1962.

Nevile, P.: *Lahore: A Sentimental Journey*, New Delhi, Penguin, 1993.

Oddie, G.A. : *Hindu and Christian in South-East India*, London, Curzon Press, 1991.

Pathak, Dr S.P.: *Jhansi during the British Rule*, Ramanand Vidya Bhawan, Delhi, 1987.

Preston, Diana: *The Boxer Rebellion*, Berkley Books, 2000.

Raimundo Panikkar: *The Vedic Experience: Mantramanjari*, Longman Todd, London, 1977.

Raja, C. Kunhan : *The Taittiriya Sarvanukramani of Yaska*, Madras, 1931.

Ramamurti, A.: *Advaitic Mysticism of Sankara*, Visvabharati, Santiniketan, 1974.

Ranajit Guha: *A Construction of Humanism in Colonial India*, CASA, Amsterdam, 1993.

Renou, Louis: *The Nature of Dharmashastra*, Walker and Co., New York, 1997.

Robson, Brian: *Sir Hugh Rose and the Central India Campaign*, Sutton Publishing Ltd for the Army Records Society, UK, 2000.

Satyapal Verma: *Role of Reason in Sankara Vedanta*, Parimal Publication, Delhi, 1992.

Savarkar, Vinayak Damodar : *The Indian War of Independence* 1857 Rajdhani Granthagar, Delhi, 1988.

Scheftelowitz, Isidor : *Die Kasmirische Rezension von Katyayanas Sarvanukramani,* Zeitschrift fur Indologie und Iranistik, 1922.

Shukla, D. N.: *Vastu-Shastra,* Motilal Banarsidass, Delhi, 1966.

Singh, Birendra Kumar: *Early Chalukyas of Vatapi, circa A.D. 500 to 757,* Delhi, Eastern Book Linkers, 1991.

Smith, Col. J. T. : *Silver and the India Exchanges,* Effingham Wilson, London, 1876.

Strauss, L.: *Political Philosophy,* The Bobbs Merrill Co., New York, 1975.

Swami Vishnu Tirtha: *Devatma Shakti,* Swami Shivom Tirth, Rishikesh, 1962.

Talageri, Shrikant : *Aryan Invasion Theory and Indian Nationalism,* Voice of India, Delhi, 1993.

Tejomayananda, Swami: *Hindu Culture: An Introduction,* Chinmaya Publications, Piercy, 1993.

Thapar, Romila : *Ashoka and the Decline of the Mauryas,* London, Oxford University Press, 1961.

Thompson, Edward: *The Making of the Indian Princes,* Oxford University Press, London, 1943.

Trautmann, Thomas R.: *Kautilya and the Arthasastra: A Statistical Study,* Leiden, Brill, 1971.

Trimingham, J.: *Sufi Orders in Islam,* Oxford University Press, New York, 1998.

Utpat, V.N.: *Riddles of Buddha and Ambedkar,* Itihas Patrika Prakashan, Thane 1988.

Vable, D.: *The Arya Samaj. Hindu without Hinduism.* Vikas Publ., Delhi, 1983.

Vedalankar, Pandit Nardev : *Basic Teachings of Hinduism,* Veda Niketan, Durban, 1978.

Visvantha, K.: *Essentials of Hinduism,* Narosa Pub. House, New Delhi, 1989.

Wendy Doniger: *Siva: The Erotic Ascetic,* Oxford University Press, Delhi, 1998.

Zaidi, A. Moin: *Evolution of Muslim Political Thought in India,* New Delhi: S. Chand, 1975.

Index

M

N

P

Q

R

□□□